You Bet Your Life

You Bet Your Life

The Burdens of Gambling

Neil D. Isaacs

THE UNIVERSITY PRESS OF KENTUCKY

Copyright © 2001 by The University Press of Kentucky
Scholarly publisher for the Commonwealth,
serving Bellarmine University, Berea College, Centre
College of Kentucky, Eastern Kentucky University,
The Filson Club Historical Society, Georgetown College,
Kentucky Historical Society, Kentucky State University,
Morehead State University, Murray State University,
Northern Kentucky University, Transylvania University,
University of Kentucky, University of Louisville,
and Western Kentucky University.

Editorial and Sales Offices: The University Press of Kentucky
663 South Limestone Street, Lexington, Kentucky 40508–4008

05 04 03 02 01   5 4 3 2 1

Library of Congress Cataloging-in-Publication Data

Isaacs, Neil David, 1931–
    You bet your life : the burdens of gambling / Neil D. Isaacs.
        p.   cm.
    Includes bibliographical references and indexes
    ISBN 0-8131-2195-7
    1. Compulsive gambling. I. Title
    RC569.5.G35   I82   2001
    616.85'841—dc21   00-012279

This book is printed on acid-free recycled paper meeting
the requirements of the American National Standard
for Permanence in Paper for Printed Library Materials.

Manufactured in the United States of America.

To my brother Phil,
who has backed my play all the way

and to Jessica and Ilana,
a jackpot of joy
for a grateful grandpa

Contents

Acknowledgments

A number of people (besides my brother, who read every version) read drafts of all or part of this book, saving me from egregious errors of fact, fallacy, inference, and phrasing (any persisting errors are of course my own). Many thanks to Paul Ephross, Rich Drozd, John Howard, Clyde Taylor, George Ritzer, Larry Malley, Seetha Srinivasan (and her anonymous reader), the University Press of Kentucky's two anonymous readers, Jerry Klinkowitz, and Irv Yalom. I am grateful to generations of students and clients, plus a host of anonymous informants, all of whose contributions and confidence I appreciate and respect. To my two clinical supervisors, Joyce Winston and Bonnie Rick, I am indebted for their teachings and wisdom. Along the way I called on many others for help—answering queries, supplying leads, making connections, opening doors, arguing issues, supplying technical expertise, sharing experience, and more. I want to thank Dick Comer, Gerry Strine, Mort Olshan, Bob Martin, Chet Forte, Corky Devlin, Clark Hudak, Susan Darvas, Valerie Lorenz, Jack Higgs, Mike Olmert, Bob Coogan, Joe Miller, Ellen Isaacs, Ian Isaacs, Rita Isaacs, Linda Cottler, Charles Wellford, Charley Rutherford, Senator Paul Simon, Congressman Frank Wolf, Lynne Hamilton, Janelle Haskell, Timothy O'Brien, Mike Cuthbert, Marge Lenane, Morris Freedman, Paul Freedman, Stephanie Kaufman, Ron Cacciatore, Harvey Cohen, and Daryl Bullock. And for fifty years of learning at their tables, special thanks to the guys in the games at New Haven, Hanover, Brookline, Providence, Knoxville, and suburban Maryland, with a bonus nod to the Book and Poker Club of Arlington.

Like fam'd La Mancha's knight, who launce in hand
Mounted his steed, to free th'enchanted land,
Our Quixote bard sets out a monster-taming,
Arm'd at all points, to fight that hydra—Gaming.

David Garrick,
Prologue to
The Gamester, a Tragedy
by Edward Moore

The gambling industry in the United States has grown
tenfold since 1975....The rapid acceleration in the growth
of gambling begs a host of questions.

Executive Summary
of the National Gambling
Impact Study Commission

Introduction

A Roadmap Through a Minefield

You don't have to be a sophisticated analyst to recognize how extensively Americans are involved in gambling. Not when weekly news magazines run cover stories calling the United States a "gambling nation" or gambling the "new national pastime." If you travel a 500-mile stretch of I-64 between Charleston, West Virginia, and St. Louis (arguably a representative segment of mid-America), billboards and roadside signs inform you of opportunities and urge you to take your chances at video slots (West Virginia), a dog track (West Virginia), three horse tracks (West Virginia and Kentucky), riverboat casinos (Kentucky and Missouri), the Kentucky "Lotto" (with updated jackpot amount), and an "Offtrack Betting Facility" (Indiana).

We are a society of gamblers. We are taught early on to take a chance on life, on love, on romance; to cherish equality of opportunity—which means equal chances at even odds on a level playing field; to ask for an even break; to court Lady Luck; to seek our fortune—which means both luck and riches.

We are a culture of gamblers. Salient features of the American value system include not only materialism and competition but also risk as a given of marketplace thinking. Risk is a necessity of entrepreneurial capitalism: the American version of the ancient proverb "Nothing ventured, nothing gained," is as much an ingrained part of our credo as "In God we trust." Columnist Jim Hoagland has gone so far as to call the entire American economic enterprise "The Big Casino." More revealing than that grandiose metaphor is the fact that the financial marketplace has created instruments that are pure gambling, indeed, as close as you can get to point-spread betting this side of your friendly neighborhood bookie. Called "derivatives," they are traded—

1

bought and sold—though they represent neither tangible properties nor equity in a company. Together with such other vehicles of financial gambling as options and futures, they make up a substantial share of the day-to-day "action" on the market.[1]

And we are a nation of gamblers. In 1998, when more than 60 percent of adult Americans gambled, only 37 percent of registered voters went to the polls. Though there is a higher percentage of gamblers among those who do not vote, those who do vote nevertheless clearly support gambling. The only two incumbent governors who lost reelection bids in 1998 made antigambling positions central to their campaigns (Alabama and South Carolina[2]), while their fellow Republicans in Illinois and Nevada won governorships with substantial backing from gaming interests. Voters in Missouri, Arizona, and California passed gambling initiatives. Only in Maryland, where the governor opposed slot machines at racetracks, were gambling interests apparently turned back—but the issue was virtually ignored in the campaign, and the governor's rationale always stressed the importance of the state's "racing industry," that is, one of its historical vehicles for gambling.[3]

Except for Utah, Tennessee, and Hawaii, all the states sanction and promote some forms of legal gambling, and more than half the states have some form of casino gambling. In addition, the federal government has upheld and endorsed the right of Native American nations to operate gambling casinos on their (our) lands.[4] A growing segment of the gambling marketplace is the quasi-legal action on the Internet, where in addition to making the bets of your choice you are also taking your chances that the courts will not find you in violation of some existing antigambling statute—before new legislation is enacted to control (or find a way for government to benefit from) that action.

Taking all forms of legal gambling together, we are talking about a $600 billion-a-year handle—and that's just the half of it. The other half, involving at least as many people, and perhaps nearly as much money, is illegal gambling in every form, format, and forum. I am not talking about just the exotic betting vehicles like cockfights (which are still legal in Louisiana, New Mexico, and Oklahoma[5]), dog fights, crab races, frog jumping, country-club Calcuttas, and floating craps games, but also the garden-variety activities of your friendly Tuesday night poker game, your head-to-head election bets, your ten-dollar-Nassau rounds of golf, your two-bit mah-jongg games, your happy-hour liars' poker and backgammon, and your NCAA basketball pool.

It may all be illegal. It doesn't matter that the precinct houses and the state's attorneys offices have the pools, too, that the former indulge in their own version of Super Bowl pools and the latter invariably have a Master's Tournament "contest"—it still may be illegal. Tolerated, condoned, winked at, but often against the law.[6] The publicly sanctioned and promoted lotteries have not put the policy ("numbers") rackets entirely out of business. The underground forms continue to thrive in some communities because (a) the winnings are not taxable, (b) the proprietors have the option of offering credit to their players, (c) the minimum bet is smaller, and (d) they can afford to offer better—that is, closer to "true"—odds on their proposition.

Except in Nevada (and perhaps, pending judgment in a number of cases now being litigated, on the Internet), sports betting is illegal everywhere in this country; and yet it is a universally popular activity. The size of the handle (total amount of wagers) is virtually incalculable. Office pools and head-to-head betting are so commonplace that no notice is taken thereof, no accounting exists. Neighborhood bookies and organized bookmakers handle the larger and ever-larger bets, which go unmonitored, unacknowledged, and clearly unmeasureable. Bettors lay eleven dollars to win ten; bookies collect 10 percent surcharge—or "vigorish"—on losing bets, but the ability to bet on credit and the tax-free nature of winnings make the 11-10 cost of placing such bets attractive. The illegality of it may also have some appeal, just as drinking in speakeasies during Prohibition had a certain social cachet.) Moreover, given the nature of the bookmaking enterprise today, it is likely that every hundred-dollar bet provides several hundred dollars' worth of action because bookies must often lay off their bets with other bookies, who are serviced by bookies' bookies, on up the line to the seven-figure brokers. No wonder estimates of illegal gambling are at worst pure guesswork, at best partly informed, and in all probability always low-balled.

Sports betting comprises the bulk of the illegal action in the culture of gamblers. For the better part of a century, the open and accepted betting on baseball—before and after the fixed World Series of 1919—helped keep the "national pastime" in its favored position among our sports. The invention of the point spread[7]—a marketplace phenomenon if there ever was one—changed all that. Point-spread betting, along with the preeminence of football as a TV-friendly event, made NFL football the vehicle of choice for American gamblers (with college football second, though in the last couple of years the NCAA basketball tournament has come close to displacing the Super Bowl as the major single betting proposition on the sporting calendar). Whether or not illegal gambling attracts as large a handle as the combined forms of legal gambling, it is at least safe to say that hundreds of billions of dollars annually are involved in the action.

It is clear to me that much of the conventional wisdom about gambling is distorted and misleading, if not dangerous. And I believe that, despite the growing presence of gambling, there is little popular understanding of how it works, what it involves, or the great risks it poses to individuals as well as society as a whole. Habitual gambling can easily lead to what is commonly called "compulsive gambling," a condition that is itself generally misunderstood.

This book, then, provides a roadmap through uncharted though densely populated territory, the naked city of Gambling, USA. Two obstacles must be skirted at the outset. One is how little we know about pathological gambling; the other, how much we think we know about gambling in general. They are the Scylla and Charybdis of this excursion. Again and again, the National Research Council's *Pathological Gambling: A Critical Review* (1999) points to the lack of knowledge[8] in a field it describes as being "still relatively immature compared with many others and [which], as a result, does not demonstrate a coherent program of scientific inquiry" (29).

This kind of ignorance is remediable, and indeed the body of knowledge is rapidly expanding—though perhaps lacking a "coherence" in part because of a narrow channeling of "scientific inquiry." The other kind, embodying conventional wisdom, common knowledge, ingrained biases, and the like (what I have called myths) is deeply rooted in cultural attitudes and resistant to remediation. It is the kind of ignorance that is often protected by establishmentarian guardians of the status quo, sometimes with conscious cynicism or arrant hypocrisy, so that any attempt at enlightenment is branded as radical iconoclasm.

The campaign to identify pathological gambling as a mental disorder was an arduous one, and all respect is due such leaders of that (radical, iconoclastic) struggle as Robert Custer and Henry Lesieur. But there have been some unexpected consequences of that particular victory over ignorance. Old myths have been replaced with new.

It is now generally accepted that there is a single condition, commonly labeled compulsive gambling, named and coded as pathological gambling, an impulse control disorder. Having attained the high ground of diagnosis, the very forces of (re)vision have dug in as a new establishment, protecting their turf by excluding other, variant diagnoses. What I call the myth of single, exclusive diagnosis is the primary target of my own iconoclastic effort.[9] Along my route, chapter by chapter, I explore the possibilities of variant diagnoses.

In another way, the route is endangered by another kind of entrenched, establishmentarian thinking. There is a school of thought among certain social scientists that, while there is value in personal accounts, memoirs, autobiographies, and the like, no works of the creative imagination may legitimately be used "in evidence" or as "data" in exploring mental conditions. As a cultural historian I find that notion not only anti-humanistic, but narrowly anti-intellectual and even ludicrous.

The case is stated more elegantly than I can manage by Kay Redfield Jamison: "It should not be necessary, at the end of a century so rich in literature, medicine, psychology, and science, to draw arbitrary lines in the sand between humanism and individual complexities on the one hand, and clinical and scientific understandings, on the other. That they are bound and beholden to each other should be obvious. . . . For many, the aesthetics of complexity—the singular appeal of psychological case histories, especially ones laced with sociological and cultural explanations—are far more compelling than statistical findings . . ." (*Night Falls Fast*, 20).

More to the point, Bettina Knapp has said, "We have but to read writers as diverse as Pascal, Dostoevsky, Balzac, Poe, Serao, Hesse, Kawabata, Aleichem, and Xinxin, all of whom have described amply the fate of the hero-gambler, to recognize the same vulnerabilities in ourselves. Whether such encounters be painful or joyous, terrifying or serene, they will, hopefully, involve readers in the writings discussed and give them greater understanding of the role gambling and gaming played in both the collective sphere and in the home" (2).

And that is another reason for characterizing my path as being through a minefield. Of the dozens of cases used to illustrate the points of my argument along the way, about half are clinical or taken from life, and half are summarized narratives taken from the sphere of creative imagination.[10]

To serve as tour guide, I wear a number of hats, approaching the field from a variety of perspectives. I have been a gambler for more than half a century. For even longer than that I have been an observer of gamblers and gambling behaviors. As a psychotherapist (MSW, LCSW-C) I have treated pathological gamblers, consulted with other therapists when gambling issues have surfaced for their clients/patients, and taught training sessions for groups of therapists both to identify and treat pathological gamblers and to help mental health professionals understand the nature and variety of gambling behaviors. I have testified in court as an "expert witness" on gambling matters and before legislative committees as a concerned citizen for appropriate legislation. As an academician I have taught a course in "The Literature of Gambling and the Gambler." And as a writer I have devoted books, chapters, essays, and articles to various aspects of the subject.

More important, throughout the years I have maintained an interested vigilance on gambling, gamblers, gambling policies, reports of treatment and theories regarding pathological gambling, and the growing preoccupation with gambling and gamblers in our fiction, movies, television, and comic strips. It is to those media that I will often turn in the following pages to chart the prevalent misconceptions and myths about gambling and gamblers.

Finally, in a larger context, I view gambling phenomena from the perspective of a contemporary cultural historian. Twenty years ago, I addressed the phenomena of our "sports-minded" nation in such a way as to denominate it a "jockocracy." *Jock Culture, U.S.A.* (1978), however, was largely an *interpretation* of phenomena. It would require only *observations* of common phenomena to conclude that we live in a gambling culture. But the present book is not just a collection of such observations. It is conceived as a way of addressing some of the manifold problems that are pandemic in such a culture.

Certain guideposts have helped me design my route. Most of the chapters in this book provide illustrative cases. Except for examples drawn from the public record or where I have been given explicit permission to identify the person, I have consistently respected the confidentiality of my own clients and clients of others with whom I have consulted. In other words, though I have relied on clinical evidence of which I have first- and secondhand knowledge and on extensive personal interviews, I have in every case both disguised the subject by arbitrarily changing identifying characteristics *and*, more importantly, composed composite portraits. I have received formal permission from several informants, whose experience informs parts of cases narrated here, to use material they graciously supplied. It should not be possible for readers to "recognize" or "identify" themselves or people they know. I do hope, however, that the cases will help readers identify types of pathological gamblers and symptomatic behaviors in themselves and people they know.

The examples of dialogue quoted in several chapters should not be misconstrued. They are not transcriptions of audio or video tape recordings of actual sessions or interviews, nor are they reconstructions of sessions based on practitioners' "process recordings" or notes. I do not lay claim to clairvoyance—like Bob Woodward quoting "conversations" he had with Bill Casey at times when he could not possibly have been there (though I may be thought to have had access to a battalion of "Deep Throats"). Instead I have *constructed* these exchanges based on my understanding of the people involved, their personalities and methodologies, their thinking and affect, if not their style of speech.

Many of the "cases," as I have said, are drawn from literature rather than life. The examples will speak for themselves, but I have found in general that the psychological perceptions of good writers are at least as valuable as clinical reports in illuminating human conditions and biopsychosocial beings. But in any case, regardless of sources, the portraits of gamblers sketched here are constructs of my own observation, interpretation, combination, accentuation, diagnosis, and analysis. Whether taken from the characterizations of creative artists or assembled from clinical observations and/or reports, these cases as presented are several removes from "real people."

Now, to sketch a "triptik": I begin with a debunking of common "knowledge," the popular mythology associated with gambling and gamblers. There follows a chapter called "Gambling and the Irrational" that establishes some premises for what follows and suggests some of the reasons that gamblers are at risk of psychopathology.

Chapters 3–11 discuss various categories of pathological gambling behaviors. This whole sequence is structured, in general, according to that essential guidebook of the mental health professions, the American Psychiatric Association's *Diagnostic and Statistical Manual of Mental Disorders* in its fourth edition (DSM-IV). But it is a central thesis of this book that gamblers cannot and should not be pigeonholed in a single diagnostic category, as the DSM has it. The scores of cases examined will amply demonstrate the validity of this position.

Chapter 12 attempts to summarize and apply the implications of what I have found and reported. "Dilemmas of Diagnosis and Treatment" presents the suggestions which seem to emerge from the admittedly complex material, though in all candor it is my experience in amassing that material that guides my approach.

Implicit or explicit along this route are the several goals of the excursion: First, to break down the myth of a single diagnosis, a monolithic exclusivistic conception of pathological gambling as an impulse control disorder, period. Second, to escape the traps of other prevailing myths. Third, to show how mass media can reinforce mistaken or misleading myths about gambling, and how serious literature can give us illuminating insights into its true nature. Fourth, to tell a comprehensive cautionary tale about the risks of pathological gambling for anyone who has the gambling habit. Fifth, to argue for treatment of pathological gambling marked by accessibility, case-by-case humaneness, and understanding of the appeals of gambling and the many forms of abuse/pathology to which it may lead.

In a sense, the whole book should serve as a comprehensive cautionary tale, composed of a wide variety of individual cautionary tales. I believe this is important because the so-called social costs of our accelerating gambling action are rarely given appropriate or adequate attention, particularly the costs attendant on the percentage of gamblers whose habit or diversion turns pathological, not to mention the burdens placed on their families, friends, employers, creditors, and insurers.

And the costs go far beyond the numbers of people or dollars involved, to ruined lives and families, not just credit ratings. What is most frightening is not the despair and devastation presented in many of these sample scenarios; it is the accelerating growth of that population, expanding in all age groups, at all economic levels, into all demographic profiles. What's more, as we look at the phenomenal growth of the gaming industry in general, we also see a general failure to address the problems it inevitably creates. Those problems are by and large issues of public health, so this roadmap may help point the way toward better-informed public policy.

Nothing between human beings is 1 to 3. I long ago come to the conclusion that all life is 6 to 5 against.

Sam the Gonoph
in Damon Runyon's
"A Nice Price"

Seven Other Myths about Gambling

Let me be clear about what I mean by myth. For the purposes of this discussion I do not mean a story or fabulous legend that serves to explain the otherwise inexplicable. Nor do I mean, in the colloquial usage, simply a lie. I am using the word in the sense of a commonly accepted misconception, a piece of misleading "conventional wisdom" or "common knowledge." In this sense, the myth that is a main target of this iconoclastic exercise could be called a well-intentioned fallacy rather than a myth, at least in the mental health professions; but it functions as a myth in the culture at large. It is promulgated in the mass media and believed by the populace at large.

What it says is that there is a single pathological condition, "compulsive gambling." What it implies is that the condition has a distinctive pattern of symptoms and a predictable course, suggesting in turn a single appropriate treatment. Chapter 3 acknowledges and discusses that condition—technically classified as an impulse-control disorder—but also presents examples of misapplications and unforeseen consequences of such an exclusive diagnosis. My position is that, although the specific disorder exists (and in some prominent cases, at that), the diagnosis is inappropriate for many, if not most, pathological gamblers.

The bulk of this book, then, chapters 4–11, will demonstrate many other forms of gambling pathologies, thoroughly refuting the monolithic nature of this myth. But before proceeding with that refutation, I want to set aside several other misleading but popularly embraced notions. These are myths that contribute to massive misunderstandings about gambling in general, and they provide a context for the misunderstandings about pathological gambling in particular.

Myth 1. A compulsive gambler is a compulsive loser.

A complex confusion of terms marks this myth. If the common misnomer "compulsive gambler" is taken to apply to all pathological gamblers, then it should be clear that most of them are not dead set on losing. They do not intend to lose or want—consciously or deep down—to lose. Indeed, they think and believe and trust that they will win. They hope to win and they want to win.

Obviously, the more persistently they act on that wish, the less likely they are to win. Bob Martin, who for many years was the "Head Linesman" who set the point spread for National Football League games for most of the Las Vegas sports books, says that no matter how good you are or how well your "system" works, "the numbers will wear you down and you'll fall by the wayside" over time. It is the nature of all gambling that the "house" will win in the long run. It is also the nature of the human condition that, in Damon Runyon's phrase, "all life is 6 to 5 against."

It is, however, the nature of the gambler, whether habitual or occasional, to fly in the face of odds, to assert the possibility of being the exception to the rule. "Inevitable loser" or "eventual loser" is not the same as "compulsive loser."

On the other hand, if "compulsive loser" is taken as a *definition* of "compulsive gambler," then many, perhaps most, pathological gamblers will have been defined out of the category or the diagnosis. Some will remain. They will include those who gamble, knowing they will lose, as a way of justifying their preexisting feelings of "lostness" or their identity as "losers"; those who gamble, knowing they are likely to lose, as a way of calling for help, calling attention to themselves, or calling for fulfillment of certain neurotic needs; and those who gamble, wishing to lose, because they cannot tolerate having what they are setting out to lose.

This final group, a small minority of pathological gamblers, will be discussed in chapter 4. But to acknowledge the existence of this rare form of pathology in a few atypical gamblers is a far cry from accepting the blanket assertion that all pathological gamblers share that defining characteristic. The cases in chapter 4 of gamblers *compelled* to lose are exceptions that prove the rule. This myth violates the rules of experience, reason, and comprehensive knowledge.

Myth 2. Things even out: The law of averages.

Virtually all forms of gambling are governed by laws of probability. In abstract terms, probability is an aspect of mathematics; in practical terms, it is an aspect of statistics. In either application, *there is no law of averages*.

The so-called *law of averages* is, at its heart, the irrational notion that life is fair and balanced, that there is some kind of natural law of compensation, that for every misfortune one experiences there will be an equal and opposite blessing. Experience, if logic fails to supply the lesson, teaches otherwise. Yet the belief is pervasive, particularly among gamblers. In general, such belief leads to all sorts of naive notions, such as the stereotype that all beautiful blondes must be airheads, but with particular reference to gambling it is an illusion used to justify persistence and stubbornness in the face of evidence, experience, and reason.

If the chances are equal, one in two, that a tossed coin will come up heads, that does not mean that a toss of heads is more likely to be followed by a toss of tails. If heads come up fifty times, that does not mean that the next fifty tosses are likely to come up tails. It does not even mean that the fifty first toss will be heads; the fifty-first toss is—like the first—a fifty-fifty proposition. If a roll of a pair of dice fails to produce a seven five times running, that does not mean the sixth roll must be seven just because the probability of a seven is one in six or five to one (six combinations out of thirty-six). Coins, dice, cards, wheels, and the like *have no memory*.

It is axiomatic that runs of luck, good or bad, must come to an end. Sooner or later, if you bet that a streak will come to an end you will win a bet—but it is impossible to know how many losses you will have to survive before that one win. Bookmakers thrive on customers who try to guess exactly when a team or a player will end a streak, because a wrong guess suggests that the next one *has* to be right—the law of averages says so. The "wrong" guess may be repeated several times, while the "right" one will only happen once.

But there is no law. Take the use of averages in baseball. A player with a lifetime .250 batting average has historically hit safely once in every four official at-bats. Leaving walks, hit-by-pitches, sacrifice bunts, and sacrifice flies out of the equation, does that mean that if the hitter goes 0-for-3 he is likely to get a hit his fourth time up, even slightly more likely than the 3-1 against that his record seems to predict? Because he's "due"? Because 1-for-4 is his lifetime history?

Even setting aside such factors or fine tunings as matchups versus particular pitchers, game situations, physical condition, hot streaks or slumps, time of day, field conditions, weather conditions, and the like, that would be a nonsensical assumption. Batting averages are records of past occurrences and have relatively little predictive value for future events. Guess what? The batting average *changes* with every official at-bat. Even large numbers, accounting for thousands of times at bat, are not in any one case predictive of performance—because the larger the number, the more thorough the database, the more longevity and attrition will tend to make the overall average approach or reach the downward curve that drags on every batter who plays long enough.

If the gamble involves long shots, say 999-1 as in a three-digit lottery game, the belief in a law of averages could support a player's practice of picking the same three numbers every day since in every thousand plays it will surely come up once. By such reasoning, every combination would come up once and only once in every thousand times. But believers in the "law" don't carry their thinking that far, or they couldn't use it to sustain or justify their habitual behaviors. On arguably even bets, on apparently evenly matched teams or competitors, on odd-or-even, high-or-low, red-or-black bets on roulette wheels (forgetting the horrible house zeroes), reliance on the "law" might well produce short-term gains. But it is probability that dictates that success, not averages—and probability also insures long-term losses since the chances of averages being sustained over any significant extended play are slight.

In the "How to Think" column in the *Washington Post's* "Horizon" section, discussing "Why the Lottery Is a Bad Bet," Robert Hershey tried to explain: "If you flip a coin 200 times, you [may predict that it's] going to come out fairly close to 100 heads and 100 tails. If you flip it 2,000 times, it's going to come out even closer to 1,000 heads and 1,000 tails." One attentive reader, Ferdie Wang of Bethesda, caught the flaw in the reasoning or at least in the explanation:

> No, no, no! This is precisely what many people understand to be the "law of averages," but it is totally incorrect. . . .
>   Many people believe that, if you've gotten a lot of heads, tails must start coming up to even things out. The gambler who has suffered a long run of bad luck truly believes that, because of the "law of averages," things must change for the better soon. Unfortunately, in reality things simply do not balance out in raw numbers; they balance out only *in relation* to the total number of trials.[1]

"The sun will come out tomorrow," Annie says, no matter how many days it rains. But if you "bet your bottom dollar" on the mythic law of averages as a basis for meteorological forecasts, you better have a Daddy Warbucks around to pay your losses.

Myth 3. Gambling is intrinsically evil, immoral, sinful—indeed, one of the Seven Deadly Sins.

> Sometimes I think it's a sin
> When I feel like I'm winning when I'm losing again.

Gordon Lightfoot

Dispelling this myth requires historical perspective.[2] The thinking of the late Middle Ages, when much of the morality of Christianity was codified, was characterized by a sense of order and orderliness, with a premium on such qualities as symmetry, balance, and neat hierarchies, arrangements that would impose rational structure on an apparently chaotic, meaningless universe. If there were Seven Deadly Sins, for example, there must also be Seven Cardinal Virtues. The septet of Pride, Avarice, Gluttony, Wrath, Covetousness, Lechery, and Sloth persists in our cultural heritage, though perhaps not as vividly as that of Doc, Sleepy, Sneezy, Grumpy, Bashful, Happy, and Dopey, which may suggest that historical Christianity is not the sole source of mythical heptads.

Dante is probably our best model of the medieval mindset, with his organized circles of the damned in the Inferno, but perhaps our best enactment of the ways sin could be depicted—prior to Breughel, at least—is in the *Canterbury Tales* of Geoffrey Chaucer. There we have a sermon-cum-exemplum delivered by the Pardoner to illustrate the text *radix malorum est cupiditas* "avarice is the root of [all] evil."

"The Pardoner's Tale" concerns three "revelers" whose downfall is the direct result of their greed, but they are characterized as comprehensive sinners, whose wanton behavior includes lechery, blasphemy (a type of wrath), overindulgence in food and drink, and idleness typified by gambling. What the tale ultimately shows, with Chaucer's characteristic irony, is that it is pride, after all, not avarice, that kills the revelers because they set out to destroy Death: the presumption of taking on the function of Christ is the deadliest of the sins. (The Pardoner's own pride is thus revealed to be his most damnable flaw, worse even than his hypocritical sermon against his own arrantly avaricious ways.)

Chaucer's revelers are guilty of sloth, as idle gamblers, but it is guilt by association—the taverns they frequent being the natural venue for gambling as well as drinking and wanton carousing. But how did sloth (accidie, *acedia*) subsume gambling as a type of sinful idleness? The fact is that the church fathers had a hard time with sloth. A common observation, particularly among sardonic observers, is that it shouldn't be considered a sin at all, since the truly slothful person couldn't be bothered with committing any of the other sins. Anomie is a bulwark against sinning and a barrier to visiting the occasions of sin. In order to give sloth its due as a deadly sin, medieval churchmen took the common association of gambling with idleness and made gambling a type of sloth, balancing the gravity of that sin with the other deadlies by the weight added to less illustrative practices of laziness or anomie.[3]

In a remarkable exercise of revisionist history, they assumed scriptural authority for their balancing act in the report found in all four gospels of the Roman soldiers dicing for the raiment of the crucified Jesus. It is, clearly, a scene of horror that evokes moral indignation. But in context, the horror comes not from the act of playing with dice—a commonly accepted practice, a minor perquisite for soldiers who drew the undesired duty of execution—but from the fact that they are oblivious of the sacred quality of *that particular* clothing worn by one who was not one of the common thieves whose fate he shared. Indeed, that is part of the tragic irony of the greatest story.

In the Old Testament there is at least one example of gambling that carries anything but moral disapprobation. The story of Samson as told in Judges involves a substantial wager placed on a riddling game (a motif common in many traditions from Hellenic to Celtic and Germanic) at his first wedding to a daughter of the Philistines (not Delilah but "she of Timnah," as Milton calls her, the gentile wife who inspires Samson's parents to ask, "What, you can't find a nice Hebrew girl?").

Medieval rabbis did not condemn Samson's gambling, even though the stakes were so high that in order to pay off his loss he had to slay thirty men of Ashkelon. The woman's wheedling of Samson's secrets from him and her betrayal of them to her countrymen, actions that prefigure Delilah's perfidy, are examples of *crooked* gambling: the bettors win dishonestly, and that is what is seen as evil here. But the risk, the staking of wagers on a contest of skill or art or wit (especially as the fixed outcome of the game preserves Samson's belligerent allegiance to his people and his god), is no less honorable than the bets laid on the chariot races during the funeral games in the *Iliad* or the implicit wagering on the celebratory horse races in *Beowulf* (has there ever been horse racing without betting?).

It is only by false analogy, guilt by association, the aesthetic standard of symmetry, and the deletion of explanatory context, then, that gambling itself was labeled a sin by churchly fiat. Its sinfulness is not intrinsic but conditionally imposed. If idleness is the occasion of gambling, so is it potentially the occasion of reading or meditating or even of prayer. Occasions for sin may also evoke kindness, charity, mitzvot, or genuine godliness.

Despite the medieval codification, Christian churches have acknowledged in many ways the potential benefits, if not virtues, of gambling. The most obvious example is church-house bingo (whether for "charity" or society or profit). Another example is an annual occasion of dicing on the altar of All Saints Parish Church of St. Ives in Cambridgeshire, England (from 1675 to the present[4]), with each of six winning children being awarded a Bible for their luck/skill. Finally, consider some colonial history in North America. The Jamestown, Virginia, colony was itself financed by lotteries. And Puritan New England, where the prevailing attitudes condemned and prohibited any activity that provided earthly pleasure or excitement, including gambling, nevertheless resorted to lotteries in order to finance not only public roads and buildings but also to endow such educational institutions as Harvard, Yale, Dartmouth, Brown, and Williams (more southerly campuses, such as Princeton, Penn, and North Carolina, were similarly endowed).

It is in the corruption of gambling, the subversion of the fair or sporting chance, that evil or immorality or sinfulness may be found. Gambling per se is found innocent of inherent taint, however commonly it may lead to evil, immoral, sinful side effects or by-products. And however widely disseminated, the moral judgment against gambling is doctrine without essence, dogma without appropriate authority, that is, an artifact of pure myth.

Yet it is a myth that has retained powerful currency in our culture. In 1988, John Rosecrance's monograph *Gambling without Guilt* described a significant shift away from that attitude, but the very need for such a study suggests the persistence of the myth. Once regarded as a proper activity for upper-class gentlemen and nobility (see Castiglione's *Book of the Courtier*, that Renaissance handbook for de rigueur behavior and curricula), gambling became emblematic of the moral degradation of the aristocracy in eighteenth-century and Victorian England. George Eliot includes the theme in her encyclopedic novel *Middlemarch*, probably the richest artistic rendering of Victorian values and attitudes, while in recent years both Charles Palliser's *Quincunx*, an elaborate and witty re-creation of nineteenth-century conventions, and Thomas Pynchon's *Mason & Dixon*, an elegant tour de force that outdoes its own eighteenth-century models of fictional sophistication, employ the motif to good (tragic, comic, and melodramatic) effect.[5]

Perhaps the best modern example occurs in Malcolm Lowry's masterpiece, *Under the Volcano* (masterfully brought to the screen in John Huston's 1984 version with Albert Finney's stirring performance as the Consul, Geoffrey Fermin). The tragic downfall and moral collapse of the hero takes places in a remote Mexican brothel, where the ultimate depravity to which his alcoholism has led not only brings together drunkenness, prostitution, betrayal, fascism, and murder in vividly degenerate forms, but also features cockfighting with wildly exuberant betting.

That myths are perpetuated in cultural conventions, however, is no argument for their historical or philosophical authenticity, only for the staying power—and artistic utility—of the beliefs they embody. Moreover, cultural conventions typically outlast the underlying beliefs themselves. (Virgil and his audience no longer literally believed that the gods, in a variety of disguises, interfaced with humans, but he used that notion to good effect in *The Aeneid* and his audience appreciated the device.) The belief in the inherent evil of gambling has its utility, too—not only artistic, but political and perhaps social as well—but it is based on a myth and its derivative cultural conventions.

Myth 4. Gambling means *getting something for nothing* and is therefore dishonest and immoral.

> You have to play to win.
> **Advertising slogan** for the Maryland Lottery

This misguided notion may be seen to underlie both the moralistic and the legalistic condemnations of gambling as sin and crime. On the other hand, it may be a *reductio ad absurdum* that derives from those condemnations. I see no way to resolve such a chicken-egg question, nor is such resolution necessary to demolish the myth itself.[6]

There is no gamble without risk, stake, investment. The ancient proverb "Nothing ventured, nothing gained," assumes new authority, validity, and appropriateness for American capitalism. It is a perfect refutation of the something-for-nothing nonsense. To take a gamble is to "put your money where your mouth is," that is, to put *something on the line* rather than the empty boast (the "nothing") of the non-gamble. "Put up or shut up" is a challenge to gamble. The something that is to be put up may be money itself (or credit), a token that represents actual money, or something tangible that may be measurable in money. But it may also be something else, intangible and priceless, like reputation, integrity, honor, expertise, loyalty, et al.

Moreover, there are likely to be other components of the "something" that refutes the assertion of this myth. To take a chance, to make a bet, to gamble at all, may very well involve an investment of time, thought, energy (both physical and emotional), hope, or even a perception of one's happiness or future. Take the most extreme case, where a person buys a single lottery ticket on the chance of winning many millions of dollars, a very considerable something for *practically* nothing. I would argue that the fleeting moment and the trivial amount of the purchase constitutes only part of what is "put up"; that there is also an investment of a piece of oneself, a staking of elements of belief and value systems.[7]

Such a gamble is not entirely "throwing away" a small amount of money. It expresses acceptance of the notion that "someone has to win, why not me?"—that is, a belief in long-shot possibilities on level playing fields. It is also, however minuscule, an expression of belief in the integrity of a (bureaucratic) system and (implicit) acceptance of and reliance on the official rationale for such a system. It is much more accurate in this case to talk about getting nothing for something than vice versa.

Indeed, "getting nothing for something" is the applicable phrase for losers in gambling, while winners get something for the multiple somethings of their gamble. "Something for nothing" is applicable to "windfall profits" or "found money" or unforeseen inheritances (though forgotten good deeds may have been big somethings in such cases). To name gambling "something for nothing" is a misunderstanding, a misguided, misapplied, misdirected mistake—a misnomer of monstrous mythic proportions.

Myth 5. Gambling and crime are inextricably interconnected.

Like other broad generalizations, this one is valid in occasional, specific applications. But it flies in the face of reality in many aspects.[8] I have isolated five mistaken notions that derive from the seminal myth:

A. Legal policy and precedent, along with the criminal justice system, have consistently enforced reasonable legislation against gambling.

B. The war on crime includes a campaign to eliminate illegal gambling.

C. Legalizing certain forms of gambling effectively eliminates illegal gambling.

D. Organized crime controls illegal gambling, so that every time you place a bet with a bookie the money you lose ends up financing drug trafficking, prostitution, white slavery, loan sharking, money laundering, labor racketeering, truck hijacking, and jewelry heists (what? no terrorism or illegal campaign contributions?).

E. Gambling is a victimless crime.

Myth 5A. Gambling legislation and jurisprudence make sense. In *Milton's Teeth and Ovid's Umbrella*, Michael Olmert cites a plaque on a pub wall proclaiming a warning from the Betting, Gaming, & Lotteries Act of 1963: "With the permission of the manager only cribbage, dominoes and certain games *of pure skill* may be played for small stakes" (94). Olmert calls this not "merely a sign of the times" but the compression of "most of the history of wagering into 21 words, most important the notions of controlling the stakes, prescribing the games to be bet on, and hammering home the distinction between games of skill and games of chance."

That distinction is frequently made but not with any consistency or clear definitions. In the United States, Olmert points out, "the bias at gambling resorts is against games of skill and toward chance" (96). He cites the example of casinos attempting to bar card counters from their blackjack tables because they turn "what the law says should be a game of chance . . . into a 'game of skill.'" Even more bizarre are the legalized poker houses in some California jurisdictions where varieties of *draw* poker are sanctioned as games of skill but varieties of *stud* poker are banned as games of chance.[9] By contrast, the poker game chosen for the World Series of Poker in Las Vegas is Texas Hold 'Em, a variety of seven-card stud with two cards dealt down to each player and five common cards turned face up.[10]

Thomas M. Kavanagh has described the way such distinctions were made in France, where between 1643 and 1777 no fewer than thirty-two "royal and parliamentary edicts" prohibited gambling, an exercise in futility since there was gambling everywhere, especially in the capital:

> In Paris action could be found in any number of different settings. Because they were ideal for police surveillance and justified as a kind of public safety valve, there were ten authorized *maisons de jeux* in the capital where . . . gambling was allowed so long as it was on what were considered *jeux de commerce* as opposed to *jeux de hasard*—games such as piquet, trictrac, triomphe, and mediateur, in which the skill of the gambler was seen as playing a larger role than the purely chance-driven turning of a card or picking of a number. In fact, the *jeux de commerce* usually served as little more

than a front for the far more lucrative *jeux de hasard*—basset, pharaon, biribi, lansquenet, loto—played in the backrooms of the same establishments. (30)

Plus ça change, plus c'est la même chose.

The Dutch psychologist Willem Wagenaar found that the "public's ability to distinguish games of chance and games of skill is irrelevant when the attractiveness of games is more determined by the reward structure, than by the mechanism by which the winner is selected" (85). If distinctions between skill and chance seem arbitrary anyway, what are we to make of the accompanying class distinctions? While the authorities attempted to control and limit public gambling in Paris, the court at Versailles was a scene of continuous, high-stakes action. Louis XIV is alleged to have encouraged nobles to lose fortunes—in appropriately courtly good grace—in order to minimize the risk of revolt. In successive regimes, queens, dukes, and princesses instituted their own games as regular features of their daily routine. Nobility at large seized on the royal model and instituted private games at home where they thrived on the house take from hoca, biribi, pharaon, and cavagnole—the very games prohibited to commoners in public.

Historically, the laws have had little effect in controlling the action. Some lotteries are legal (typically when they benefit the royal treasury), some illegal (private enterprise, venture capitalism), but lotteries are ubiquitous. Anyone looking to Daniel Defoe's *The Gamester* (1719) in hopes of finding the author of *Moll Flanders* exploring in prose fiction the popularity and corruption in London's eighteenth-century gambling culture will be disappointed. Instead, *The Gamester* will be found to be an eighteen-page pamphlet, with the elaborate subtitle, "A Benefit-Ticket For all that are concern'd in the Lotteries; or the Best Way how to get the 20,000 l. Prize Together with Some necessary and reasonable Remarks on the Schemes of Insurance relating to the present Lotteries."

There follows a statistical analysis of the probabilities of winning, while calculating the unfavorable option of selling shares in tickets to "insurance" speculators. The implied market for such a publication, however, suggests the prevalence of lotteries, while more effectively suggestive is a remark of Defoe regarding the "Follies and Vices of the Age": "The most reigning and predominant one amongst us, which in most Places of publick Resort ever occurs to View, and tends most to debauch our Manners, and ruin the Nation, viz. Gaming."

Prominent among the follies of our age is the popularity of official (state-run) lotteries. The prevalence of illegal numbers or policy rackets in the cities has suggested the presence of a consistent, ready-made source of revenue. That the lotteries do not *replace* the numbers will be addressed in Myth 5C below, but their discriminatory nature is relevant here. In the first place, it has been clearly demonstrated that, except for the enormous payoffs of the multi-state lotto drawings that generate heavy middle-class action, the lotteries are a form of regressive taxation. Working-class and underclass people participate far out of proportion to their ability to supply funding for education, infrastructure, sports authorities, or whatever rationalization supports the enabling legislation.

But what seems never to occur to those who equate lotteries with "policy" is how integral a part of inner-city cultures the numbers rackets may be. The daily deposit of quarters or even dimes on the chance of a favorite lucky number paying off is often a localized ritual, similar in some ways to regular collections of burial insurance and some forms of religious tithing, supporting community identity and community-based operations.

No, finally, it is safe to say that consistency, coherence, and rational distinctions are conspicuous by their absence from the laws concerning gambling. Neither here nor abroad, neither now nor at any time in history, have I found really sensible legislation or edict enacted, never mind enforced.[11]

Myth 5B. The war on crime eliminates illegal gambling.
Law enforcement has typically taken an ambivalent attitude toward gambling. In the first place, wherever and whenever gambling laws have been enacted they have been selectively enforced. In the second place, such laws are inevitably accompanied by corruption; both the laws and the gambling activities they legislated against have therefore been favored and indeed courted by law enforcement agencies. On the other hand, honest law enforcement personnel have been indulgent toward gambling—in part out of consideration for the relative innocuousness of the "crime"; in part because of cost-benefit considerations of detection and prosecution, as well as the leniency of the courts in conviction and sentencing; and in part because of a sense of the hypocrisy that accompanies the unenforceability of such laws.

Police, then, either wink benignly at gambling or are paid off to allow gamblers the privilege to operate. Either way, the attitude is "no harm done." Political reformers sometimes campaign on promises to crack down on illegal gambling. In many a jurisdiction in two-party heartland America, this has brought about a curious cycle in which gambling is banned in a town but flourishes in the same county outside city limits—until the reformers take hold countywide, whereupon the sheriffs banish it from the county only to see it resurrected inside city limits. I know of one local bookmaker who maintained two offices and two sets of phones, so regularly was he required to move his operation between county and town.

A third facet of the ambivalence relates to the federal "war" against organized crime. Though enforcement of local laws against gambling is reserved to the sovereign states by the Constitution, the Crime Control Acts of 1968 and 1970 gave the federal government the right to enforce such laws by expanding its wiretapping capabilities. Add the expanded definition of interstate commerce to include the dissemination of "gambling information" across state lines by electronic means, and then the proliferating spawn of so-called RICO laws (Racketeer Influenced and Corrupt Organization Acts), and law enforcement agencies have potent weapons to wage that war, if they so choose, against illegal gambling operations of any kind.

But skirmishes of this nature are often considered Pyrrhic victories by law enforcement agencies. Insofar as gambling has been a function of organized crime, it has also served as the easiest way to penetrate the mobs and their criminal practices and plans. I have it from reliable sources both inside the law enforcement community and among their presumed targets that it had long been a practice of the FBI, for example, to cultivate gambling "connections," virtually guaranteeing them the privilege of continuing operations in exchange for access to useful information about more serious criminal activities. To shut down the gambling was to close the window of opportunity for successful prosecution of hard-core gangster activity.

"Vice" crimes are typically manipulated in this way, as in the employment of prostitutes and low-level drug runners as informants on heavier street crime. Overt corruption is one thing; vested interest in keeping selected criminals in business is another. The war on crime sometimes involves actions against gamblers (and some of those times involve the need for easy convictions), but it is in the larger interests of that war and those who wage it to allow illegal gambling to continue—and to maintain a legal system that keeps it criminalized.

Myth 5C. Legalized gambling drives out illegal gambling.   This notion is actually still used by proponents of new enabling legislation for legalized gambling, when experience demonstrates that it never works that way. The record is clear, with the American evidence replicating the results in Britain and Australia.[12] Wherever and whenever gambling is legalized, instead of illegal gambling being reduced, it in fact increases.

In some jurisdictions, apparently, the initial offerings of government-sanctioned and -operated lotteries have made temporary inroads on the illegal numbers or policy rackets. But within a short time the illegal operations are handling as much action as ever.[13] And wherever and whenever gambling in some form is newly legitimized or decriminalized, other forms of illegal gambling inevitably experience a heightening of interest and activity.

In his famous essay "Where the Action Is," Erving Goffman wrote, "Strangers in town can ask the local cabby where the action is and probably gain entry when they get there" (200). With two friends I was able to verify that claim on a first Saturday night of May in Louisville, Kentucky. After the Derby and dinner, we hailed a cab and asked the driver to take us where there was some action. He asked no questions, announcing that the biggest games in town were at a large (chain) motel, but we were disappointed to find nothing going on there. Undaunted, he drove us across town to a used car dealership where a large mobile home housed a lively craps table. A hundred thousand people had come to Churchill Downs for legal parimutuel wagering that day, but a substantial number of them would also be engaged in illegal forms of gambling before the weekend was over. Derby weekend in Louisville, after all, was the setting for high-stakes billiards play in The Hustler (in Robert Rossen's movie; in the original Walter Tevis novel, the action is in Lexington after a day at the races at Keeneland).

Racetracks are favorite haunts for bookies, who often do business there. Even in these days of simulcasts from other tracks with parimutuel betting, many tracks will show football games on Saturdays and Sundays on some of their TV screens. Do you suppose that crowds of race-going horse players do not bet, at least among themselves, on those games, that they do not know the point spread, or that there are not people available to take their action? In some cases, the operators of racetracks will condone or actively encourage bookmakers to set up shop in the grandstands and clubhouse (chapter 3 tells of a parallel case of this kind of activity, though not at a racetrack). In this way, they can connive at controlling the payoffs on certain races by having some of the handle not recorded in the tote machines. There is also a more general principle involved, one which is demonstrated by certain street corners where four different gas stations are clustered or certain strips where every fast-food burger chain is hawking its wares cheek by jowl with the competitors.

Gamblers will go where the action is, and the more action available, the more interest there will be in those sites. The current trend is toward the installation of slot machines at racetracks. Maryland has kept slot machines from its tracks so far, but the action generated by slots at tracks in Delaware and West Virginia is drawing customers across state lines and draining resources from Maryland racing. Instead of siphoning money from the racing tote machines, the slots generate business directly and indirectly: they draw more active gamblers to the track, they generate the circulation of money, they often contribute to the maintenance of an appealing ambience at the track, and they allow the tracks to increase purses and thus attract more entries of higher quality animals, in turn making the races more attractive betting propositions.

In Nevada, where sports betting is legal, illegal bookies are ubiquitous. Given the accessibility of sports books and their casino-backed ability to handle huge wagers, is it any surprise that when bookies lay off bets and bookies' bookies lay them off, the end of the layoff chain is Las Vegas? The size of the legal handle on sporting events in Nevada is overwhelmingly dwarfed by the illegal handle throughout the gambling land. The national line is set in Las Vegas, but when Vegas moves the line it is in response to money pouring in elsewhere and from elsewhere on one side of a proposition.

Bookies operate successfully in Nevada for some of the same reasons that legal gambling does not drive out illegal gambling elsewhere: illegal numbers can offer better odds and accept smaller denominations of bets; bookies, like numbers runners, can offer and accept bets on credit; and winnings can go unreported and untaxed. (For some people there is an added frisson to certain action *because* it is illegal.) Casinos take markers from high-rolling players, but they expect timely payoffs. They may also indirectly extend credit, by serving as vendors for credit card companies—but there is generally a hefty, discouraging service charge involved. Unless and until legalized forms of gambling can match or exceed the services, pleasures, and advantages offered by illegal gambling operators, the latter will continue to thrive wherever the former may be, whether in their shadow or in their face.

Myth 5D. Illegal gambling is a subsidiary of organized crime.
There may have been a time when organized crime outfits maintained their own bookmaking operations, along with the ancillary activity of loan-sharking. There may also have been a time when bookies paid off mobsters for the privilege of operating in their "territory" or for protection or for access to layoff centers. (Ironically, they may also have been paying off the police for some of the same services.) But that, as they say, is history.

In my files is an eleven-page letter from a literate bookmaker (not an oxymoron, stereotypes to the contrary notwithstanding) of my acquaintance, which says, ". . . there are very few 'bookies' left. By 'bookies' I mean those who, by virtue of the fact that they have two-way action on a game, can have the vigorish going for them on each and every game, and, therefore, are sure of the ten percent going for them. In other words, the 'bookie' will make a profit on every game." He went on to say that most people who take bets "these days" are in fact gamblers, who benefit from the vigorish as always but are always at risk of being inundated by bettors on the "right" side of any game because their action is typically one-sided on almost every game. This is partly the function of most bookies operating as small-time independent operators, partly the inhibitions against laying off bets due to the interstate antigambling legislation, and partly because no "institutionalized" syndicate stands behind them in proprietary, silent-partner, or avuncular positions. Besides, a significant percentage of bookies is made up of gamblers who take bets in order to support their own habit, like addicts who deal drugs.[14]

In all candor I should say that this letter was a more than gracious response to my request that the bookie evaluate a draft of the chapter ("The Serpent in the Garden") concerning point-shaving scandals in my history of college basketball (*All the Moves*). More to the point, the letter is dated 1973. In the more than a quarter century since, the trends that he identified have continued and expanded. There may yet survive some old-timers with "family" allegiance who answer to and are patronized by some vestigial organized crime outfits. (I heard rumors of one just recently, an octogenarian operating a handbook in Staten Island after his release from Attica.) But almost all the illegal sports betting action now is handled either by independents or by organized gambling networks—as distinguished from organized crime mobs. If you want to open an account with a bookie now, you don't have to ask who is bankrolling him; as linesmaker Bob Martin says, "The only thing you need to know is does he pay off when he loses."

There are many reasons for this. One is the relative unprofitability of bookmaking, compared to drug trafficking or the many quasi-legal scams and businesses that organized crime has become involved with. Another is that sports betting is so widely tolerated and so openly practiced that serious criminals cannot risk involvement in known, readily accessible (though illegal) operations.

Remember that the Boston College point-shaving scandal of a few years ago came to light because of an ongoing investigation into an armored-car heist. As a result of that inadvertence, at least three ongoing investigations of point shaving in other parts of the country had to be terminated because criminal sources suddenly ceased providing information. Sports betting and serious felonious activity are no longer natural bedfellows. In fact, they are in opposing corners. Criminals may want to corrupt sporting events and athletes, but bookies' business is based on credit, trust, and faith—hardly the value system of crime, organized or other.

Bookies must depend on the integrity of the games; if they are going to be caught on the "wrong" side of a game, at least let it be an honest game. The latest pair of well-publicized cases of college basketball point shaving (Arizona State and Northwestern, both in 1994) are instructive here. In both cases, the fixers got to players who had run up big debts betting on games; and in both cases, the point shaving came to light not through law enforcement or institutional vigilance but because bookmakers identified unusual betting patterns and alerted the authorities.

At least two widely held beliefs stem from this surviving mythology. One is the stereotypical bookie with his guaranteed profits (and his leg-breaking goons to intimidate welshers). He may yet be found, but most likely on the big and little screens from Hollywood scripts and in the comic strips. Yet even so sophisticated an observer of sports betting as George Ignatin falls into this fallacy. Noting appropriately that "amounts wagered with bookmakers are usually underestimated," he goes on to say that "the net income of bookmakers is typically overestimated" (168). The latter point is no doubt accurate, too, but Ignatin supports it by a mathematical accounting that is based on the myth of *balanced action*.

The other residual notion based on some mythologically projected image of bookies is that their betting lines, their point spreads, are *predictions* of the outcomes of games. Through their networks of inside sources and information, they can "handicap" a game so accurately as to provide equal sporting opportunities on either side. But a linesmaker succeeds or fails not on the basis of his game predictions but on the basis of his ability to predict how a point spread will divide the betting action. He is the merchandiser of a number. The goal is to protect the bookmaking establishment, to approach the rarely achieved ideal of a nationally balanced book.

That is why, to give a famous historical example, the line that Bob Martin put out in Las Vegas for Super Bowl III made the Colts a seventeen-point favorite over the Jets. After two weeks of betting, the game kicked off with Baltimore at -18. As a prediction, that was as far off the mark as one could get, but Martin was justly proud of the number because the public bet with both hands—on both sides of the proposition. Martin knew that Namath's Jets were much better than the line suggested, but what he had *predicted* was that the number he posted would protect bookies from having to gamble on their biggest-action day of the year. There was no coup for organized crime, no matter how many gamblers frequented Broadway Joe's saloon. But it was a nice payday for bookies, who approached the ideal of a five percent profit on their total handle.

Myth 5E. Gambling is a victimless crime.   If gambling is a victimless crime, so is war. Combatants who engage in the conflicts more or less willingly are not the only casualties. Civilian casualties, in terms of family members alone who are victimized by an individual succumbing to pathological gambling, are many times greater in number than the gamblers themselves. The family structure itself is often threatened, weakened, or totally destroyed. But there are other victims as well: clients or patients of professionals, associates of businessmen, employers themselves in terms of lost worker-hours and in many cases of direct losses by theft, embezzlement, even purloined ("borrowed") payrolls. Bankruptcy leads to losses by creditors.[15] Social costs also include diminished services, dilution of funds, and so forth. The damaged lives may be measured not narrowly by the number of suicides, derelicts, prisoners, the institutionalized, and the impoverished, but must broadly include multiples of others. Once it becomes clear that many innocents are victimized by the affliction of a relative few, appropriate attention may be given to examination of causes and prevention of pathological gambling. As with cancer, early recognition and treatment are key. Just as warfare inevitably produces civilian casualties, the saturation level of gambling in our system necessarily claims victims who, willy-nilly, directly and indirectly, suffer the booby traps of prevailing customs.

So, is gambling a criminal activity? Well, yes, some kinds, sometimes, in some jurisdictions. But there is no necessary correlation between gambling and criminality, except when it is defined as such at specific times in specific places for specific purposes. The other way to answer the question is to say, well, in general, no. And in general, the criminal justice system doesn't have a clue about how to get a handle on it.

Myth 6. The mirror-extremes of motivation:
Gambling is always just about money.
Gambling is never just about money.

> It is no vice to play at dice and cards, unless a man pay it so much attention that he neglects more essential things, or else play for the sole purpose of getting money, or to trick his

friend, or—when he loses—he fumes and carries on so that one would take it as a sign that he gambles only out of greed.

Baldassare Castiglione,
The Book of the Courtier (my paraphrase)

All I want to do is break even—because I need the money.

Popular gambler's lament, a mantra against greed

This myth seems to offer only two polarized, absolute possibilities for explaining why people gamble. Aside from the logical fallacy of the excluded middle, it would seem to contain several affronts to common sense, not least of which is the insistence on a globalizing *always* or *never*. The question of why people gamble—a question raised by the virtually universal presence of gambling in all cultures, times, and places—seems to evoke simple, simple-minded, single-directed answers.

Those answers often reveal the overriding biases and attitudes of the answerers. Basically, they fall into two broad categories, those who (embracing myths 3, 4, and some aspects of 5 above) simply reject gambling as acceptable behavior and those who believe that it has nothing to do with greed or money. The latter category subdivides into those who believe the money stands for something else and those who find other motivations entirely.

Is gambling an expression of universal greed? It is only very recently in the history of gambling that money came to be an issue of any consequence at all. At different times, gambling has been part of religious and other ritual celebrations, has been "play" (precisely in Huizinga's or Caillois's terms), and has been—as Castiglione's codification of courtly behavior advises—simply a gentlemanly thing to do, a diversion, a pastime.

During the Enlightenment, the monetary possibilities intrinsic in gambling, even as a means of redistributing wealth, took on greater significance. Two particular transvaluations that took place during that period are crucial here: the development of probability theory and the "invention" of credit. As much mathematician as philosopher, Blaise Pascal was instrumental in the former movement (he is also often credited with the invention of the modern roulette wheel). The ancient and Renaissance icons of the blind goddess Fortuna and the Wheel of Fortune would be replaced by the ascendant mythos/ethos of science/empiricism/knowledge, that is, Reason.

A masterful summary of this development appears as the first chapter, "The Triumph of Probability Theory," in Kavanagh's *Enlightenment and the Shad-*

ows of Chance. What is most instructive for us is how often the exercises and applications of this theory related to games of chance (dating all the way back, a century before Pascal's correspondence with Fermat, to Galileo's treatise on dice) on the way to the ascension of what Kavanagh calls "the more imperial demeanor of statistics" (9) in the nineteenth century.

Commercial credit, as developed throughout the eighteenth century along with the creation of stock companies, is another concept that replaces the Wheel of Fortune as a vehicle for expressing human hopes and fears. The rise of nationalistic capitalism, beginning in the England of the Restoration (brilliantly contextualized in Rose Zimbardo's *At Zero Point*), yields, among other products and by-products, manifold means for redistributing wealth. The trading of notes of credit as a kind of paper money is itself a kind of gambling, but it also incidentally provides "chips" to be played with in games of chance themselves.

Credit and probability cohere, appropriately, in the career of the Scottish gambler John Law, who, plying his trade with probabilistic precision at Dutch, Italian, and French gaming tables, acquired both a fortune reputed to exceed 100,000 livres and a reputation for astuteness and even prescience. After the death of Louis XIV in 1715, Law persuaded the Regent to accept his financial plan to replenish a depleted treasury by issuing bills based on property rather than gold, ironically a new form of credit to bolster the *ancien régime*.

During the period his System was in operation (1716–1719), Law, as proprietor of the Banque Generale, monopolist of the Compagnie d'Occident (popularly known as the Mississippi Company), and finally comptroller general of finances for France, was responsible for a frenzy of speculations. Fortunes were made and lost. When an attempt to devalue the paper currency cost him and his System their credibility, the colossal gamble of the experiment was terminated, and Law, discredited, disgraced, and in despair for his life, fled the country. He could still support himself through gambling until his death in Venice in 1729, but most of his time was devoted to composing justifications for his System and rationalizing its collapse.

Law's ideas may have failed eighteenth-century France and permanently damaged the old order of landed nobility, but they are the direct ancestors of the operational principles of contemporary finance. As Kavanagh says, Law's cardinal principle of economics—that money is not an end in itself but a tool the value of which increases according to its ability to generate activity (its own volatility, in effect)—is perfectly consonant with "the gambler's disregard for money as money" (75).[16] Credit may be simply the "illusion of wealth" (72), but the phrase may be applied with equal force to money's role in gambling.

Twentieth-century psychological theorists have consistently looked beyond greed to analyze the motivations and mechanisms of gambling. They have made associations with sexuality and pointed to oral fixation, masochism, and anal fixation.[17] Outside the rarefied world of academic theory, popular symbology, too, has suggested that a stack or pile of chips in front of a gambler may sometimes stand for a penis or feces, depending, I suppose, on how they are arranged unconsciously by the player.[18]

An interesting view is that of Kusyszyn, who employs humanistic-existential theories of motivation to conclude that gambling is healthy adult play and that people gamble in order to "confirm their existence and affirm their worth" (136). The question here is whether that *worth* can be measured in terms of money. Can every aspect of the gambler's identity, affect, self-image, and behavior when gambling be quantified in dollar amounts?

It is impossible to say, finally, that gambling of any kind anywhere at any time is just about money or that greed is the exclusive force that drives any gambling machine. It has been argued and demonstrated that people gamble for many reasons: honor and ego, excitement and boredom, values noble and skewed, attitudes healthy and neurotic, concerns public and private, fixations penile and fecal, and more, much more. Besides, winning, in and of itself, may have a value or gratification unrelated to the stakes won—as in a "gentleman's bet," for example.

But to say it is never about money is to ignore the last three hundred years of the history of ideas in western civilization. Whether any gambler, in fact, is motivated by need, greed, or wish for money, or whether the money has some secondary, extraneous, or symbolic significance may be unanswerable in any given case. And that assumes that the question is an either-or proposition to begin with.

Given the multifaceted nature of gambling phenomena and behaviors and the multitudes of personalities who engage in it, the explanations of motivation would have to be nearly infinite—including both pure greed and the complete absence of any greed whatsoever. Sometimes, at least, one would think, a cigar may be just a cigar.

In the movie *Rounders*, the character Knish (John Turturro), a professional poker player, explains his principles of conservative play to the hero, Michael (Matt Damon). "It's all about money," he says. "I've got rent to pay, alimony, child support." Those costs may inevitably *mean* something more or other than money, but Knish's whole purpose in playing and his modus operandi at play are the product of his belief that, in this time of his life, money is just money.

For some, like Vince Lombardi, winning is the only thing. We may also say that, for some, winning means nothing more or other than winning money. We must conclude then that the global assertion that gambling is never just about money must be false. The same reasoning leads us to conclude that the converse globalism—gambling is always just about money—is equally false.

If the result of the game is not important to the play, why do we keep score? In gambling, we keep score in money. But keeping score is not the sole purpose of the game. If, as Wagenaar argues, most gamblers lose and indeed often expect to lose, that does not mean that gambling is never just about money. Yet winning *against all odds* defines a satisfaction that surpasses that of merely gaining money. The persistence of the twin towers of absolutes in this myth underscores the power and appropriateness in Wagenaar's use of the term "paradox" in his title.

"The biggest paradox of gambling," he concludes, "is that gambling exists at all, and that so many people engage in it voluntarily, without consideration of the negative expected value" (117). There is also an apparent paradox in an attempt to explain such paradoxical behavior by one of two mutually exclusive absolutes. These two are so much alike that they fail identically under rational analysis. They are the Tweedledum and Tweedledumber of gambling mythology.

Myth 7. The United States is officially aware of and concerned about the proliferation of gambling in the country and is in the process of working toward establishing an informed, comprehensive public policy.

> Six blind men encounter an elephant for the first time. The first touches its side and says it's a wall. The second touches its trunk and says it's a snake. The third touches its tusk and says it's a spear. The fourth touches its ear and says it's a fan. The fifth touches its leg and says it's a tree. The sixth touches its tail and says it's a rope. A wise rajah comes along and tells them, "It's an elephant, a very large animal, and you must put all its parts together to find out what it's like."

> **Redacted from** Lillian Quigley's version of the ancient Indian folktale *The Blind Men and the Elephant*

Sometimes a myth is promulgated by political rhetoric, that is, propaganda. More than ever, gambling issues have become prime subjects for public posturing, moralistic charges and countercharges, exercises in hypocrisy and disingenuousness—with little regard for developing an informed citizenry or for clarifying the public interest. From local option to federal planning, when it comes to gambling, a climate of cultivated ignorance would seem to be the order of the day.

The Gambling Impact and Policy Commission was established in 1995. It was supposed to express the federal government's determination to take a comprehensive view of gambling. This time the movement to establish a National Commission on Gambling was spearheaded by the introduction of S. 704 by Senators Simon (D-Illinois), Lugar (R-Indiana), and Lieberman (D-Connecticut) and H.R. 497 by Congressman Wolf (R-Virginia). Following the lead of several states, Congress acknowledged the magnitude of the situation and determined to take the necessary steps toward understanding, remedying, and perhaps regulating.

Nonsense! What the enabling legislation did, in effect, was form a committee in order to avoid taking action, to accept the status quo (including elements of free-market laissez-faire, states' rights, and local self-determination), and to perpetuate both the prevailing hypocrisy and the ostrich-like posture implicit in its cant. At no time did the discussion and debate around this legislation even acknowledge the existence of illegal gambling. And yet it should be clear that no public policy that is limited to (and attempts to rationalize) the proliferation of legalized gambling—even if the "social costs" were to be comprehensively addressed, as they have never officially been in any jurisdiction—can make sense without attention to the pervasive presence and pandemic effects of illegal gambling in this society.

All that is necessary to demolish the Pollyanna myth that the federal government is engaged and involved with the realities of gambling in this gambling culture of ours is to examine the results of the National Gambling Impact Study (which Steven Crist, editor of the Daily Racing Form, called a "two-year road show of hearings and reports that failed to produce any meaningful conclusions or recommendations") as published in 1999 in its Executive Summary.

The Commission acknowledges that gambling is a substantial staple of this society but strangely regards it as a very recent phenomenon in cultural history. The National Research Council, by contrast, begins its Critical Review with the observation, "Gambling in America has deep cultural roots" (1).[19] Over and over the Commission seems to throw up its collective hands in the face of gambling issues "so fraught with ingrained moral and philosophical dichotomies and unresolved social questions that no disposition . . . can ever come close to being universally accepted" (9). The "pragmatic" solution? Leave gambling policy up to the states.[20]

Among the Commission's many recommendations, covering a variety of subjects, is a ban of "cruises to nowhere" that are blatant vehicles to escape mainland jurisdictions for gambling purposes. Limited as it is, such a proposal highlights an inability to fathom or deal with the mushrooming opportunities for gambling on the Internet (sports betting, casino gambling, electronic card games, and—perhaps most frightening of all—day trading on the world's financial markets).

Those opportunities, typically with offshore bases, are at best quasi-legal, at worst intricately defended against any monitoring, regulation, or even legislation. But worse still is the Commission's ostrich-like attitude toward illegal gambling. There is no instrument for measuring the extent of illegal gambling activity (unmonitored, untaxed, underground). Estimates range from one third the size of legal gambling's total to its equal. Arguably, when the quasi-legal activity is included, it may be even greater. But where public scrutiny, control, and an enormous taxable business could be the result of legalization, political expediency precludes even a consideration of that option.

What is generally acknowledged, however, is that sports betting comprises the bulk of illegal gambling activity. It is one of the staples of the American sporting/gambling scene. Yet the Commission trivializes it by mentioning it only twice, in reference to its concern for countering an alarming growth of gambling among adolescents. This seems to be a deliberate refusal to acknowledge the significant place of sports betting in our cultural history.

Here is a summary from the authoritative history, *The Games They Played: Sports in American History, 1865–1980*, by Douglas Noverr and Lawrence Ziewacz:

> Another factor that must be considered in the growth of sport from 1865 to 1900 is the role of betting. Americans had been notorious for betting on cockfights, bullbaiting, and ratbaiting. . . . With the development of baseball, a legitimate sport, one could now bet on an event without the fear or threat of arrest. Bets could be placed in any number of places, such as saloons, cigar stores, factories, and ballparks. Betting on sports was a natural extension for urban subcommunities that were rife with gambling. (15)
>
> Betting [on games of the National Association of Professional Baseball Players, established in 1871] was heavy, with bookmakers often having their

booths out in the open. Players were often accused, and sometimes rightly so, of dropping games because of bribes. (21)

In the [nineteen] sixties football replaced baseball as the most popular national sport. . . . The football pool with its obsession on the point spread became a fixture in offices, factories and bars across the country. (260)

One need only add basketball and its NCAA tournament to bring this summary up to date.

These are but a few of the signs of the Commission's inadequacy. When the time comes that government, keeping the social welfare, the protection of the rights of individuals, and the satisfaction of people's needs always in mind, accepts its appropriate roles with respect to gambling as legislation, regulation, taxation, and education, then we may find a way to formulate a coherent public policy. Government's roles in instituting, managing, and promoting gambling operations may then be brought to account under the general question of why governments should be in the gambling business at all. Until then, this myth will be perpetuated, and the people will continue to be told that government is comprehensively concerned with protecting them from the evils of gambling, though in some forms it is all right and may even be encouraged.

Collectively, these myths embody the prevailing state of common "knowledge" about gambling in the culture at large and the conventional wisdom that presides over our attitudes, values, and practices. They must be seen as the empty vessels they are if we are to get a grip on the situation. (My metaphors suggest a kind of cultural hand-eye coordination.) As a nation we gamble more and more, not really knowing what we are about, what risks we run. The more we understand what gambling is, how it works, and what it involves, the better will we be able to guard against the risks it poses to individuals, families, and the society at large. It's not going to go away; it's an integral part of our systems and institutions. We must learn to live with it; to be informed, aware, and vigilant; to guard against the pathologies it engenders or signals; and humanely to treat those who fall victim to it. That plural form—pathologies—signals the primary thrust of the following chapters, a debunking of the myth of a single condition that has been mislabeled compulsive gambling.

Gambling is the only thing where nothing depends on nothing.

Dostoevsky

Nothing will come of nothing.

King Lear

The gambler's life is a rhythmic tale of numbers, premonitions, symbols and dreams. He worships magic, and is magic's willing victim. But within all these cycles and prismatic mysteries, he must fight to maintain a fingerhold on ordinary reality.

Don DeLillo

Gambling and the Irrational

 G ambling, which by definition depends on risk and uncertainty, necessarily involves the irrational. Chance, luck, random occurrence—these are not the stuff of reason. Nor, for the purposes of the distinctions I am making here, is belief in some unknowable system of fate or preordained pattern or predestination. Clearly, belief in any of the myths enumerated in the first chapter is itself a matter of irrational faith. Probability, on the other hand, is another matter entirely: "the house" (the proprietors or purveyors or operators of any gambling activity, with the odds on their side) is a rational entrepreneurial entity, not a gambling venture, which profits from the irrationality of the gambling customers, the players, the bettors, the wishers, the wannabe-winners, the punters and plungers.[1]

In many of the courses I have taught in recent years (including "Literature of Gambling and the Gambler"), I have stressed the distinctions among cognitive processes. Early entries in students' journals in those courses typically use constructions like *believe, suppose, accept on faith, have been taught, have the opinion,* and *understand* as interchangeable with *think.* I try to teach my students to think about their thinking—so that when they think they are thinking, they should be aware of the presuppositions, implications, and consequences of what they say they are thinking. I try to get them to consider what they mean when they say they *know* something. And I urge them to try to distinguish between active and passive thinking, so that constructions like *it seems to me, it popped into my head, it suddenly dawned on me,* and *it came to me in a flash* (not to mention *a little bird told me* or *I have always known*) are understood as qualitatively different from "I have reasoned my way to the tentative conclusion that. . . ."

It is not my intention, here or in my classroom, to make value judg-
ments about cognitive processes, to establish a hierarchy of "thinkings." I do
not mean to denigrate faith any more than I would dismiss the enrichment
of human experience by such irrational cognitive processes as inspiration,
dreaming, insight, hoping, meditation, acceptance of paradox, et al. The immediate purpose is to demonstrate the essential connection between gambling and the irrational, the better to understand why and how irrationality
may cross the line to pathology. Wouldn't it be surprising if gambling behaviors, related as they are so substantially to the absence of reason, did not ever
go past the point of "loss of judgment" to the begetting or representing or
exaggeration of an inherent potential for mental pathology? If gambling is
based on irrational states, those states may become unhealthy.

Aspects of irrationality to be considered here move from the elementary
belief in luck to such prevalent accoutrements of gambling behaviors as superstition, ritual, and paraphernalia. This train of thought will lead to considerations of "magical thinking," "primary process thinking," and "ideas of
reference," all universal parts of human mental functioning, but clearly unhealthy when excessive or dominant. Common phenomena of gamblers'
mental states also include feelings of prescience, omniscience, and even
omnipotence, which remind us again of the various applications of the verb
"to know" in our human arsenal.[2]

I do not intend in this short chapter to explore the many varied and
storied enactments of neurotic states in gambling behavior (though some of
them will necessarily be touched on in later chapters), nor will I take examples from those gambling behaviors which evidence psychotic states, where
gamblers are totally out of touch with reality (the focus of chapter 7); what
I am interested in suggesting at this point are the ways in which "normal"
gambling behavior is irrational.[3] Along these lines, I will address two additional subjects. One is the array of common phenomena that show gambling
as a ritual enactment of aggressiveness. The other is the commonly perceived
phenomenon of timelessness, or being unaware of the passage of time, in
gambling.

So pervasive is the assumption that gambling and gamblers are irrational
that it is readily accepted in popular culture and mass media as a basis for the
ludicrous, the inane, the zany, the comic—in attitude, behavior, personality,
and incident. No better example comes to mind than the 1989 Paramount
movie Let It Ride, directed by Joe Pytka from a screenplay by Ernest Morton,
which follows very closely its source, the 1979 novel GoodVibes by Jay Cronley.

The book's title suggests the feel-good mood of the movie as it follows the main character, Trotter (Richard Dreyfuss), through his day at the track. "Fugue for Tinhorns" from *Guys and Dolls*, that playful-artful anthem to horse-race handicapping is the music over the credits at the start of the movie, as we are introduced to a habitual losing gambler and his cronies. Trotter's loving marriage to Pam (Teri Garr) has been put at risk because of his gambling, but in an early scene at a Chinese restaurant he pledges to mend his ways. After his night shift as a cabdriver, he's going to be allowed to come back home and they will start over—without gambling.

Unfortunately, his fortune cookie says, "Sometimes you could be walking around lucky and not know it." Later, on a doughnut break, his best buddy, another cabby and racetrack regular whose other habit is to secretly tape the conversations of his passengers, plays a segment for Trotter. It turns out to be a plan for a fixed race on the next day's card, so Trotter must go to the track after all, regardless of his well-intended pledge to Pam.

The movie necessarily omits or severely telescopes some background material from the book, but some of Cronley's musings are instructive. Trotter's "rational" rationalization in the novel can evoke the comic anticlimax that stands the intended explanation on its head in a kind of conceptual slapstick: "The thing about gambling that is so appealing, in addition to control— after all YOU get to pick—and in addition to the possibility of a nice score, is that with gambling you can make a bet even though you don't have a boot to piss in. Gambling functions on the honor system whereby a person gives his word to pay if he loses, then if for some reason he doesn't, somebody comes by and kidnaps his kid or beats up his wife or pulls his ears off, depending on what he owes" (22).

Trotter is clearly a pretty bright guy, like many comic protagonists or rogue heroes too smart for their own good. He *knows*, for example,

> all about gamblers and why they gambled. Some guys . . . gambled because they were shy and couldn't make friends the conventional way, like shaking hands instead of palming some bookie a hundred. Some guys gambled because they had trouble at home, or at work. Gambling, you see, is a major diversion, kind of like sex, only with gambling you never know who's going to win. Also, with gambling, as opposed to with sex, you can make a comeback. As an extra bonus, you can do it all day.
>
> When you have a pretty good load on a horse, like at 10-1, and he's hanging on there at the top of the stretch, NOTHING matters, not the rent, not a headache, plus you don't have to worry about the horse getting pregnant.

> Every person, Trotter learned, gambles for a serious reason.
> Trotter was told that he gambled because he was self-destructive, and that he had a compulsive desire to lose, which pissed him off so much, he bet the guy who had said it a hundred dollars. He offered to take a lie detector test to prove losing was the LAST thing in the world he wanted, that he wanted more than anything to win. (41)

To save his marriage, Trotter has agreed to attend self-help-and-therapy sessions at "Gamblers Limited," which seems to operate like Gamblers Anonymous (GA) with the addition of some Custer-style therapy. There Trotter acquires the additional information about why people gamble, and the notion is reinforced that habitual gamblers are losers. This context gives Cronley another opportunity to run a comic riff of one-liners about gambling in general and Trotter in particular:

> Most habitual gamblers gambled for a very specific reason. Trotter gambled for ALL the reasons.
> He was not satisfied with his job, thought he was overqualified, and gambling provided the opportunity, theoretically, to get the money he deserved. His marriage was less than stable. He enjoyed gambling. He continued to gamble despite the loss of many thousands of dollars. When all this was put before Trotter in the group session, he had to agree, he was a little nuts.
> Addictive gambling . . . is different from other illnesses because . . . you don't go through any physical torture, with the possible exception of starvation. . . .
> Withdrawal from gambling doesn't hurt at all.
> That's why it's so hard to quit.
> It's like quitting smoking after a good lung X-ray.
> It's only a pain in the figurative ass. . . .
> Anybody who is reasonably fond of money has to quit.
> What you miss is the action.
> Action is fun. (61–62)

In the movie Trotter argues that he's not gambling when he bets on the horse identified on the tape from the back of his friend's cab. Gambling involves risk, chance, uncertainty, he says, but this is a sure thing. His friend, however, doesn't bet on that horse, pointing out plausibly all the reasons the information could be unreliable while using totally implausible factors to support his own choice in the race. Indeed, their many acquaintances at the track have their own superstitions, rituals, incantations, hunches, triggers, associations, numerologies, charms, and "systems" to help determine their picks.

As the movie plays out, Trotter's early lament that "God hates me" turns into the joyful paean, "God really likes me," while he goes around between races chanting, "I'm having a very good day." Trotter takes the big score from the fixed race and sends it all in on the next. His subsequent bets are all made in the absence of rational analysis. He gets shut out on the one bet he would have lost, getting to the window too late because he's been detained by mistake by track security officers.

One of his wins is based on a tip from the original fixers, whom he locates in the stable area to thank them, as if they could be trusted; one is based on a "sign" from the horse itself; and another is based on a "poll" he takes of fellow bettors. He asks for their picks and then eliminates those numbers, arriving by that process at the one horse nobody else has picked. The reasons given for the choices by his polling sample range from the absurd to the fanciful, but all are ludicrously irrational. His own choice is the least sensible of all, with no reason to support it other than its unpopularity. A random sampling yields the unlikeliest of results, and he eliminates logical choices because the reasons given for the choices are foolish—as if the right choice couldn't possibly be made for the wrong reason.

Trotter's winning begets opportunities for a variety of comic effects: social satire, as he moves up into the jockey club; slapstick action; and sexual farce, as he becomes the object of the amorous attention of three women of different generations.[4]

The gambling itself is travestied in multiple ways. For example, when Trotter persuades Pam to join him at the track, she becomes the stereotypical innocent, asking why people can't just enjoy watching the horses run without betting. Another example is a different sort of neophyte, Evangeline, a teenager brought to the track by one of Trotter's cronies. She has a juvenile tantrum after a difficult loss and says, "I may go to the bank, get my savings, come back with some money, and get back what we lost. I'm pretty mad."

This is the attitude described in the theory of the chase propounded by Henry R. Lesieur in his 1977 book, *The Chase: Career of the Compulsive Gambler* (revised in 1984, streamlined in his 1979 article, "The Compulsive Gambler's Spiral of Options and Involvement"). Next to Robert Custer, Lesieur has been the most important figure in psychotherapeutic treatment for pathological gambling, and as editor of the *Journal of Gambling Studies* (originally *Journal of Gambling Behaviors*), his views carry great weight and have been constructive, instructive, and helpful throughout the field.

In Lesieur's view, losses—especially after impressive winnings—beget losses, in that the accompanying loss of judgment is heightened by increased excitement as the stakes rise. And all in the pursuit of getting even. That drive, what he calls the chase, reflects not only a concentration on the amount of money involved but also the conviction that only by escalating the action can the gambler restore himself to his proper estate, thus making it possible for him to stay in action.

Bill Barich says that "all gamblers share a common experience, a nostalgic longing for a condition prior to habituation" (44). For Lesieur, that would be a condition prior to losing. But set aside the "all gamblers" thinking implied by both; what I find astonishing is that the full meaning of "getting even" has been ignored. The phrase refers not only—perhaps not even primarily—to a balancing of the gambler's books, but to a process of exacting vengeance. It is an expression of anger, a direction of rage at projected targets, the "causes" of the losses. Betting well and winning is the best revenge. When Evangeline expresses her anger at her racetrack loss, she is talking not only about the money she has lost but about *getting back at* whoever or whatever is responsible for the injustice of that loss.

One climax of *Let It Ride*, leading to Trotter's reconciliation with Pam, occurs when he realizes, "It's not my gambling you hate, it's my losing." Trotter becomes hero-for-a-day at the track, less because of his phenomenal winning streak than because he continues to bet all his winnings on his next pick. Crowds part for him and he is welcomed with applause. In the final race of the day, he transcends the tumultuous racetrack excitement around him, attaining a state of benign and confident calm, knowing that he will win a photo finish.

The comic theme of irrationality is climaxed when Trotter offers all his cronies in the grandstand bar the opportunity to pool their money with his for the last big plunge. One by one they back off. Rather than accept the illogical magic of Trotter's winning streak, they find reasons out of their own illogical convictions to back other horses. Early in the day, one of them has used as an argument for his choice in that race the familiar sports absurdity "He's due," to which a skeptic with his own chop-logic responds, "So's Jesus." The ironic point of this is that for gamblers the prevailing notion is that my irrationality is better than yours. It may be irrational but it's mine. And even a blind pig can find an acorn sometimes.

I take my next example from the tedious "fiction" of Charles Bukowski, who, to the persistently voyeuristic taste of his faithful following, never tires of relating episodes the purpose of which seems to be to brag about his sexual, drinking, gambling, and writing prowess. (Unlike Henry Miller, his obvious model, Bukowski has to keep telling us he is really a writer; Miller shows us, at every turn of phrase.) In *Hollywood*, amid the predictable episodes of his narrator persona's "life," there is a brief passage in which a couple of movie types enact a caricature of gambling at the epicenter of irrationality.

The Bukowski character is supposed to be writing a screenplay for Jon and François, the latter being so preoccupied with gambling that he carries his own little roulette wheel and wins millions with stacks of his own chips. Jon reports that the two of them "went to Vegas the other night," and François proceeds to tell the story of their night. "Listen to this. I am five thousand dollars ahead, I am in control of the world, I hold Destiny in my hand like a cigarette lighter. I know Everything. I am Everything. There is no stopping me. The continents tremble" (21).

The megalomaniacal feelings, with delusions of grandeur and a belief in his own prescience, omniscience, and omnipotence—the hypermanic rush that can come with a winning streak—is interrupted by Jon, who wants to go to the Tab Jones show in the casino. Telling about the show, François reexperiences the rage he felt at the time:

> Here is this Tab Jones. He sings. His shirt is open and the black hairs on his chest show. The hairs are sweating. . . . He's got on tight pants and he's wearing a dildo. He grabs his balls and sings about what he can do for women. He really sings badly, I mean, he is *terrible*. The women are *screaming*! *They* think he is real! . . . Then this Tab Jones turns and shows us his behind. I can see behinds anytime, anywhere, and I don't even want to, and here we have to pay MONEY to see this fat, soft, ugly ass. (21–22)

The furious outburst carries him—and his narration—back to the wheel.

> I am five thousand ahead and we have seen the dead dildo sing. My concentration is broken. Who is this Tab Jones? . . . What are these numbers? What are these colors? The little white ball leaps and buries itself in my heart, eating from the inside out. I have no chance. I leap in with a rush of chips. I see my skull already in the stupid casket. . . . I lose. I don't know where I am. Once the concentration is broken, once you begin to fall, there is no return. Knowing I had no chance, I played all the chips away. I made all the wrong moves as if an enemy had taken over my body and my mind. I was finished. And why? BECAUSE WE HAD TO GO SEE TAB JONES? I ask you, WHO IS THIS FUCKING TAB JONES? (22)

Exhausted from reexperiencing the mad flight, François pours more drinks, lights a fresh cigar, and calmly says, "Shit, I probably would have lost anyhow. A gambler without an excuse is a gambler who can't continue" (23).

This is about as amusing, in its offensive way, as Bukowski ever gets, and yet he has detailed a striking cartoon with elements of extreme irrationality. Delusional thinking, ideas of reference (the objectifying of abstract forces as having personal relations with one), explosive anger, superstitious beliefs, fetishes, mojos, satanic possession, and the like: all are glimpsed here. Less florid, but no less irrational, are the touches of compulsion and obsession, and the way François embraces the certainty of losing. Even the garbled or inverted aphorism of his last quoted remark is irrational. "Show me someone who has an excuse for losing," the saying goes, "and I'll show you a loser." François has been given such an enormous excuse for losing, however fake or ugly, that rationally he must not continue playing. Yet the remark acknowledges gamblers' characteristic facility for rationalizations that justify their continued action. (This irrationally garbled aphorism is reminiscent of what William Blake scholar John Howard once said at a poker table: "I'd rather be lucky than dumb.")

These two examples may be overbroad or heavy-handed in their comic approaches, but there is something inherently funny or provocative of satire in such irrationality, even in its milder forms. My wife, for example, who is not a gambler but is a sports fan, will say, "Maybe I should stay out of the room," if the Orioles score when she is away. And we'll smile at the silliness of it—but if the O's need more runs, she has been known to leave the room to "help" it happen. I've seen my brother, who does gamble, kick the seat in front of him at a jai alai fronton when his player has dropped the pelota from his cesta and say something like, "Why are they doing this to me?" I may or may not laugh, but he does not think it's at all funny.

Do casinos themselves take the irrationality of gambling seriously? Or do they mock it? When players are having exceptionally hot streaks at the blackjack tables, why does the house, in the person of the pit-boss, impose a change of decks and/or dealers? Do they thereby indicate that they share the players' beliefs in luck or magic? Or are they disingenuously pretending to share the nonrational thinking of the gamblers in order to perpetuate it? I suspect that it's not an either-or proposition, that there may be some cynicism involved but that the house has seen so many streaks and bizarre improbabilities that it must give grudging acknowledgment to the reality of luck as opposed to random occurrences.[5]

All kinds of irrationality will be found in the historical and literary cases to be discussed in following chapters, but I would offer one more example here, though not a comic one. This is from a novel by George Garrett, an artful and astute observer of cultural history whether his story is set in the mid-twentieth-century or in Elizabethan England. This story is that of Johnny Riche, the narrator and rogue hero of *Which Ones Are the Enemy?* who announces in an early chapter, "Poker was my doom and downfall" (79).

The story is set in and around occupied Trieste in 1952, where Riche has been assigned to a remotely based field artillery unit after being released from military prison. The plot takes him, inevitably, jailward rather than deathward, and the narration, while telling his individual story in compelling detail, also presents a picture of the irrationality not only of army life, with characters and incidents that sometimes mirror the absurdities of *Catch-22*, but also of Cold War political/ethnic attitudes and behaviors.

George Core, in his appreciative introduction to the novel's 1994 reissue in *The Old Army Game*, says, "The troops in the Nth Field Artillery are chiefly misfits, has-beens, ne'er-do-wells, madmen of one kind and another, and, make no mistake about it, criminals" (xi). But Core's critical acumen does not extend to diagnostic expertise when he says, "Our man Riche, as both actor and observer, is a *psychopath* [emphasis mine], a man who is unmoved by moral considerations and who is fixated helplessly and finally upon himself and what promotes his self-interest" (xii).

In the first place, Riche's egocentric ways of thinking and acting are plainly rational or at worst rationalized. Even when he gets carried away into emotional responses, caught in the tide of events over which he has no control, he sees them clearly and even acknowledges his contributions. He is keenly in touch with reality, not just external reality (which he views with a comprehensive cynicism) but even his own inner reality with its idiosyncratic and sometimes bizarre or paradoxical elements (which he views with a kind of indulgent comprehension).

Riche, then, is one of that wide range of people classified as personality-disordered, people who are typically very difficult for others to tolerate but who are content with the tics and foibles that delineate their selves.[6] The appeal of such a character as a protagonist may be recognized in the way audiences identify with loner types, rebels, solitary adventurers. They "do it my way" and sustain involvements only long enough for an episode to play out, then move on to the next town, island, or frontier. The picaro may be a rogue, but he is often a self-sustained, self-confident, self-satisfied, even self-unquestioning rogue-hero.

The rogue-hero is close kin to the Trickster, a virtually universal figure of folklore and mythology.[7] Lords of Misrule, imps of Dionysian if not diabolical power, Tricksters are everywhere regarded with awe as embodiments of the irrational, the unreasonable, the unfathomable, the unpredictable. In *Continental Drift*, Russell Banks describes the loa Ghede in Voudoun as "the cynical trickster, the glutton, he who foments not death but dying, not salvation but consumption, not fucking but orgasm. . . . He derides wordly ambition . . . he parodies materialism . . . clown and trickster . . . trickster become transformer, the clown become magician . . . he who can change men into beasts and who, properly placated, can bring the sick and dying back to life" (321). In short, he is the god, the tutelary deity, the ego-ideal venerated by the gambler, who emulates the Trickster in his value system and behavior.

Riche's personality underlies his gambling behavior, but the gambling sets the plot in motion. For our purposes, however, the gambling provides an expression of symptoms, and it touches on many of the points of irrationality mentioned in this chapter. It begins, of course, on a payday when "everything seemed to go right":

> I walked right out of the pay line and got myself in a fast little game. I was just killing time. I couldn't have cared less whether I won or lost. I picked up the first hand and luck kissed me and called me her boy. I could feel it happening. I had been in many a card game before and once in a while I had had a streak of good luck. But only once on a troopship one time had anything like that happened to me. I hadn't been playing a half hour before I could feel the same thing coming over me. It must be a kind of craziness. You get taken over by a spirit, like a prophet. You can win with any hand you've got. For once you are among the touched, elected, chosen, blessed. (79)

Signals of pathological gambling or irrationality are plentiful in this paragraph, including the notion of killing time (theoretically the unconscious goal of all addictive behavior, a phrase that can translate to "filling the void"), the value of playing as opposed to winning, the embrace of a personified power, possession by a spiritual force—all under the general heading of "a kind of craziness." In the series of words for the special few at the end of the paragraph, the first is a word that has a secondary slang meaning of "crazy."

As Riche's day goes on, more symptoms are exhibited. He loses track of time and place. The faces of other players are no more real to him than the pictures on the face cards in the deck. And when the game breaks up—he has "broken" the game by winning all the money at the table—he goes off to a bigger game, egged on by Corporal Stitch, a "no-good guy" who becomes his crony and partner in crime. They go to the engineers' barracks where "there was always a lot of action" and "where the big games took place. By now most of the money would be in the hands of a few guys. They would have already done the dirty work for me. . . . I knew I was still hot" (80).

Here are the timelessness of gambling action, the nearly "fugue state" of dissociative experience, the sense of omniscience and prescience (here also clairvoyance) and omnipotence, the sense of superiority to the eliminated losers (the "ribbon-clerks," as small-timers or "pikers" are called in old poker lingo), and the idea that others have done the "dirty work" of setting him up for the big kill (like picadors preparing the bull for the matador's moment of truth). This last item suggests both the aggressiveness masked as competitiveness for the gambler and the expression of antisocial tendencies of doing whatever it takes to beat or punish or get something from others.

By midnight he has cleaned out the bigger game, too, "like a string of fish" (a punning image, since "fish" is gambling jargon for "sucker"). And yet Riche knows, "I would have to come back soon and give the boys another chance at it. And I knew they would get most of it, maybe all and more too. That's the way luck runs. But already I was starting to itch all over with the feeling of having all that money with me. I was bound I was going out and spend some of it before I had to lose it back" (80–81). The "have to" sounds compulsive, and there's a fatalistic tinge about the losing to come that rationalizes it in advance. It also goes with the physical sensation of the tangible winnings and the need to spend it, get rid of the "itch," to scratch the pressure of the "scratch," if you will.

Only then does Riche start to drink: "If I get going in a serious game, especially if the cards start to fall good, I won't touch a drop. For one thing gambling makes me kind of drunk anyway, all sort of breathless and set loose from myself. Then I've got to admit I'm superstitious about it. When my luck is going right with anything, not just cards, I feel like I've got to give myself up to that and nothing else. I owe luck that much" (81–82). The intoxication of gambling, again the dissociation, the element of superstitious belief that smacks of obsessiveness, and the rationalized "morality" of the behavior are further suggestions of irrationality. And yet there is nothing in the entire chapter from which these passages are taken that stands outside the realm of normalcy in gambling.

George Garrett has it just right. In the context of what follows in the novel, the only egregious abnormality in Riche's behavior is his refusal to show normal feelings to anyone else, especially those in authority or those who might temper their judgment of him with pity. He acts foolishly, impetuously, deviously, and criminally. And he falls in love, in spite of himself. But all along he is in touch with reality, aware of what he's doing, mindful of consequences though willing to take great chances, and in touch as well with feelings he refuses to show others. If this be psychosis, make the most of it.

From the poker games, however, Riche proceeds to higher risks and greater gambles. That he relishes the play is symptomatic of his disordered personality; that he suffers great losses (the woman he loves, his freedom, such as it is) is the essence of the plot-and-character construct; and that he is true to the self that will not give outward signs of guilt, remorse, loss, or conscience (such as that is) is his triumph. We, the audience, can see and feel those inner processes in his narration, so we know he's not a sociopath.

He is, however, impulsive in the service of his aggressive nature. Virtually every risk he takes is a way of "putting his money where his mouth is," a phrase that may be taken as an emblem of irrational aggressiveness in gambling.[8] Riche's personality disorder would make him resistant to therapy: the personality-disordered are difficult projects for any change-agent because of their typical self-satisfaction (as we shall see in chapters 10–12 below). But his overt aggressiveness is the salient feature of his gambling behavior.

Buried deep in the brain's anatomy, the so-called reptilian brain is the seat of the aggressive instinct, as it is the locus of autonomous physical functions and the fight-or-flight response. This structure precedes, in evolutionary terms, the primitive mammalian brain (limbic system) and the modern mammalian brain (neocortex) and thus any cerebral or cognitive functioning. Although we understand now that these systems work together, integrating simple signals and complex information, it may be said that aggressive behavior is regression to preconsciousness. Much gambling behavior, then, as I understand it, is an acting out of primitive functions.

The challenge, the dare, the call to immediate and finite determination, the put-up-or-shut-up mentality are all vestiges of the irrationality of aggressiveness. In another sense, Freud taught us (and this may be the most enduring of Freudian doctrine beyond the very existence of the unconscious) that aggression is at once an expression and a masking of the self-destructive impulse, highlighting another intimate connection between gambling and the irrational.

In poker, for example, a bluff, however canny the bluffer, is a challenge issued without the rational materiel to carry it through. It resembles the boast of the epic hero as much as the toss of the gauntlet, the dare-to-duel signal. In that regard, bluffing is a ritual of aggressiveness; to call the bluff is as much an irrational acceptance of the invitation to enter the lists as it is a rational decision or reasonable guess that the bluffer is acting irrationally. And to fold in the face of a bluff is as much the irrational but self-protective urge to flee as an act of prudence that devalues a particular guess.

Oddly enough, in the grip of such irrationality as instinctual aggressiveness, not only do gamblers struggle to rationalize or intellectualize what is going on with and around them, but they also may be seeking some rational explanation for what is going on inside them should they be experiencing otherwise inexplicable feelings. One of the most terrifying, complicating, and incapacitating aspects of mental illness is that the stricken individuals—almost by definition—cannot fathom what is happening to or in themselves.

Common, everyday events become inordinately stressful, inchoately ominous. They find themselves plunged into the depths of despair without even having an occasion for sadness in their awareness. They rush out of a place where they have normally felt comfortable without knowing why now they cannot tolerate another second there. Successful achievements are accompanied by feelings of helplessness and hopelessness. What normally gives pleasure is joyless or shunned; sleep and diet are disrupted, social relationships both intimate and casual are altered or avoided. And they don't know why.

It is one thing to ask, What is more natural than for something which is essentially irrational to give rise to a pathology of the mind? It is another dimension of the connection between gambling and the irrational to ask, What is more natural than to find an apparently rational, objective explanation for otherwise inexplicable feelings? Thus, mood swings, variations from what has been known as normal or familiar states of mind, sudden fears, surges of grandiosity and sublime confidence, flashing prescient visions of horror or triumph, and the like may all be chalked up to wins and losses—or anticipations of them and attributions to the consequences thereof.

The final element of the irrational in gambling that I would discuss here is its relationship to time. There is perhaps no clearer indication of the rational mind's enterprise of imposing measured "objective" order on human experience than the concept of chronological time. Great energy and resources have been expended to monitor and regularize this universally accepted phenomenon—with our mean solar time at the meridian of Greenwich, our chronometric ability to measure microseconds, our periodic adjustments to account for minuscule discrepancies, and so forth. And I suspect that the difficulty an ordinary human mind has in comprehending such concepts as relativity theory and the time-space continuum is that they seem to contradict our "rational" comprehension of time.

Gambling tends to oppose all that, at the same time flying in the face of instinctive time coordinates like circadian rhythms and digestive cycles. Traditionally there were no clocks in casinos, but I suspect that their occasional presence is hardly able to counteract the sense of timelessness experienced by those actively involved in the gambling.[9]

In *Underworld*, Don DeLillo observes that "the lure of every addiction is losing yourself to time" (319). From my own experience I can cite two examples of gambling taking me out of time. As an undergraduate poker player, I was involved in games that ran day and night or "around the clock" (meaning both "continually as the hands circled the dial" and "outside whatever impositions clock time imposed"). Class schedules became irrelevant, and so did mealtimes. We would eat periodically—without interrupting the flow of cards—and we did not sleep. No amphetamines were required to keep us awake and functioning, and it was only in retrospect that we might realize that we had played as "long" as we had.

I remember being more surprised than others who heard about it that one stretch of play had lasted seventy-two hours (and at least a dozen fresh decks of cards). We had entered into that mysterious state of timelessness called mythic time where everything that happens is "always" happening. (That is why, incidentally, there is such a thing as the "lyric tense"[10] in poetry, an ever-recurring present, and why we talk in the present tense, regardless of the tense of the narration itself, about what happens in works of fiction—because it is always happening in mythic time.)

On another occasion, years later, I was in Las Vegas on a writing assignment and checked out of my (casino-)hotel in the morning before driving to Los Angeles, both to continue my project and visit some family. I decided to spend a little while at the dice table—perhaps an hour—before crossing the desert. I was a small and patient player; those were the days when even the big places on the strip had five-dollar minimum tables; and when I went to cash in my chips I had the sense of having idled away a brief break in a busy schedule, at virtually no expense. When I went out the revolving door to claim my air-conditioned midsize rental car, it was full dark outside. My "hour" had multiplied elevenfold, while my bankroll had stood still.

To escape from time is to embrace the irrational; stepping outside time is a denial of mortality, a natural wish to escape the inevitable. Human awareness of the process that marks the limits of our time, from birth to death, may be the most intimidating consequence of consciousness and rationality. Both the process and the appeal of gambling have something to do with escaping the consequences of time by willing suspension of rationality. Perhaps it is appropriate to say that it is not unreasonable to resort to the irrational, after all.

Of all the passions of which human nature is susceptible, a passion for gambling is inconceivably the most pernicious. Once indulge in it, and you are inevitably hurried forward to irretrievable ruin. . . . There is a sort of fatality in it; its victim has no free-will of his own. . . . With the confirmed gambler . . . his judgment already condemns his conduct; it pronounces him to be a madman, and yet his will impels him forward in his career.

James Grant
The Great Metropolis

The High-Profile Profile

When I met Corky Devlin in 1993, he could have posed as the middle-aged poster boy for the prevailing myth of compulsive gambling. His personality profile matched the one described by Robert Custer, Henry Lesieur, and others; the story of his life followed the standard scenario; his symptoms met the DSM criteria; and he had even been treated by Custer himself. In conversations over a period of several months, he told me his story in some detail, and we discussed the possibility of working together to put that story into book form. At the time, Corky was working for a public relations firm in the Washington, D.C., area, but he died suddenly in 1995 during a sojourn at a monastery in Kentucky.

I knew Corky Devlin as a bright, articulate, effusive, energetic, good-looking man whom no one would identify as an ex-con. His candor was a testimonial to his years of therapy and acceptance of GA's concept of self-inventory. I believe, in good conscience, that I have his posthumous permission to tell parts of his story. And I tell it for several reasons.

Corky's story serves as an example of the seriousness of the impulse-control disorder, as a record of successful recovery, as a tribute to an approach that identifies and treats the disorder, and as a demonstration of how persuasive that approach can be. Other stories that serve similar purposes will follow. But before the chapter ends, I will offer certain counter-tales to show that what is valid for some is not necessarily valid for all, that to try to force all pathological gambling into a single diagnostic category does not make practical, theoretical, or logical sense.

Corky's first job, as a boy in Jersey City, was as a "shabbos goy" hired to come into Orthodox Jewish homes and perform ordinary tasks which are forbidden during the sabbath to strict adherents of the ritual laws. From Jersey City he came to Washington, where he was a hot-shooting basketball All-American at George Washington University. In the late 1950s he was a journeyman NBA player. His gambling did not begin until his athletic career was over.

For a vigorous competitor, betting seems an almost natural substitute for involvement in sports once active competition has ended. This seems to account for the timing and direction of Devlin's career. He plunged, at first successfully, into horse race betting. But when he started to lose, his action escalated until he went broke.

The cycle repeated itself, until he was "forced" to turn to crime to pay off debts and—more important to the already addicted gambler—to stake further action. The path he was on could very easily have led him to suicide; instead it led to incarceration, hard time as a convicted felon in California's Soledad prison. Either way, his life had been apparently lost, as his marriage and children had been. As soon as he was outside again, he was inside the addiction, in rapid-fire sequence renewing the cycle of quick fix and plummeting, desperate losses. At this point, suicide was imminent. In fact, Corky was on a train, intending to tie up a few loose ends before killing himself, when he met therapist Bob Custer.

Fortunate, perhaps even miraculous as Corky came to view it, the presence of Custer on that train saved his life. Custer persuaded him to give treatment one last good shot and admitted him to his inpatient program. The success of the program in Corky's case made him an active booster for the Custer methodology, which involves intensive group and individual therapy along with an ongoing twelve-step program. When I last saw him, he was still completely abstinent, enthusiastic if humble about the way he was living a constructive life, and hopeful about a reconciliation with his daughter.

No matter what else Corky was doing in his last years, he was a proactive proselytizer for Custer's program, particularly with high-profile cases where his own reputation as a prominent athlete gave him credibility and cachet. He was involved, for example, in getting Art Schlichter into (repeated and, alas, unsuccessful) treatment. And he had been a prominent member of the team effort to get Pete Rose into treatment.[1]

Custer was a hero and savior for Corky, as he was for many others. Custer's pioneer efforts in establishing the first inpatient treatment program for pathological gambling, in a VA hospital in Ohio, paved the way for other programs and inspired other practitioners. He was the key figure in defining the condition and its diagnostic criteria for the American Psychiatric Association and having it included in the third edition of the DSM in 1980. His book *When Luck Runs Out* (written with Harry Milt) remains, along with Lesieur's *The Chase: Career of the Compulsive Gambler*, probably the most influential work in the field. I think also of Arnie Wexler in New Jersey and Valerie Lorenz in Maryland who, following Custer's lead, have made significant differences in the lives of many pathological gamblers.

The Custer/Lesieur approach to pathological gambling is the model that prevails in the mental health professions. The condition is classified in the DSM-IV under "Impulse-Control Disorders Not Elsewhere Classified," along with such conditions as Kleptomania, Pyromania, and Trichotillomania (self-destructive hair-pulling). Custer provided ample evidence in case histories of people whose experience followed a common pattern, a repeated course that tends to justify a single program of remediation. Lesieur's complementary contribution of a common set of psychological processes, neatly summarized as the "chase theory," is strong support. Moreover, the relative success of Alcoholics Anonymous and derivative programs in dealing with addictions has provided additional support for the viability of the approach.

Keep coming back. It works. It really does. Indeed, it is only fair to say that nothing seems to work better—as long as the gambler fits the profile. But for all its practical successes, the approach fails as a theory because of the many types of pathological gambling it does not encompass. It is too limiting, exclusive, restrictive, even tunnel-visioned. For example, Lesieur's persuasive analysis identifies as central to the behavior of an addicted gambler his wish to "get even," that he is compelled to chase harder and faster after this elusive goal on the perceived pretext of a need or wish to be able to stay in action. But "get even" is not simply the equivalent of "break even"; another powerful sense of the phrase—perhaps its primary meaning in the vernacular—is a reference to revenge: "getting even" is an expression of primitive aggressive rage. And when many cases that do not fit the profile are examined, it should become clear that certain gambling behaviors may well be misdirected expressions of irrational anger.

The Custer/Lesieur/GA model is very useful, particularly by calling attention to the great need for treatment and the possibility of recovery. But it is not the be-all and end-all of the matter. Nor is it new. In the very first year of Queen Victoria's reign, James Grant's *The Great Metropolis*, a remarkable survey of London from which this chapter's epigraph is taken, describes the career of pathological gamblers with a scenario that predicts in precise detail the Custer/Lesieur script.

That script begins with a character profile with elements of high energy, fragile ego, and oversensitive moods; and upon that profile are etched specific environmental factors of parental insensitivity and skewed societal values. Inevitably, the condition follows a course through phases of winning, losing, bail-out, and desperation. Without intervention, the bottom line is ruin, prison, or suicide.

I cannot deny that certain pathological gambling behaviors suggest a particular syndrome, but I will demonstrate that in many cases the gambling may be seen as symptomatic of other conditions. About thirty years ago two psychiatrists, Darrell W. Bolen and William H. Boyd, argued persuasively and demonstrated that "it is an oversimplification to place the [problematic] gambler in any particular diagnostic category. . . . We have found pathological gambling to be associated with many types of psychiatric abnormalities. It has been more useful for us to view pathological gambling as a complex symptom and defensive maneuver present in a wide variety of psychiatric disorders rather than to regard it as a diagnostic specific disorder" (627). I find substantial evidence to accept their conclusions about "wide variety," but I would reject the implicit either-or thinking in their argument. After all, despite the wide variety, there may also be a specific diagnostic category—just not an all-inclusive one.

What makes the case for the Custer profile/scenario so convincing, besides the proportion of favorable results from treatment according to his (medical) model, is that famous people whose stories are widely known (or assumed) match the profile and have enacted the scenario. Leonard Tose, for example, the former owner of the Philadelphia Eagles of the NFL, is commonly thought to have been the kind of "compulsive gambler" who couldn't stop the action. Having gone through many millions, and gone many millions more into debt to the Atlantic City casino operators who loved and courted Tose's action, he was rumored to be within one losing night of using his football franchise as collateral when he was forced by the league to sell the team. Imagine the dilemma of a professional sports team being owned by professional gambling establishments.

Others who seem, from sketchy details bruited about in the media, to match the profile include Gladys Knight, John Daly, Wilfrid Hyde-White, Lenny Dykstra, Albert Belle, Nicky Hilton (who left Elizabeth Taylor's bed on their wedding night to go gambling), and perhaps even the great iconographic hero of our time, Michael Jordan. The evidence is hardly conclusive and may not come close to being convincing in these cases, but the point is that conventional wisdom has only one way to identify people with possible gambling problems. They are "compulsive gamblers"—or they're not.

Perhaps the best publicized example is that of Chet Forte, whose case is therefore worth examining in some detail. It is the story of a man who went from lifelong winner to colossal loser, a violent turn on the wheel of fortunes. As a 5' 9" basketball player at Columbia, Chet the Jet was first-team All-American, third in scoring nationally (behind Elgin Baylor and Wilt Chamberlain), and UPI consensus player of the year in 1957. Subsequently, his honors as an undersized athlete were dwarfed by his world-class performances in sports television: nine Emmys as director and producer for ABC, from Roone Arledge's *WideWorld of Sports* to his *Monday Night Football* concept. People in the business generally believe that it was the perfectionist drive of Forte's personality and his intuitive athlete's genius as a director that were largely responsible for making those Monday night telecasts the benchmark of televised sports productions from 1970 on.

But Chet Forte had already started betting on games by that time. It made no difference if he was in the booth for a game or not—he craved that action. It is also a tribute to his integrity that his rooting (betting) interest never impinged on his presentation of a game, though the *appearance* of conflict of interest is unavoidable. Despite his insider's knowledge, access to late-breaking information, and athletic/analytical acumen, he rarely won his bets. And the more he lost, the more he bet, seeking the elusive comeback in a full card of college basketball games or in six-figure action at Atlantic City blackjack tables. He was the kind of bettor who had to lose because he would bet every race at the track, every fight on the card, every game on a full slate of any sport.

He made a lot of money in those days but lost a lot more than he made. He knew how to spend, too, so that there were accumulated assets he could borrow against and, eventually, sell, like his lavish home in Saddle River, New Jersey, and his daughter's pony. When it was all gone, when his huge debts to relatives could not be paid, when his enormous debts to bookies forced them to shut him off, he sold out on his ABC job as well. The old Roone Arledge gang was gone anyway, so he took the buyout on his contract—not to pay off the bookies, the bank loans, or the overdrawn credit cards, however, but to bet some more (while pursuing more funding as an independent TV producer).

The banks and the IRS were closing in. Chet had misstated his assets and liabilities in applying for loans, and he was eventually indicted for bank fraud. By that time he could be represented only by a public defender. And he lost the case as well. The lonely route from the top of his profession, the achievement of intelligence and ambition in a competitive meritocracy, to the quicksand of white-collar crime completed the stereotypical scenario. When Chet Forte quit gambling, completely and without relapse, he determined to let his story be known publicly as a cautionary tale. With the help of GA and his pathological-gambling guru Arnie Wexler, his recovery seemed to be reinforced by the notoriety his career generated in the mass media.[2] That is all well and good, but unfortunately the publicity has also served to reinforce the public perception of the stereotypical "compulsive gambler."

My own acquaintance with Forte followed the renewal of his career in broadcasting, as cohost of a sports-talk radio show on XTRA in San Diego. He gave my book *The Great Molinas* a rave review, and we talked on and off the air a number of times, mostly about sports and gambling. I'm proud to say that we had mutual admiration and respect, and I'm sad that the recurrence of his heart disease killed him long before he could fulfill the promise of his talent and honesty.

Chet chuckled when he told me a story about Jack Molinas that wasn't in my book. After Chet had failed to make the NBA in his single training-camp attempt, he had played on weekends in the Eastern League, on Molinas's team in Williamsport, Pennsylvania. One night, driving to their game, Molinas was surfing the radio dial when he found a college basketball broadcast of a game that had tipped off at 7:00. "Shit!" he yelled, "that game was supposed to go at 7:30." And he wheeled off the road to the nearest public phone to make a call.

"I didn't know a thing about betting then, but all of us in the car are roaring," Chet said, "because we all figure Jack is trying to get a bet down on a game already in progress, to 'past-post' some sucker of a bookie."

That's when I gave Chet a new punchline for his story: "Well, you all got it wrong. Molinas was calling Joey Hacken [his partner in a bookmaking operation] to make sure they weren't getting past-posted." (See chapter 10 for a discussion of Molinas's pathology.)

In retrospect, what is interesting about this story is Chet's naiveté about gambling at that time. Move forward some years to another anecdote I heard recently, from a firsthand source. Chet was producing the telecast of the Thomas Hearns–Sugar Ray Leonard fight in Las Vegas, and he and his director were getting paid $15,000 each for the show. They decided to bet it all on Leonard, a 3-1 underdog. For most of thirteen rounds, Hearns was clearly dominating the fight, and the climate in the control booth was glum. But then Leonard turned it around with a late knockout, and the director started jumping up and down and shouting. But he turned to find his producer sitting still, still glum.

"Chet," he yelled, "what's wrong with you? We just won forty-five thousand each."

"You don't understand," he said. "I had three baseball losers and I'm out sixty thousand for the night."

One more example that supports the wisdom of the conventional stereotype is one I hope will become widely known because of the context in which it appears. It is the story of "Evan Peters," recounted pseudonymously in his own words in Timothy L. O'Brien's recent book *Bad Bet*. A splendid overview of the condition of this society's fixation on gambling, *Bad Bet* is especially strong in the chapter that sees Wall Street as driven by gambling action in its ever heavier reliance on options, futures, and derivatives.[3] I also found O'Brien's accounts of the historical backgrounds for contemporary gambling venues in New Orleans and San Francisco, and the segments on thoroughbred racetracks and Native American reservations, lucid and illuminating. But I am uncomfortable with the perpetuation of the "compulsive gambler" notion in the Peters passages, and I regret the absence of precise distinctions between or definitions of "problem gambling" and "compulsive gambling."

It is not difficult to read the thirteen or fourteen pages of italicized text in which Peters tells his story as yet another scenario according to the Custer model. The former policeman who turns to crime to pay gambling debts or provide a stake for reentering the gambling arenas, the man who values his action above family and wives, the prisoner who dreams of freedom in images of being able to gamble again, the person who rationalizes every inevitable relapse despite oaths of abstinence, the player who tells of his "bad beats" (memorable, dramatic, enormous, or exceedingly unlikely losses) with more effusive expression than his biggest wins—all of that etches the stereotype in bold lines.

Yet a careful reading of this life story suggests other possibilities of diagnosis. What we are given is, first, a self-diagnosis by the subject/patient. And then the writer accepts that diagnosis, which matches his preconceived idea of what the diagnosis should be.[4] I cannot concur on the basis of this circular presentation, though I can rely on O'Brien's careful reporting. The details can be framed in other ways. For example, the extreme mood swings Peters describes as associated with his gambling or as providing a context for his gambling sound suspiciously bipolar to me. Again, the self-image projected through his own language and the attitudes and values implied therein are strongly suggestive of a personality-disordered person.

I would never want to base a diagnosis on what amounts to less than a single session's worth of remarks by a person, made in a context which lacks the discipline or the safe "holding environment" of a therapist's consultation room. Still, those remarks raise suspicions that I would want to pursue in great detail, with careful questioning and appropriate probing, before I would make even tentative conclusions as to diagnosis. I would certainly want to rule out manic-depressive illness and consider the symptoms of Narcissistic, Borderline, and Antisocial Personality Disorders (in accordance with conventional practice, official names of DSM disorders are capitalized to distinguish technical from colloquial usage) before labeling Evan Peters a compulsive or pathological gambler with impulse-control issues as his primary diagnosis. (See chapters 6 and 10 for examples of cases where therapy penetrates the superficial symptoms of pathological gambling behaviors to approach underlying, core conditions.) It is well to note that, so far as we know from his remarks in *Bad Bet*, Peters apparently has never been adequately treated—or medicated.

These pages present a man who seems to justify unconsciously (rationalize) his relapses so that he has an excuse to gamble again. Yet one may reframe the account to say that Peters is using his condition as "compulsive gambler" to explain away his criminal behaviors, his rage, his abuse of women, his inability to sustain interpersonal relationships, his power tripping, his manipulativeness, and so on. Such a vicious cycle of thinking is not likely to be interrupted by acceptance of the "compulsive gambler" label; a more comprehensive examination of the psyche or personality or behavior of such a person is clearly in order.

I think O'Brien's book has made an important contribution to public awareness of the enormous and growing problems in this society from pandemic gambling. But I fear that its very comprehensiveness and stylistic/rhetorical/reportorial strengths may serve to perpetuate the monolithic myth of compulsive gambling. That myth is supported by high-profile cases that capture public attention and fit the generalized description of "compulsive gambler" very well. Conventional wisdom facilely accepts this condition as the condition. It is a sensational, compelling, dramatic narrative, with a familiar and conventional protagonist and recognizable episodes.

But it is a simplistic scenario. No doubt the condition as outlined does exist, and it is predictable in its course. Its origin may not be discernible, its etiology remains unknown, but its progress conforms comfortably to the well-known pattern. I have found, however, that it accounts for only a minority of pathological gambling cases.

The image of the compulsive gambler has the virtue of getting attention, of raising public awareness and alarm, and therefore of facilitating funding for study and treatment. The assumption of a single condition, then, is the basis for much, perhaps most, of the research into, reports on, and studies of the issues.[5] And one should never discount parsimony as a valuable principle of the scientific method. But faulty application of parsimony can be counter-productive, leading to simplistic conclusions, as I believe it does in this case. It becomes an example not of active thinking but of passive acceptance of prevailing popular notions. And it may have problematic consequences for treatment of pathological gamblers (as most of the cases examined in the rest of this book will demonstrate). The conditions at the core of the pathology may be missed, and symptomatic behaviors mistaken for the disease.

The popular culture provides numerous examples of how simplistic, stereotyping notions become facile formulas for action, mood, character, and melodramatic plotting. In his Matt Scudder detective series, for example, Lawrence Block, an otherwise sophisticated and capable observer of the scene (cultural historian, if you will), says, "Here and there I saw a face straight out of any OTB horse room, one of those knobby, on-the-come Broadway faces that only gamblers get. But there weren't too many of those. Who bets prize-fights anymore?" (29).

Here (in Eight Million Ways to Die), in 1982, Scudder is typing the people of the crowd in Madison Square Garden's "Felt Forum," sounding a bit like Dostoevsky stereotyping gamblers and nationalities in the casino at Roulettenberg; but it is the dismissive, reductive "only gamblers" that catches the eye. Fifteen years later, in Even the Wicked, Scudder is still at it, describing a topless bar as "probably sad at any hour, deeply sad in the manner of most emporia that cater to our less noble instincts. Gambling casinos are sad in that way, and the glitzier they are the more palpable in their sadness. The air has an ozone-tainted reek of base dreams and broken promises" (119).

A more egregious example is Playing to Win, advertised as "A Moment of Truth Movie," made for TV, that appeared in prime time on NBC on February 11, 1998. Here, a bright, talented, sweet-natured, over-achieving, exemplary-in-every-way teenager becomes entangled with a new boyfriend who takes her on quick visits to a casino and a racetrack. Virtually overnight she is hooked on gambling (urged on by the addicted boyfriend) and transformed into a loathsome creature who lies to and borrows from her kid sister and her best friend, sells or pawns family property including her widowed mother's wedding ring and other jewelry, steals money at her fast-food job and cash from her mother's failing business, forges a check, throws a championship soccer game, and participates in armed robbery at a golf course.

She is even drawn to the twin destructive peaks of prostitution and suicide because of her affliction. She is spared the obligatory motif of a physical beating at the hands of evil bookies/loan sharks, but the audience is not—it's the boyfriend who is beaten.

Gambling has become a serious problem in later adolescence, particularly among sports-minded students, but the *reductio ad absurdum* of such a simpleminded scenario is hardly the way to encourage appropriate public attention. Indeed, in telescoping the progress of the monolithically conceived disease, such a rendering might tend to debunk the myth by exposing it to ridicule. Granted that this was a well-intentioned fable, its formulaic abridgment of a frequently documented set of symptomatic behaviors may at best be called misguided.

NBC has much to answer for along these lines. In the episode of *Profiler* aired on March 14, 1998, the team discovers that a series of murders are the result of a plan to pit a pair of desperate men to fight one another to the death while an elite group of enthusiasts watches the performance on closed-circuit television. The script develops the various reasons for these men to be willing to take part. Predictably, one of the victims had become a compulsive gambler, and this was the one "honorable" way that he could pay off his debts. What is totally ignored is that the raison d'etre of the whole plan is to provide a novel vehicle for gambling among the gathered aficionados—a human cockfight, as it were (like the pitted or caged combatants in the *Road Warrior* or *Mad Max* movies). That's where, in an examination of the variety of appeals for members of the gallery, a useful examination of gambling problems might have been undertaken.

NBC is not alone. Other networks have attempted to make use of simplistic formulas of what the producers must perceive as the public perception of pathological gambling. The Mark Harmon character on CBS's *Chicago Hope*, for example, is a "recovering compulsive gambler," whose habit has been shown from time to time as dramatically interfering with his otherwise promising medical career. Complete with codependents and enablers and GA and a lot of "talking the talk," the series has made this motif a featured component of its ongoing soap opera material.

In the March 18, 1998, episode, however (it must have been the hot topic of that sweeps season), four of the featured docs, including Harmon, attend a convention in Las Vegas. While Harmon, GA-and-therapy-schooled, avoids the lures of the casino, the other self-righteous three fall prey in their own innocuous ways to the manifold garish temptations of the environment. Harmon, however, fails to avoid one occasion of sin, an adjunct gambling venue, a prize fight, because his godson is fighting. The young man is accidentally killed in the ring, but neither the shock nor the ensuing depression drive the Harmon character to gamble. Yet when he sees the boxer-killer enjoying himself, in victory, at the tables, his rage sends him into action—no doubt to "get even."

There follows a plunge into accelerating symptoms even more precipitous than those of the high schooler of *Playing to Win* (the obligatory hot streak followed by more excessive losses, all telescoped into screen time measured in seconds rather than minutes, that is, telescoping more typical of commercials than of serious drama). Finally, out of resources and methods to borrow or steal, he forces himself into a chump-change craps game on the street, winding up mugged and beaten within an inch of his life. He has taken a knockout punch very nearly lethal (flashing back to his own boxing career)—an archetypal "hitting bottom" for this talking-the-talk sequence of clichés.

At least one TV series, the original British version of *Cracker*, has seemed to break the stereotyping mold, as we shall see in chapter 10. Another pop-culture treatment also seems to be nudging open the envelope of clichés about pathological gambling: James A. Halperin's futuristic novel *The Truth Machine*. One of its main characters is David West, who becomes president of the United States in 2028. He is first introduced as the fourteen-year-old son of compulsive gambler Bruce Witkowsky, who is cashing in a winning $300 lottery ticket that he had spent over a thousand dollars to get.

We are told that "David was smart enough to know that everything his compulsive gambler father touched was eventually lost. . . . Bookmakers, loan sharks, the cops, were all on Bruce's trail" (31). But two years earlier, twelve-year-old David had been busted for fencing stolen property to pay off a fourteen-year-old bookie in the eighth grade. Halperin says, "Maybe David had a gambling problem too, or more likely, he'd just wanted to be like his dad." A kindly judge, impressed by the boy's intelligence and initiative, gives him a break, on condition that he put his acumen to work earning money by lawful pursuits rather than gambling. The Solomonic decision spurs David into a variety of youthful business enterprises that accumulate enough money for him to escape from his father, taking his mother and kid brother along with him.

Even while working hard to achieve that escape, however, he finds time to attend Gamblers Anonymous meetings, "more to understand his father than to help himself" (32). He even convinces Bruce to show up for a session: "He had watched that night while Bruce took over the meeting and told everyone that his father had been murdered when he was still a baby and about his own attempts to go straight. David had watched his dad cry and hug all the participants after the meeting. But he knew if there was a fast horse running at Santa Anita, his dad would steal the credit cards from those he now embraced and turn them into cash" (32–33).

As the story unfolds into the future, projecting a dystopian world, Halperin describes the state-of-the-art treatment for addictions in 2026: "During the 20th century, before the cure for alcoholism was discovered, compulsive gambling had been far more difficult to treat than alcoholism. Even in 2026, gambling addiction was incurable . . ." (199), and again in 2045:

> There are literally hundreds of compulsive and intermittent mental disorders known, all requiring different combinations of therapies. . . .
> Workaholics were addicts, just like David's compulsive-gambler father. MediFact had long ago discovered that both addictions occurred more frequently among highly intelligent people who had lacked certain kinds of parental discipline as children. The newest cures for those pathologies had an unfortunate side effect of slightly lowering the operative IQ of the patient, and therefore were used only as a last resort. Generally, long-term therapy was preferable to the cure. . . . (233)

It is gratifying to see at least one genre novelist reject the cliches of conventional wisdom. I would hope that such "long-term therapy" would itself reject facile diagnosis. The negative consequences of adhering to a monolithic, simplistic concept of the condition, whether it be called "compulsive gambling," "pathological gambling," "problem gambling," or "impulse-control disorder," are manifold. The recognition of certain specific symptoms may lead to failures in appropriate diagnosis in the effort to assign the single label: individuals in treatment almost always suffer when their "profile" forces them into a group with which they fit only with great difficulty.[6] A lack of understanding of the various conditions that may be subsumed under the general heading (whichever rubric is employed) is almost certain to impede preventative measures, education, and public policy. Misdiagnosis may also have unfortunate consequences in the criminal justice system, as in the following case.

The man I'll call Herman was court-ordered to treatment for pathological gambling. That treatment—along with community service, a fine, and one year's regular attendance at weekly meetings of Gamblers Anonymous— was a condition of probation for him. Though he had been convicted of a felony for the second time, on several counts of betting, gambling, book-making, and racketeering (under his state's loosely drawn and broadly applied RICO legislation), he would at least not serve any jail time so long as he fulfilled those conditions for probation.

The judge's diagnosis and sentence were made without benefit of professional forensic-psychiatric counsel, but they might well have been justified by the court's reading of the diagnostic criteria in DSM-III (the existing authority at the time of Herman's trial). Under criterion A, the court saw Herman as "progressively unable to resist impulses to gamble," in part because even during his trial and again prior to sentencing he would spend weekends in Aruba, San Juan, Las Vegas, and Atlantic City. Differential diagnoses of Manic Episodes and Antisocial Personality Disorder were not apparently appropriate (criterion C). But most crucial to the court's determination was its interpretation of criterion B, which calls for evidence of three of seven indicators. It should be instructive to examine the details of his case, to see how the conventional psychiatric wisdom furnished the judge with the tools to force a square peg into a round (pigeon)hole.

Did Herman's gambling "compromise, disrupt, or damage his family, personal, and vocational pursuits"? How could it not if he was willing to continue gambling at the risk of going to prison? His first marriage had ended in a relatively amicable divorce in which his gambling behaviors played no part (indicator 3 misapplied); and if he had semiretired from his business, which was now managed by his children, this was hardly "loss of work due to absenteeism in order to pursue gambling activity" (indicator 6). The third "match" for the judge's case was indicator 5: "an inability to account for the loss of money or to produce evidence of winning money." Any such evidence could have strengthened the prosecutorial case against Herman, contributing to convictions on gambling and bookmaking charges. Had such evidence existed—and none was discovered in a warranted search of his home—he would have been foolish not to destroy it. Yet its absence was taken as a sign of pathological behavior: a catch-22 in the jurisprudence of gambling.

The other indicators could not be made to fit at all. In his long gambling career he had apparently never defaulted on his financial responsibilities (nor welshed on a bet, for that matter); and he had never, so far as anyone knew, had to be bailed out of a desperate financial situation (indicators 2 and 7). None of the criminal charges designated in DSM-III had been part of his indictments, despite the efforts of investigators to prove—and by the special prosecutor to imply—income tax evasion; and the racketeering (RICO) indictment itself bore not the slightest trace of dealings with loan sharks (indicators 1 and 4).

I should note at this point that the guidelines for diagnosing the condition have been significantly revised in the fourth edition of the DSM. Still, a present-day judge who is *au courant* could well come to the same judicial conclusion and diagnosis, finding "maladaptive gambling behavior" evidenced in items 1, 2, 4, 6, 7, and 9 on the current list of ten diagnostic criteria (five are required).

Herman, then in his early fifties, had been gambling since he was twelve, spending much of his time as a teenager around racetracks, betting parlors, sports venues, and "social clubs." He left college to open a retail business which proved to be successful, and he never overextended despite several expansions. Gambling winnings and gambling associates may have provided some of the initial investments, but caution in operational matters was key to his success. Happily, that success allowed him to gamble at higher levels, but always within an affordable range.

At the time of the trial he apparently remained on good terms with his ex-wife, and their children were all supportive and concerned. His second wife, who actually shared Herman's enjoyment of gambling action, wondered why he wasn't taking the trial more seriously and teased him about his unwillingness to stop gambling for even a short time, that is, the duration of the trial.

Like most pathological gamblers, Herman exhibited a heavy reliance on denial as a defense. When he was first made aware that he was a target of investigation, he denied the existence of a prior felony conviction on his record. Then he rationalized that denial by recalling how the conviction had been the result of a plea bargain that he had misunderstood, thinking it meant the felony would be expunged from his record. Then he denied the seriousness of the present situation, finding the charges laughable. Sure, he took bets from ten or a dozen acquaintances on a regular basis, based on the point spreads published in the local newspaper, but he wasn't a bookie by any professional definition of the term.

When his attorney succeeded in making him aware of the very real possibility that he could be convicted and that he faced the attachment of his property and a maximum of fifteen years in prison, Herman took appropriate action. He divested himself of many of his assets and plunged into a concerted effort to cooperate with the attorney in preparation for trial. He maintained his right to certain forms of (legal) gambling, but cut back on the proportion of his time spent on it. Still, his preoccupation with gambling was untempered. On the evening between the two days of his trial, he entertained a guest at dinner with a long dissertation on his system for winning at craps tables in casinos, calmly discoursing about odds, about obligatory plays, and about a single remaining obstacle to perfecting his system.

When the jury returned a verdict of guilty, Herman felt affronted, betrayed by the judicial system. The jurors had ignored a careful defense and with his conviction had completed a perfect record for the special prosecutor. Sixty-four defendants had been charged after an elaborate undercover state police investigation over a two-year period, and sixty-four guilty verdicts had been returned.

Nevertheless, the court had apparently accepted some of the defense's argument, and Herman gratefully accepted the sentence of community service, fine, GA meetings, and treatment as conditions for probation. But when he met with his therapist, he told her that he was there because he had to be or go to jail. Gambling had caused problems for him, he said, but he was not in any way, shape, or form a problem gambler. The therapist, while unwilling to accept the court's diagnosis at face value, was also unwilling to reject it out of hand on her patient's assurance. Here was a man patently unable—or unwilling—to resist the impulse to gamble, but the question remained as to whether it was unreasonable and therefore pathological.

I do not want to be perceived as opposed to, not to mention demeaning of, the process of diagnosis. Indeed, this is a case where careful attention to the process produced beneficial, timely results—thanks especially to the multiaxial approach that is at the heart of the overall DSM concept.[7] Herman's therapist took note of his obesity, shortness of breath, and high blood pressure. She explored the relationship of these Axis III factors to the habits of the gambler's life. She explored Axis IV issues of psychological and environmental problems in the recent past, namely, effects of arrest, trial, and possible disastrous consequences thereof, as well as business and family issues of the more distant past. And she also explored, on Axis V, levels of functioning, adaptation, and defenses.

The health issues remained ambiguous. While it was clear that Herman's physical condition would benefit if he had a better exercise program than occasional dice-throwing, a better diet than his arenas of activity afforded, and so on, it was also clear that he would not necessarily eat, drink, sleep, exercise, or reduce stress any more therapeutically if he never placed another bet. The other factors, however, suggested either that his adaptation to conditions was more or less realistic and sound or that he had maintained an adequate set of defenses—or both.

Exploration along the lines of Axis II provided interesting results. She found hints of several personality disorders (Narcissistic, Avoidant, Borderline, Paranoid, and Compulsive, in declining order of significance), but they were no more than hints. No clear pattern emerged to justify a differential diagnosis. Most impressively, of the one Axis II diagnosis that is consonant with the single-syndrome profile of problem gambling, Antisocial Personality Disorder, not a sign could be seen.

Herman had always felt that society's attitudes, laws, and practices concerning gambling were misguided at best, hypocritical for the most part, and vindictive and manipulative at worst. He had developed early on a cynical view of the whole situation, accepting it and going on with his own ways in and out of the system. Now, as a result of his trial and conviction, he was enraged by what he felt was his victimization, and he felt diminished and insulted by the sentencing—even though he was grateful it had kept him out of jail. Rather than a protracted and expensive appeal, he had made the intelligent gambler's choice of cutting his losses, but he was still enraged at the game.

"Focus, if you will for now, on your first conviction."

"It was a joke, and I can actually laugh about it. The owners of the local sports franchises knew me as a fan who liked to bet on games. They approached me at the racetrack one day and asked me if I would be willing to take bets at the arena where the basketball and hockey games were played and where they occasionally booked a boxing card. They wanted to use the betting opportunities to stimulate interest and attendance, badly needed at the time, and they said they'd back me against the possibility of major losses.

"I said sure. I loved the idea. There was practically no risk. The action was good and so were the winnings."

"You're smiling now, but obviously there was some risk. What happened?"

"Someone dropped a dime on me, you know, blew the whistle. It could have been a disgruntled loser, or it could have been someone involved in an attempt to buy one of the franchises. Whatever. The owners were in no position to come to my defense. I was out there on my own. If I wanted to continue gambling—and if I wanted to stay healthy, too, I suppose—I had to accept their silence and go for the plea bargain the prosecution offered."

"So why is it that you can laugh at that now, while you can only rage at the present case?"

"I got caught in a stupid police sting," he said, in a tone of utter contempt. "They were at it for over a year and my nickel-and-dime action is the biggest illegal betting operation they could have come up with? There are three or four big-time bookies in town, with hundreds of clients, and out in the county there are guys running big action at the Legion and the VFW both. Me? I took bets from a dozen friends, I used the line in the paper, and when I had one-sided action I never laid it off. I'm just a gambler. Sure I took the vig, but that was in return for giving my buddies the privilege of picking either side. And they called this *racketeering?* What a joke!"

"But you're not laughing at this one. Let's see if we can figure out why, what the difference is, especially now."

It took months, but a clear explanation did emerge. The rage and resentment were provoked by the interruption of what Herman felt was the best time of his life, that he had paid his dues to get to. He felt overwhelmed by the injustice of it. He gambled within his means, he won more often than not, and he enjoyed being "comped" as a high roller whenever he took a vacation or a junket to a casino. He felt that he operated within the spirit of the law if not its letter, and that nobody got hurt by what he did. The pursuit of happiness, which he felt entitled to, had been substantially fulfilled in recent years and he had had it taken away on phony technicalities.

The therapist considered not only the DSM's distinctions among social, professional, and pathological gambling, but she also applied what she knew of Custer's categories. Herman had been, it seemed to her, at different times the serious social, the relief-and-escape, and the professional gambler. But she was unable to discern either a pattern of compulsive behavior in the gambling or an underlying disorder which the habitual behavior masked. Finally, she focused on reality testing to verify her growing feeling that the court's diagnosis was either (judicial, injudicious) error or a nearly humane, face-saving device on behalf of a system that had convicted her patient.

Herman acknowledged that he had to be more careful about stretching the envelope of "legal" gambling. The prevailing social, political, and legal standards might be misguided, but he did not need to flout them since he had enough legal avenues open to him to satisfy his chosen lifestyle. He concluded that his sentence was actually a "blessing in disguise" and that he could even learn from what he heard at GA meetings—a whole new set of negative modeling for losing, self-deceiving, self-defeating gambling. Maybe when he bent the law, he had been following a losing strategy of his own.

For the therapist, her conclusion that treatment was no longer necessary produced a quandary. How could the court's order be satisfied? Herman proposed a solution. He'd continue to attend weekly GA meetings and check in with her at least once a month—at least until he was off probation. She thought this was a reasonable nonterminating termination agreement, and she accepted it. Herman responded with another acknowledgment.

"You know, I usually felt good when I was gambling, but I've *always* felt good *about* my gambling. Now I see that it has really gotten me in trouble, and maybe because my success always made me feel that I was, you know, impervious."

Now that he knew he'd be able to gamble again, though with less grandiose expectations of happiness, he was able to let go of his rage and resentment. He added his recent trial and tribulations to the core of his amused cynicism. The therapist, for her part, was determined to continue to monitor the relationships among Herman's habit, his health, his affect, and his adaptation. At the end of his nonterminating termination session, Herman turned at the door and said to her, "Is this a great country or what?" He was entitled to his irony. His gambling had gotten him into trouble, but the trouble was not what the court, laboring under the prevalent popular mythology, judged it to be. Nevertheless, the misdiagnosis had led him to helpful treatment.[8]

As a final example for this chapter, I turn from a case at law to the judgment of a literary case—from the work of Irvin Faust, one of our most underappreciated writers of valuable fiction. His portraits of complexly intriguing characters in novels like *The Steagle*, *Willy Remembers*, and *Jim Dandy* are exemplary demonstrations of the way cultural history, political events, and prevailing social attitudes impinge upon individual lives. Among the treasures of his short stories is "Bar Bar Bar" from the collection *The Year of the Hot Jock and Other Stories*. As the slot-machine allusion of the title suggests, it is a story about gambling, and it has particular relevance for this discussion.

Howard Fu is a widower, retired from his Queens laundry, who regularly takes the bus to Atlantic City to gamble, despite the concerns of his son and heir (who has changed the business to a "French" rather than Chinese laundry) about losing and addiction. Widowed Carrie Greenbaum, who used to take her husband's shirts to Fu's, is on the same bus one day, taking her first trip to Atlantic City in forty years—and not to gamble. They exchange pleasantries on the bus, then meet again when Howard goes into Bally's after a losing blackjack run at Resorts. As he watches, she makes her first bet, a quarter in a slot machine, wins five quarters, reinvests three of them and hits bar bar bar, plays three more and hits a cascading jackpot with seven seven seven. They have lunch, he loses some more in the afternoon at Playboy while she wins some more at the slots, and on the bus ride home, while he explains to her "the maddening intricacies of blackjack and the absolute treachery of roulette" (36), they plan to come back together the next day.

From daily trips to the casinos or to Belmont Park, their camaraderie escalates to a four-day junket to Las Vegas and a week at Saratoga. Their children express growing dismay and concern, not without ethnic stereotyping regarding money and gambling, but when they convene a summit conference and confront their wayward parents with the question of whether they are considering marriage, Howard jumps to the idea "like he had just hit a 50-1 shot" (51), proposes, and Carrie accepts.

With comic relief from the resistant families and the hapless religious figures they summon for help, the happy couple settles on a plan to go to Reno where a justice of the peace will perform the ceremony. But on the eve of their departure Howard has a stroke, leaving him speechless and paralyzed on one side. Carrie's response is to go rigid and mute at his bedside with apparent catatonic shock, and she is admitted to the same hospital floor just two rooms down from his. Around midnight, however, she slips out of bed, down the hall, and into his room. There, instructing him to respond to sample gambling situations with eye blinks, she proves to them both that they can go on with their lives together, happily gambling, standing pat with two blinks or boldly hitting another card with one blink.

"Bar Bar Bar" is the stuff of romantic comedy, from the "cute meet" of the unlikely couple, through the obstacles to their coupling, to the sentimental, unlikely, or zany conclusion. The gambling context is the distinctive feature (along with the irrepressible wit of Faust's style), and the gambling itself is described knowledgeably and benignly, though with comprehensive appreciation of conventional wisdom. In this case, gambling is seen as a good thing, a companionable activity that gives new meaning—not to mention a meaningful relationship—to two declining, depressing lives.[9]

"Bar Bar Bar" found its way onto my syllabus for "Literature of Gambling and the Gambler." It gave me a chance to introduce Faust to my students, to show that stories of gambling were not absolutely required to be cautionary tales, and to provide emotional relief amid the dark visions of Dostoevsky and DeLillo, of Pushkin and Peri Rossi. And then, to my astonishment, several students discussed this story in their journals as if it were an account of Howard Fu's and Carrie Greenbaum's descent into addiction and madness.

The pervasive mythic scenario of the high-profile pathological gambler, the persuasive conventional wisdom of seductive excitement and destruction, had been imposed on this delightful story of two sympathetic characters who overcome opposition and convention to be enjoyably together. Forcing these well-rounded characters and their uniquely pegged narrative into the square slots of a dominant myth about gambling is virtually the same process as imposing the grid of a monolithic diagnosis of "compulsive gambling" onto the case of anyone whose gambling behavior seems pathological, dangerous, problematical, or in any way unusual.

People like Carrie and Howard, who have made habitual gambling central to their lifestyle, are surely susceptible to having their habit become pathological in times of stress or in the event of trauma. A paralyzing stroke could indeed trigger maladaptive changes. That's the higher risk involved; that's the argument for awareness, caution, and vigilance. But worst-case scenarios are not inevitable. In the case Irvin Faust has given us here, so far as we are allowed to see, the potentially destructive habit is found to be benign, even constructive.

She lost. She felt so light, an airy, dragon-fly wing of feeling. It was always like this when she lost. She felt such guilt and fear after she had lost that she did not imagine she liked losing, and yet this sensation always came with it, and once, seeing the carcass of a grasshopper all eaten out by ants, only its delicate and papery form remaining, she had recognized, in that light and lovely shell, the physical expression of this feeling she had when losing.

She shed her money, sloughed it off.

Peter Carey
Oscar and Lucinda

The Compulsion to Lose

The myth of the pathological gambler as a compulsive loser was given authoritative support with the publication of Edmund Bergler's *The Psychology of Gambling* in 1957. His psychoanalytical approach, based on scores of cases from his own practice but rooted in Freudian theory, posited a model of orally fixated neurosis. Pathological gamblers are compelled to lose because the punishment of defeat and humiliation is more tolerable (or masochistically satisfying) than guilt-ridden suffering inflicted by unconscious conscience. The pathological gambler's experience, then, resembles—or substitutes for—a cycle of masturbation and remorse.

Bergler's view found some support in the apparent validity of his observations of repeated, characteristic symptoms. That his theory has failed to be persuasive over time, however, seems to be the result less of the passing of Freudian thinking from fashion than of the increased attention paid to the perspectives and examined experiences of the gamblers themselves. Lesieur, for example, stressed the nearly universal sense of excitement that gamblers experienced from the action, which typically contained both pleasurable and painful components. Moreover, both the concentration on money and the aggressive desire to get even, in Lesieur's more widely accepted analysis, argue against Bergler's conclusions.

The one-size-fits-all thinking that characterizes both these authoritative views, however, raises great practical problems when one tries to apply them to particular cases. What are we to make, for example, of the common clinical phenomenon of *changes* in the experience of habitual gamblers? Can we shift from one psychology to another in order to account for the sudden emergence of pathology? Must we account for such behavioral changes by recourse to environmental shifts? external stressors? life cycles? the weather? May an anally fixated gambler turn overnight into an orally fixated gambler?

Such questions are triggered by the recent movie *Rounders*, in the character of the protagonist Michael (Matt Damon). Having begun his gambling career as an adolescent, with marked signs of emerging Antisocial Personality Disorder (an outsider who cheats, scams, or schemes at every opportunity to get over on people and/or institutions), he is now seen as a risk-taking, void-filling, highly competitive winner, honorable rather than unscrupulous.

The movie pays deliberate homage to Robert Rossen's *The Hustler* (1961), with playing poker rather than shooting pool as the focus of the action. Michael is a player who at different times has been a hustler in the sense of dissembling cheater, hustler in the sense of one hurrying to defeat, and hustler in the sense of clever competitor searching for angles but eager for action and confident in his skills. The depiction on screen may not be persuasive for either therapists or poker players, but neither a Berglerian nor Lesieurian approach could account for such a "life story."

The two cases of gamblers compelled to lose presented in this chapter, one from life and one from literature, resemble the *Hustler* and *Rounders* scenario only superficially. In these cases the gambling habit is put to pathological or irrational use, though only in one does such use represent a radical change. Idiosyncratic and extraordinary, these cases suggest the rarity of this kind of pathology while they argue for a case-by-case approach to a condition not well-suited to the strictures of any one definitive theory.

Dr. Morris "Moose" McQ. consulted with a psychiatric colleague when he became alarmed at the recent changes in the gambling behavior of his friend James, a thirty-year-old assistant professor of history with a recently minted Ph.D. from Yale and a pregnant wife. Moose and James had been classmates and habitual gambling buddies during their undergraduate years at Brown. They had spent many afternoons together at Narragansett Park, Lincoln Downs, Suffolk Downs, and even Rockingham Park, not to mention evenings at the dog races at Taunton and Wonderland and the harness races at Foxboro. They had traveled as far afield as Monmouth and Saratoga for a day at the races. Back on campus in Providence, they had spent hundreds of hours together over their four-year membership in a virtually perpetual poker game down the hall from their dormitory rooms.

From the beginning of their acquaintance, Moose had learned how closely parallel to his own experience James's gambling history had been. They had both started at age fourteen, playing gin rummy (progressing over four years from a tenth of a cent a point to ten cents a point) and betting three-game baseball parlays at five bucks a shot with the local handbook at a corner snack shop. Moose considered James's gambling acumen very nearly equal to his own. Both were known not only for their skills at cards and handicapping, but also for being available for almost any kind of action at any time. The net results over the years, extending through graduate school for the one and medical school for the other, were a great deal of action and pleasure without significant profits or losses. The gambling had not impeded academic achievement for either of them, and so far as Moose knew it had not threatened James's marriage, either.

What was particularly alarming to Dr. McQ. was a dramatic change he had observed in James's recent gambling behavior. He reported to his colleague that with James's acceptance of his first full-time academic appointment, he and his wife had become financially independent from their families—if marginally so—for the first time in their lives. And James had eagerly reunited with his old friend Moose in a weekly, table-stakes, pot-limit poker game.

According to McQ., James could win or lose a quarter of his annual salary in this game, and in fact he had done so on four occasions, three of the four being losses, in his first four months in the game. Even more than the stakes, however, there were three other things particularly disturbing to McQ.: that James was not playing with his customarily confident skill; that he had asked to borrow money to play in next week's game; and that he had proposed a bizarre, high-risk betting strategy for a trip to the racetrack.

Moose confronted James with his observations and concerns, called his attention to his apparent acute anxiety, and strongly advised him to call a psychiatrist. James had denied that there was a problem and said he could cover the loan if necessary by cashing in some CDs he was holding. But when Moose made seeing a therapist a condition of the loan, James agreed and promptly called for an appointment. The psychiatrist had received Dr. McQ.'s thorough briefing, with James's permission, prior to the scheduled session.

Almost immediately, James acknowledged that there was indeed a problem and that he didn't understand it at all. Dr. F. said that he thought they could work toward some understanding but that there were two conditions for treatment.

"I want you to agree to stop all gambling immediately, perhaps for the duration of treatment, or at least until we get a handle on the situation."

"Yes, I can do that," he said. "In fact I assumed that would be the case, and I welcome it."

"The second is that you begin to attend meetings of Gamblers Anonymous."

James demurred, arguing that he couldn't accept the premises of the program, particularly the spiritual component, and that he didn't think he belonged in such a group.

"Think of it as a structural imposition on your schedule," Dr. F. said. "You don't have to buy into any of it. You just have to do it—because it is a condition of treatment with me."

James agreed, Dr. F. believing he could detect some relief along with resistance in the slightly delayed acceptance of the terms.

Therapy moved very briskly through an initial phase. As James described his gambling experience, Dr. F. discerned a clearly dichotomous pattern. On one side, there were the accounts of James's history, which he would narrate in fondly nostalgic, low-key terms. He'd tell amusing anecdotes about other gamblers, about incidents enriching the gambling contexts, about memorable wins, about unusual games or ventures or individual plays, and about memorable losses as well.

In the historical material, the dollar amount of the action seemed to have no bearing on James's attitude toward the experience. Unlike many pathological gamblers who have a tendency to seriously underestimate—or deny—the measurable degree of the gambling in terms of money and/or time, James seemed to be a reliable and accurate reporter. Unlike other pathological gamblers, he neither boasted nor expressed aggressive satisfaction in stories either of wins or of "bad beats." Most striking, there were several self-deprecating anecdotes, like the time he had to leave his car in the parking lot at the track because he had gone broke and lacked the change for the toll booth on the return trip.

In contrast, on the other side, there were the stories of the present poker game and reports of gambling ventures he had been projecting in recent months, all of which were attended by clearly anxious or depressed affect. James acknowledged that one reason he had been happy about his academic appointment was that he thought it would make it convenient and feasible for him to play in this particular poker game, which he had been hearing about from Moose for a couple of years. He had been looking forward to it with pleasure ever since getting his degree and the appointment, but the game itself had turned out to be a nightmare. It became the focus of his thinking. His whole week was structured from game to game, the time between the last deal of one week and the first deal of the next week a period of anticipation, replaying of mostly losing hands, planning of strategy, recalculating of probabilities, and mounting excitement. But none of it was pleasurable.

For the first time in his life he was having trouble concentrating on his work, or thinking about anything but the game (this is what Frederick Barthelme calls "the jones" in *Bob the Gambler*). Most dismaying, he knew he was playing badly, making what he called amateurish mistakes, calling bets he knew he had no business calling. In the past he had felt he always had an edge in poker games that lasted long hours because he had the ability to sustain his concentration while others became fatigued and careless. Now, after just an hour or so, he found himself unable to remember cards dealt and folded in stud poker. If he got behind early in the evening, instead of getting more conservative as had been his prudent habit, he started taking longer chances. And as his losses mounted, he began scheming about other ways to recoup. His last loss had virtually exhausted his whole stake, all the money he had saved while living the Spartan existence of a graduate student.

At this point, with the extensive and readily accessible background on record, Dr. F. turned the focus of the treatment to the vital question, Why now? What else had changed, besides the gambling behavior and attitudes toward it? Had the gambling simply exhausted James's tolerance for it and passed over the threshold of addiction? His ready acceptance of abstinence and GA meetings argued against this, except that James made it clear that he hoped to return to action as soon as he figured out what had happened, why it had gone bad. He missed it, or at least he missed the old self he had been when he could gamble happily.

Well, then, what else was going on in James's life, what other changes accompanying the alteration of a long-standing pattern of behavior, in which an avocation he felt good about had turned into a disturbing obsession? In this phase of treatment, Dr. F. set aside any direct attention to the gambling per se and explored the recent major changes in James's life: the end of his identity as a student; the arguable loss of freedom as a married man; the start of a professional career with its accompanying stresses and pressures; the end of dependence on his family; and, perhaps essentially, the responsibilities of becoming a parent, the giving of hostages to fortune. Clearly each direct change was likely to have indirect effects both on his gambling behavior and on his attitudes toward it.

James examined these issues carefully. He still thought of himself as a student and looked forward to maintaining that identity throughout a career as a publishing research historian, with several projects already in mind; he had simply entered a new phase of his academic life and anticipated continued success, measured by acceptance of his work and the possibility of receiving funded grants, which he was already being urged by his distinguished mentors to pursue. There had always been time for gambling, and he didn't see why there couldn't continue to be some.

As for his personal life, he seemed genuinely pleased with his marriage, and the expected child had been planned and was eagerly anticipated. They both had always wanted children, wanted to have them while still young, and had thoroughly explored the consequences to their lifestyle and relationship entailed in such a development. Jenny enjoyed an occasional gambling foray herself (there was an anecdote about their honeymoon), had expressed no negative feelings about his gambling (never even asked for an accounting), and seemed to approve his choice of diversion.

The only warning sign in this picture was that he hadn't told her about the recent developments or the extent of his losses. She had no problem with his being in therapy, had never asked about his reasons for starting treatment, and did not know about the GA meetings. Unless James was uniquely masterful at rationalization/intellectualization defenses, which seemed unlikely at this point in treatment, Dr. F. concluded that he would have to suspend the hypothesis that major life passages were the proximate causes of the problem. But he did make some notes questioning Jenny's passivity and challenging James's assumption of her innocence about his activities.

It was only when Dr. F. turned his attention to an exploration of relationships within the families that there emerged a crucial clue to a valid solution of the mystery. Long before he was fourteen, James had observed his parents, some of his aunts and uncles, and many of their friends taking pleasure in playing cards for what seemed to be moderate stakes. And there had often been vacation trips and cruises that included visits to racetracks and casinos; but there had never been suggestions of difficulties arising therefrom. Jenny had had no such experience in her family. Finding no particularly useful information in these answers, Dr. F. asked an offhand question, perhaps more out of curiosity than therapeutic insight.

"How did you and Jenny manage to save so much money in the first place, when you were a graduate student and she had never worked?"

"Well, as soon as I started college, my folks put me on what they called an 'allowance'—more than enough to pay for tuition and bare living expenses. And they insisted on continuing it all the way through graduate school, even though I began to receive fellowship and then assistantship stipends.

After we got married, it was enough for Jenny and me to be comfortable, so that we could put away what we got from her folks."

"What was that, a similar 'allowance'?"

No, what it sounded like, after James struggled to explain it, was an old-fashioned dowry. It was not a wedding gift; it took the form of annual checks, made out to James, over a period of five years, by which time he should have earned a degree, a position, and a livable salary.

When Dr. F. used the word "dowry," James responded with chagrin and contempt, unusually strong negative affect for him: "He was paying me to take his daughter off his hands. The two of us sat alone in his study after dinner and worked out the deal. I had no intention of refusing whatever offer he made. I would have married Jenny without a penny, but I saw no reason to turn down a relatively modest amount from a rich man."

"That sounds like a reasonable position, now, perhaps a healthy rationalization. But I wonder how you felt about it at the time."

"As a matter of fact, even then I knew that I was rationalizing. I can remember feeling for a couple of uncomfortable minutes that I was being bought and even stronger feelings about the man—that he was anything but generous, that there might be unseen strings attached to anything he gave, and that he was probably getting more than his money's worth of pleasure out of humiliating me in this way. But I set aside all of those feelings, took the deal in my eagerness to get on with what mattered—marrying Jenny."

"And what did she think of it?"

"We didn't discuss it. It was between me and him, and it was understood from the start that I would handle all financial matters."

"So it never came up?"

"Not for a couple of years. Then there was some kind of argument between her parents about the way her father had been treating her mother's family, and Jenny said that he liked nothing better than to lord it over people, to throw in their face that they might be better educated than he was but that he was the one who made money. One of his favorite boasts—Jenny said she'd been hearing all her life—was about the Ivy League graduates he could buy and sell. And I'm one of them, I said to her, and finally told her the details of that session. She wasn't at all surprised or disappointed. She said there wasn't any point to denying him that little pleasure out of some false pride or foolish principle."

"Maybe there was some point," Dr. F. said.

"What do you mean?"

"Maybe, now that you can get along without it, you have been divesting yourself of unwanted funding from a source you despise."

"The word my mother-in-law uses is 'loathe.' Let me tell you what she told me during the family celebration after I got my degree. She took me aside and said she hoped I'd never again have to accept any money from 'that man.' It was her husband she was talking about, and she said that his money was all 'blood money.' His business success had begun in a series of ventures, both wholesale and retail, in which he'd cheated a succession of partners, beginning with his own family, and then he had collected an enormous insurance claim from a fire that he had hired an arsonist to start. That's how he got the capital to start his present occupation as a second-mortgage man, operating at the margins of the law, taking advantage of troubled people. He seemed to specialize in loans likely to default, so that he could foreclose on property he saw potential value in.

"She called him a clever and ruthless man, said she loathed him, and angrily told me she was disgusted with herself for staying married to him after learning the extent of his cruel and even criminal behavior."

Almost incomprehensibly, James had "forgotten" this confession until this session had triggered it. He had never shared it with Jenny and hadn't given it, he said, a moment's thought—"at least consciously," he added, with a bit of an embarrassed smile for Dr. F.

James wholeheartedly embraced the hypothesis that he had used the high-stakes poker game to cleanse himself of his father-in-law's filthy lucre and perhaps the guilt of having accepted it in the first place. His habitual gambling had indeed become compulsive, in the sense that compulsive gambling is compulsive losing, and he had rushed eagerly into a gambling situation far beyond his means, losing what he felt he had to lose, but also losing his enjoyment of gambling itself. That money had been a burden; the unwanted "bundle" was baggage that he had found a way to jettison.

Over time that hypothesis held up, and James's treatment was quickly terminated. He went back to modest recreational gambling, at a level he could afford. He began to keep a written record of his action to monitor his performance, and this scrutiny allowed him to eliminate the kinds of gambling that netted losses (NFL football was his worst field), in turn making him a consistent, modest winner, especially in the small-stakes poker games that are common in academic communities.

James and Dr. McQ. remained close friends (as did Drs. McQ. and F.), but the only gambling they did together was on occasional visits to the racetrack. On those occasions, however, at least until the advent of computerized wagering, they always went to different windows. Nevertheless, Moose always paid close attention to the recommendations of his clear-thinking, keen-handicapping, small-betting friend.

For a habitual gambler like James, whose recreational habit feeds a substantial involvement of interest and time, there is always the danger that situational stressors or transient traumas will push habit over the line into pathology. Keeping careful records can be a defense against potentially devastating escalation, just as the sudden change in the shape or texture or color of a mole can signal the emergence of skin cancer in what had been for many years a benign blemish.

The obsessive record-keeping of a habitual gambler, however, is not necessarily a symptom of pathology. This was the inappropriate premise of an episode of the short-lived TV series *Murder One*, where a client's meticulous accounts were themselves presented in court as evidence of a pathological condition. The character was a pathological gambler, all right, well on his way to self-destruction and harming others along the way. But it was not his obsessiveness that made it so, nor was his compulsiveness driven by a need to lose. His pathological need was for the action, and there were apparently no limits to what he would do to finance his continued play.

For a more "compelling" fictional representation of the need to lose that characterizes this rare form of pathological gambling, I turn to Peter Carey's *Oscar and Lucinda*, which includes a richly detailed portrait of this condition. There are hints of it in several other gamblers profiled in other chapters, especially in the gambling folie à deux of Ray and Jewel Kaiser examined in chapter 9, but it does not appear to be the primary feature of pathology.

Nevertheless, it is prudent and practical for a practitioner to rule out this condition; if it can be established that this particular pathology is indeed at work, then successful treatment is likely. Like other, one-dimensional, guilt-fostered neuroses, the compulsion to lose is remediable through standard insight therapy, cognitive-behavioral approaches, or modalities based on "existential," "self-psychology," "ego-psychology," "object-relations" theories et al. For Carey's Lucinda, however, the "cure" comes from the experience of exhausting the need to lose and eliminating the substance of what must be lost.

Lucinda Leplastrier is an heiress to wealth she does not want, knows she does not deserve, and feels belittled by because she has not earned it. She grieves and is conscious of guilt because only another's death could make her wealthy. She identifies herself closely with working-class origins and has fierce loyalties thereto, but she is constrained by the Victorian value systems of her time and place from fully expressing that identity. And her acquired wealth imposes an idleness upon her, great expanses of time she is unable to fill with constructive effort or productive energy.

When Lucinda, with her proto-feminist values, her enterprising nature, and her energetic brightness, discovers gambling (cribbage, fan-tan, dice, poker—anything), she finds both pleasure and purpose in the days of her life. Gambling occupies her time, preoccupies her mind, diverts her attention, discharges her energy, and allows her to divest herself of the unwanted wealth. If, at the novel's end, she beseeches Miriam to get some of that money back, we may understand it as a matter of right and justice—since Miriam's inheritance is hardly a reward for virtue or in any way the intended consequence of Lucinda's losing bet—as well as an indication of the dire straits into which Lucinda has fallen ("an impoverished woman" who "walk[s] the streets of Sydney" [428]). She has lost not only her fortune but, more important, her "beloved."

The anomaly of a Victorian-era woman frequenting the seamy sites of gambling (and other) degeneracy adds poignancy to the depiction of Lucinda. In this accomplishment, Carey has been anticipated by William Gibson and Bruce Sterling in their portrait of Lady Ada Byron in The Difference Engine. She has "rubbed shoulders with very ugly company—sharpers, low clackers, loan-makers, and worse" (189). Unlike Lucinda, however, Ada suffers visibly from the ravages of "this gaming-fever":

> What vivid, unnatural hope and fear, joy and anger, sorrow and discontent, burst out all at once upon a roll of the dice, a turn of the card, a run of the shining gurneys! Who can consider without indignation that all those womanly affections, which should have been consecrated to children and husband, are thus vilely prostituted and thrown away. I cannot but be grieved when I see the Gaming Lady fretting and bleeding inwardly from such evil and unworthy obsessions; when I behold the face of an angel agitated by the heart of a fury!
>
> It is divinely ordered that almost everything which corrupts the soul, must also decay the body. Hollow eyes, haggard looks, and pale complexion are the natural indications of a female gamester. Her morning sleeps cannot repair her sordid midnight watchings. (408–9)

Lucinda, on the other hand, survives (or recovers?) to become a person of significance in the Australian labor movement, a kind of Down Under Mother Jones, achieving a well-directed fulfillment of her energy and values without benefit of her fortune, her love, or her glassworks. She has lost all. She has no further need of gambling action, having dispensed with the unwanted cash and invested herself in social action. The speculative acquisition of the glassworks has clearly been a rash and impulsive gamble. And the climactic bet with Oscar, which she desires with all her heart to lose, becomes the fullest expression of her love (though Oscar, in his own blind devotion to her and his total ignorance of "what normal is" when it comes to emotions, misconstrues it).

At the heart of the novel there is a scene where they discover, in her stateroom en route to Australia, their common experience with gambling in all its forms and their mutual enjoyment—or addiction or obsession or curse. He has come ostensibly to hear her confession, and it becomes something quite other than what either of them contemplated. "Where is the sin?" he asks, when she has given an abbreviated history of her polymorphous indulgence in action. "Our whole faith is a wager . . . we bet that there is a God. We bet our life on it. We calculate the odds, the return, that we shall sit with the saints in paradise. Our anxiety about our bet will wake us before dawn in a cold sweat" (218).

The anxiety of the gambler is all Oscar's (see chapter 5); Lucinda is serene and joyful at play (beautifully caught on screen in Cate Blanchett's performance). They play poker. She loves the way he plays, legs jiggling all the while. She loses, rejoices, raises the stakes, and loses her way into blissful anticipation of more losses to come. The passionate attachment between them is born over the cards and achieves its only consummation in the mad, impulsive, risk-all bet she offers him later on. Guilt-ridden as he is, Oscar must accept the wager, obsessively misunderstanding its meaning, resigning himself to the phobic ordeal and traumatic stress he must endure to play it out.

Oscar, in anguish, plays to win the bet, believing it will mean his ultimate loss. Lucinda bets, hoping to lose, even stacking the deck to achieve that loss, believing it will make her an ultimate winner. Both are right, though ironically not as they foresee the payoff. In Lucinda's case, the compulsion to lose—found but rarely in the lives of problem or pathological gamblers—leads her to a life of accomplishment in which her independent values are triumphant though her hopes for a passionate paradise are lost.

It is for such rare cases that I would reserve the use of the word "compulsive" in characterizing a gambling pathology. For what shall it profit a gambler who sets out to lose the whole pot, unless there is a payoff of freedom to act without the burden of the unwanted buy-in stake? Once understood, the pathological and irresistible power of the compulsion may be lost as well.

Anything can happen in a horse race . . .
there's ten thousand ways to lose.

A thoroughbred trainer
in William Murray's
Getaway Blues

Gambling and Anxiety

Anxious affect often is apparently present in gamblers, but this is no more than would be expected in a highly energized, excitement-filled, tension-charged activity and atmosphere. That does not necessarily mean that gambling produces, characterizes, or expresses symptoms of anxiety disorders, nor does it mean necessarily that the observable signs of various anxiety disorders in common gambling behaviors are typically masking, or serving as acceptable self-explanations of, underlying disorders. Yet certain particular cases suggest that that may be exactly what is happening on some rare occasions.

Jerome L., a thirty-six-year-old psychologist, had made a substantial success in his hometown. His consulting firm had won exclusive contracts with both the city and the county school systems to administer all psychological testing for them. And his clinical staff received most of the referrals from the school counselors for both their students and the dysfunctional families of those students. His wife, a former member of his clinical staff, was content now to be a full-time homemaker for their two small children.

As a couple, Jerome and his wife had a social life that revolved around a group of his friends from high school days. In a tightly knit (minority) ethnic community, most of them had never left home, typically working in family-owned businesses. Jerome himself had been away only during graduate school, and on his return he had picked up his old associations as if he'd never left—the weekend get-togethers, the Sunday touch football or softball games, and the poker games every other Wednesday night.

For nearly twenty years the group of six or seven men, with a constant nucleus of five, had been playing cards together, and though their life situations had changed over time the stakes they played for had not risen commensurately. Jerome didn't consider himself a gambler anyway. In fact, this poker game was his only gambling action. The other men often made fun of him because, though he was among them perhaps best able to sustain whatever moderate losses the game could inflict, he would constantly complain. He would never sit still at the table: his knees seemed always to be rhythmically knocking together, and he'd frequently jump up between hands to get a bite to eat or to refresh his soft drink.

"I ain't got no mazel," he'd whine, like a mantra, when he drew cards, whether it was a losing hand or in anticipation of losing the hand. "Ain't that a bitch?" he'd say, when he won one, as if his luck was sure to go bad again. A win meant that Lady Luck was setting him up for a bigger loss. As for a "poker face," forget about it. His countenance revealed a constant series of tics, winks, smirks, moues, and grimaces. In terms of results, Jerome, over the years, was probably as close to even as laws of probability allowed, given his relative level of skills and the cutting of pots to cover the cost of refreshments. Nevertheless he persisted in declaiming his ill fortune.

Jerome sought counseling at the insistence of his wife. For months, she told him, he hadn't been himself. He didn't seem to be able to focus on anything at home or at work, complained of fatigue and soreness and tightness, while what she experienced was a shortening of his never remarkable patience. She had heard that one day recently he had walked out in the middle of his own staff meeting without a word of explanation. Moreover, she drew his attention to her observation that his behavior was at its worst just before and after the Wednesday night game.

"It's that damned poker game, Jerry," she had said, finally, when she gave him no choice but to seek help, along with a remark along the lines of "Physician, heal thyself."

"Why now?" Jerome was asked at his first session. "Has anything changed in recent months in your life?" Then, in the absence of any positive response, "Has anything changed in the poker game?"

Indeed, the nature of the game had changed, in part because of "new blood," three new players, somewhat younger men, two of whom were latecomers not only to the group but to the community itself. Instead of breaking up at midnight as they had always done, they often played on into the night, sometimes even quitting just in time to go out for breakfast. Instead of every other week, they were now playing every Wednesday, and a couple of times they had actually shot dice after the last round of poker had been played.

Jerome professed to enjoy the increased action but felt he was "too preoccupied" with it. He anticipated the next game as soon as the last one was over and planned his week so that he would be well rested for Wednesday evening and then be able to recover from Wednesday night. He was aware of being preoccupied with the game, but he also realized that he was losing more than he won and was making uncharacteristic mistakes of judgment. The losses didn't concern him—he could well afford them—so he couldn't understand his increased agitation. His self-esteem wasn't keyed to winning at poker. He also experienced, when he won, a kind of "postcoital tristesse" that could last a couple of days.

"Sue's right," he said. "It's the damned poker game. But I don't have a gambling problem. I wouldn't get into the craps games, and when the gang organized a group junket to Las Vegas I wasn't the slightest bit interested or tempted."

"Have you thought about quitting?"

"Of course. But I don't think I'm ready to do that. For the last month, I tried something else. Regardless of what the others would do or say—which has never bothered me anyway—I would quit at midnight and play only every other week."

"And?"

"It was worse. I had two full weeks to dwell on the game. On the off Wednesdays I'd fantasize hands. By the time the next game came around I was so keyed up I was a basket case. And playing the game itself was no fun at all."

For Jerome L., himself a mental health professional and a generally bright man, a shrewd diagnostician with quick insight and a logical turn of mind, treatment moved very quickly.

The focus on the poker game provided no ready explanation for the changes of mood, deterioration of normal functioning, or escalation of habitual behaviors over the past six months—although the inner changes paralleled the changing conditions of the game. No other factors in his family, professional, social, or sexual life could be discovered.

Clearly there were issues associated with the Young Turks in the game. They were aggressively seeking to carve their own niche in a long-standing social structure and actively take on roles of new leadership. It presaged a genuine changing of the guard, and Jerome felt some resentment about it, as did some of the other old-timers. But Jerome had the wit, the wisdom, and especially the ego strength to deal with these factors. If tinged with sarcasm, his attitude toward the younger men was rather avuncular than bitter—no sour has-been he.

"Suppose the poker game were taken out of the equation," the therapist suggested, "what then?"

It was as if a lightbulb suddenly gleamed in a balloon over his head. Jerome not only grasped the concept but seized on the validity of the application to himself. The poker game was incidental, coincidental, or peripheral—though the occasion for the dramatic emergence of symptoms—to the matter. He quickly diagnosed his own condition as Generalized Anxiety Disorder, and referred himself to one of his own adjunct-staff psychiatrists, who prescribed a moderate dose of Xanax. He responded favorably, with no apparent side effects over the next nine months, and the symptoms of Generalized Anxiety Disorder disappeared.

Even though it was neither the problem itself nor the proximate cause of the problem, despite his wife's perception and his own concurrence, Jerome decided to give up the poker game. He neither needed nor enjoyed it anymore. He maintained his friendship with the gang, however, and occasionally filled in when they needed a hand if one of the regulars couldn't make it. He had to remind himself to intone, "I ain't got no mazel," just to get a rise out of his old buddies and the new guys as well, but this at least provided the frisson of enjoyment that for him the actual play lacked.

Jerome concluded that he had been using the regular poker game to mask the "prodromal" symptoms (precursory or premonitory signs before a latent or developing condition emerges) of anxiety all along. Perhaps it was the disorder in the process of developing into the full-blown condition that resulted in ever-increasing demands on the game to mask and/or explain the symptoms. Perhaps it was the escalation of the game that precipitated the ripening of the incipient condition. He concluded that it was impossible to know, that he didn't care which came first, the chicken or the egg, as long as he knew that he liked his eggs sunny-side up.

Clearly there may have been other forces at work in this situation. Viewing the game itself as a "system," for example, we can see that the sudden appearance of new members could have a dramatic effect on each of the old players. The nature of the system as a whole would change to accommodate and adjust to the new elements, while each of the surviving elements would be challenged to reassert its nature, function, and role or to make appropriate adjustments in them. New blood is invigorating but also threatening.

A comprehensive analysis of the dynamics and psychodynamics of the game would have to examine the competitive-aggressive nature of the game itself. It is very likely that the aggressiveness of the younger players in carving out their own niches in the game, asserting their wish for a higher level of action—raising the stakes, for example, then lengthening the hours of play and increasing the frequency of the games—was an assertion of youthful vibrancy, strength, and resilience. And this in turn would have provoked an instinctual response enacted in displaced aggressiveness, reaction formation (welcoming, nurturing, and mentoring the despised, feared interlopers), or other defenses in the older players.

In a sociological context, the nature of the ethnic community itself would have to be taken into consideration. A small, insular, self-sufficient Jewish community in a small border-state city would provide both a challenge and a haven for newcomers from large, cosmopolitan cities of the North and Northeast. And the community would be both enriched and enraged by the incursions. On this level, the poker game could have played out a microcosm of the entire socializing process.

Moreover, Jerome's very role as leader in the community, where his reputation as wisest and most-likely-to-have-succeeded was well-established, was a role played out in the poker game as well. In other words, Jerome's anxiety and symptomatic behaviors could have had their overdetermined origins in a wide variety of influences on him as a biopsychosocial organism. A persuasive scenario might very well also be posited by object-relations theorists. But the therapist had been presented with very little of the systemic or contextual circumstances to work with, and given the identity of the client it is doubtful that such material was accessible or that an enriched understanding of the anxiety-producing factors could have brought about a more satisfying outcome for a client in search of prompt results.

The pathological, disturbing behaviors ceased; Jerome happily quit the poker game. He was pleased, the therapist was pleased, and they congratulated each other on successfully achieving their goal. At termination they briefly addressed the issue of the likelihood that Jerome's anxiety would recur, perhaps triggered by possible professional reversals, by his children's adolescence, by the aging process in himself and his wife, by parents' deaths, or by other unforeseeable stressors. But both were confident that he and Susan would recognize the symptoms and take appropriate steps to deal with them. Jerome saw no reason to seek in-depth analysis to explore a hypothetical etiology, but he acknowledged the possibility, however remote, that he would change his mind about that. And he knew where to go to get whatever help he might decide he needed. Whether or not he was relieved to know that he was not a pathological gambler, he was in a way gratified to realize that his gambling behavior had led him to appropriate treatment for his anxiety disorder.

As for the poker game he left behind, I suspect that both the other individual hands and the game as a whole, whatever other pathologies might have been at work in its system, was probably relieved by the removal of the chronically anxious player. Most gamblers are uncomfortably aware of the anxiety-prone players in their midst—the knee-jigglers at the table, the white-knuckled chair-grabbers at the jai alai fronton, the moist-palmed pacers in front of the TV monitors at the track, the shaky-handed drinkers at the sports bar. Chronic worriers are a fixture of the gambling scene, players who worry about every bet, expressly anticipate losing, and even worry over winning bets because they may trigger losses to come.

Of greater concern here are the not infrequent occasions of full-blown anxiety or panic attacks associated with gambling. Behaviors that signal possible pathology are those that are often laughed at, if nervously, by other players. There may be early warning signs in the poker player who jumps from the table in the kitchen and kicks the refrigerator door or the one who throws the whole deck of cards across the den in the basement. More serious are the not infrequent spectacles of gamblers who suddenly jump up from the table or wheel or slot machine, sometimes bursting into tears or letting out a scream, but more commonly staring with glazed eyes and shocked expression and vacant affect as they rush out into the night or day or weather.

In extreme cases, such florid displays of anxiety attacks may terminate in "accidental" traffic deaths or in that ultimate act of the pathologically anxious gambler, the jump from the bridge. I remember the day that a horse player ran from Golden Gate Fields in what may have been an anxiety attack and couldn't wait to get to the Golden Gate Bridge, that most popular of all suicide sites, so he went off the upper level of the Oakland–San Francisco Bay Bridge. "Bridge jumper" is a phrase usually reserved for bettors who borrow the company payroll to bet on a favorite to show, where running out of the money means running out of time and life. I suspect, however, that the bridge jumping of some gamblers is neither a calculated suicide nor a deliberate act of picking the last desperate option, but a careening out of control from overwhelming anxiety or an uncontainable panic attack.[1]

The anxiety disorders, according to the DSM, include Panic Attack, Agorophobia, Social Phobia, other specific phobias, Obsessive-Compulsive Disorder (OCD), Posttraumatic Stress Disorder (PTSD), Generalized Anxiety Disorder (GAD), and other anxiety disorders. Theoretically, gambling behaviors may be exhibited by sufferers of all these pathologies.[2] The case I am about to present exemplifies several of these conditions at once.

The character of Oscar in Peter Carey's *Oscar and Lucinda* provides a persuasive illustration for this segment of my argument. Oscar Hopkins is first described by his great-grandson as he (the narrator of the story) contemplates a "sacred glass daguerreotype" of Oscar prominently displayed on the wall of the family home: "the ramrod back, the tight lips, the pinched nose, the long stretched neck . . . caused by Oscar Hopkins holding his breath, trying to stay still for two minutes when normally—what a fidgeter—he could not manage a tenth of a second without scratching his ankle or crossing his leg" (1).

These persistent nervous tics, suggestive of GAD, are captured very well by Ralph Fiennes in the role of Oscar in Gillian Armstrong's movie version (1997, screenplay by Laura Jones, adapted from the Carey novel). The filmed portrait of the character, however, tends to isolate only a few aspects of the comprehensive picture of anxiety disorders found in the literary "daguerreotype" of Oscar's story brought to novelistic life.

Carey's Oscar suffers several full-blown panic attacks during the course of the narrative; his childhood's magical thinking and accompanying ritualized behaviors may suggest early signs of OCD; his tendencies toward agorophobia and social phobia explain both actions and avoidance of actions central to the plot; his hydrophobia is intense (brilliantly enacted on screen by Fiennes); and the latter affliction has an explicit etiology related to his father's inflictions of serial traumas upon him, all of which are related directly or indirectly to water and the ocean (hence, PTSD). The strange child evolves into a most peculiar, afflicted, traumatized, inhibited, repressed, tormented, obsessive man. And it is his gambling that allows him to give expression to these many aspects of his identity (a kind of punning ironic twist on F. Scott Fitzgerald's notion of "character" in "action").

We see him as a small boy, early in his great-grandson's imagined reconstruction of his life, who cannot walk or run to or from his home to the bottom of the cliff at the waterside without ritually counting the number of steps he takes. He thinks (magically believes) that if he can cover the distance in exactly 365 steps it will bring about something good, though he knows not what or how. It is from that cliff that his father has cast all his wife's clothes in his melancholy madness after her death. And it is at that waterside, where Oscar is required to help him collect the specimens for his scientific study, that the father suffers a serious injury for which Oscar feels responsible.

The injury occurs in the aftermath of the single instance when Oscar has been struck by his father, a preacher of the Plymouth Brethren so austere as to consider popish and pagan any joyful celebration of Christmas. Oscar, given a taste of Christmas pudding by a kindly servant, has been physically rebuked—both for the taste and the enjoyment of it—and prays for a divine message to help him understand. After the first phrasing, "if it is your desire that your flock eat pudding in celebration of Thy birth as a man, then show Thy humble supplicant a sign" (16), gets no answer, he prays, "if it be Thy will that Thy people eat pudding, smite him!" (17).

What amounts to an "idea of reference," then, means that Oscar has caused his father to be smitten. The magical thinking and ritual behaviors intensify, leading him to believe that arbitrary occurrences are signs from God, including the results of flipping coins and the casting of a special stone on a grid resembling a hopscotch design but marked with Oscar's own "runic" symbols. In time he is thus "divinely" persuaded to leave his father's home and take up residence with the Anglican priest.

Oscar Hopkins, this friendless isolate, this obsessive observer of minute details, this overbright but bizarre interpreter, this phobic fidgeter, eventually matriculates at Oxford, where his studies accomplish no significant alteration in his behavior or personality—until the day he is introduced to the racetrack. Quite by accident, Wardley-Fish encounters him and informs him that he is known around the college as "Odd Bod." Still, rather than go to Epsom Downs alone, Fish lends Oscar five guineas and takes him along. He lectures Oscar on his system: how to handicap a race, how to manage money while betting, how to distinguish between good information and bad, and how to observe significant characteristics in the paddock—advice apparently sound, though Fish himself proceeds to ignore all of it in his fever to cash a big bet in the first race.

Oscar has his own ideas, keeps his own counsel, and proceeds to bet three guineas on a 9-1 shot, knowing that he will win, that it is God's will, and that the winnings will enable him to continue his education. It is all part of God's plan, as Oscar divines it, and both the opportunity to gamble and his own prescient gift for it are understood and appreciated as the evidence of a heavenly Providence. He wins his first bet, of course, and his great-grandson ends the chapter with the wry observation, "In the case histories of pathological gamblers you find the same story told time and time again" (97).

From this moment on, everything changes for Oscar. The strange child having become the Odd Bod, all his phobic and obsessive and anxious characteristics are expressed in his gambling behaviors. His meticulous accumulation of detail is accompanied by a belief system permeated with primitive superstition. And throughout the rest of his short but eventful life, all of his dilemmas—moral and ethical, theological and philosophical, familial and practical, intellectual and emotional—are either the direct result of his obsessive involvement in gambling or expressed in his inevitable resort to gambling. "I cannot stop gambling," he says, "cards, dogs, whatever is going—even on the sabbath," and again, "I cannot gamble . . . it is like opium to me" (a screenplay line derived from a letter of Oscar's [285]; his subsequent dependence on laudanum to counter his hydrophobia is but an incidental irony in the story).

If we look at the psyche of the character, that is, beneath the superficial movement of the plot, we find the explanation for Oscar's actions in his manifold neurotic anxieties, and just as important, we find the explanation for his failures to act in his manifold phobic constraints. The gambling, the escalating gambles of his "career," are the symptoms through which a plot, or life story, is enacted. But the underlying set of pathologies are the anxiety disorders that are themselves enacted in the gambling behaviors. Without the gambling we have no story. But without understanding the etiology of the gambling behaviors we cannot appreciate the richness of the character portrayal nor the delightful irony by which the plot is resolved. It is an extraordinary impotence, imposed and reinforced by anxieties and phobias, that produces an act of procreative fecundity.

Some of Peter Carey's most compelling imagery, as Gillian Armstrong's movie makes patently clear, takes on an iconographic eloquence, particularly the glass church drowning of its own glittering but transparent weight in the Australian backwater. The climactic adventure of the story is the result of an inevitable bet between two pathological gamblers. Together, Oscar and Lucinda have engaged in a kind of folie à deux in which they embrace a mad gamble against preposterous odds. Yet clearly neither these two nor Faust's Howard and Carrie (chapter 3) nor Barthelme's Ray and Jewel (chapter 9) qualify for inclusion in the chapter on psychosis (chapter 7) that is to come.

It is at least as clear, as this discussion of Oscar contrasted with the presentation of Lucinda in chapter 4 has demonstrated, that it would be reductio ad absurdum to use the same diagnosis for these two cases. Indeed, although Carey's (and Armstrong's/Laura Jones's voice-over) narrator calls the history of their gambling "the same story told time and time again," the dramatic power of the story derives from the very essential differences between the two.

Lucinda's gambling "makes sense" as both a sequence of acts of deliberate divestiture and as a pleasurable, satisfying, necessary, energetic activity that must be discharged before she can get on with her life, that is, get a life of her own. Oscar's gambling makes no sense at all; it must be pursued because it is the one viable way he can deal with or express his multiple

anxiety disorders (in other words, the way his creator can objectify or exter-
nalize the disordered character he has created). It is the encounter of the two
contrasting pathologies that generates their fascinating story.

What I find particularly poignant in the portraits of these two pathological gamblers is how persuasively they demonstrate in their symptomatic
gambling two such distinct pathologies: the one compelled to lose to attain
a specific defined goal, the other obsessed with the action to avoid or contain the anxiety of his fears, foibles, and fidgets. Both Lucinda and Oscar have
their sadnesses, their griefs, and their feelings of despair and hopelessness.
But their frustrations, guilts, and anxieties, not to mention their personality
constructs, identify their conditions as something other than clinical depressions. If they evidence problems of impulse control, those problems are rooted
elsewhere than in disorders of mood, and they find their flourishing expressions distant and distinct from those of one another.

Both Lucinda's "condition" and Oscar's belong in two distinguishable
categories of pathological gambling. Yet both are distinctly minor modes of
the constellation of psychological disturbances I am describing in this study.
They may be examples of tales told time and time again, but they are hardly,
alone or together, typical stories or case histories. The goal-oriented compulsion to lose and the enactment of anxiety disorders are among the rarest
forms of the pathology. In the next chapter, we turn to some of the most
common, the mood disorders.

If it wasn't for bad luck, I wouldn't have
no luck at all.

Booker T. Jones
and **William Bell,**
"Born under a Bad Sign"

Gambling and Depression

Bill Barich's *Laughing in the Hills* is the
memoir of a major depressive episode masquerading as reportage of a romantic adventure into the subculture of horse racing. Unlike William Styron's
Darkness Visible or Kay Redfield Jamison's *An Unquiet Mind*, which delve deeply
and affectingly into the turmoil of manic-depressive illness, Barich's book
projects his anguish outward onto the externalized experience. The inner
state, which he barely suggests, is instead masked, deflected, diffused, and
distracted by his immersion in the racetrack scene.

The impetus for Barich's depressed (and depressing) idyll along the back-
stretch was his mother's cancer. It came with sudden force upon his psyche,
and he consciously sought escapes from watching this much-loved woman
deteriorate irreversibly before his eyes. He took long walks, drove around his
old childhood neighborhood on Long Island, and finally, "Out of this desperation I started playing the horses" (2).

Immersed in the *Daily Racing Form* and distracted by his visits to OTB and
the peripheral, apparently whimsical betting of his family, Barich endured
the deathwatch. When he returned home to California, his grieving became
a "lingering sadness" (4), augmented by other traumas among his extended
family and especially by his wife's surgery for a suspected brain tumor. He
found himself unable to write, to live an orderly existence, to get along with
his wife—in other words, to function normally. Knowing consciously that
what he was trying to do was "to get past the sadness" (9), he left home in
mid-April to spend the rest of the spring at Golden Gate Fields in the East Bay
where the Tanforan meeting was about to begin.

It was about a year after his mother's death, but he had not adequately mourned, was still waking at night with visions of her face. So defended was he against the anxiety of profound grief that he found another "object" of loss to grieve over. Much of his dissatisfaction, frustration, and rage during this time he would direct at developmental blight: the environmental, cultural, and social decay he saw around his formerly idyllic California home county.

This is a textbook example of the defense mechanism called displacement, by definition an unconscious process. Ensconced in a motel near the track, Barich continued to lament the visible signs of decay while avoiding his own interior wounds. Recording the piling up of losses in his early betting ventures, which both reinforced and blunted the depression, he observes, "All gamblers look for signs, and I was given an appropriate one . . . when a filling from one of my molars popped out. . . .The image of emptiness should have been transported to my brain, but it was not and I kept losing steadily" (43–44).

The emptiness might have signaled the underlying issue rather than the problems he was having with his gambling. Ironically, in the same passage, Barich says that "all gamblers share a common experience, a nostalgic longing for a condition prior to habituation" (44). But he makes no explicit connection with his own nostalgic longing for a time before the developers destroyed his environment, before his wife's surgery, when he could live and write in an ordered world. More to the point, this generalized nostalgia was suggested by his drives around the scenes of his childhood, and those in turn represented his essential nostalgia for the cherished mother of his childhood, before she sickened, withered, and died. In his case, nostalgic longing was camouflage for intolerable grief.

Laughing in the Hills is a nonfiction novel of the highest order, conceived and executed with the artistry of compelling fiction.[1] The details of horse racing and of the gambling it generates are interspersed with reflections on Italy and the Renaissance. A passage on Savonarola aptly focuses not on the infamous book burnings of his reign in Florence but on his reformist persecution of gamblers (and prostitutes); and there is pointed reference to the hanging and burning that was Savonarola's lot, followed by a series of plagues upon Florence, as if to mess with established traditions of gambling was to bring down the wrath of God or Fate.

Among the people Barich encounters at the track are a trainer (the engaging Emery Winebrenner), who exhibits florid symptoms of bipolar disorder, and a "racetrack gypsy" named Richard Labarr, who says that winning a maiden race at a county fair with a horse he owned, having bet fifty dollars across the board on him at 19-1, was like "the best orgasm you ever had" (51).[2] But for the purposes of this analysis, the enactment of emotional states by other gamblers is less meaningful than the detailed, implicit account of Barich's own depression in the guise of his gambling odyssey.

By the end of the Tanforan meeting in June, Barich still had more than three hundred dollars of his original five-hundred-dollar stake. It happened to be the day Affirmed beat Alydar in the Belmont Stakes to complete his Triple Crown. But Barich's emotional books had been balanced: "I was letting go of the sadness, letting go of my mother. Living and dying, winning and losing, I sat on the stool and drank my whiskey, suddenly permeated by all the emotions I'd been blocking out. Nothing abides; no cause for alarm" (219). In Barich's case, the artifice by which a preoccupation with gambling masks depression had not been disastrous. One could argue that it was salutary, in that he survived a major depressive episode, and even constructive, in that it allowed him to break through his writer's block and fashion a memorable book from the experience. In the case I am about to describe, where the masking was at least equally conscious, the results could have wrought significant harm.

Wally's poker game was a convivial biweekly (payday) affair among a group of men who had worked together for many years. The food was good, the beer in ample supply, the play erratic and amateurish, and the men enjoyed riding one another as much as they enjoyed the action itself. When Wally brought his prospective son-in-law into the game, Vinnie was heartily welcomed. After all, the guys had seen Janie grow from an enchanting child into an engaging and accomplished young woman, and they figured they could embrace any choice she had made.

Vinnie did not disappoint them. Outgoing and voluble, he entered into the spirit of the play and byplay with good-natured energy. But after a few months, one of the men took Wally aside and wondered if Vinnie should be playing with them. "What do you mean?" Wally asked, and was told that there was a suspicion the young man had a gambling problem. "It's not so much the way he plays poker—hell, we're all lousy players and we know it—but did you hear what he said about the NFL games and the money he bets? Can he afford that kind of wager?"

Wally said he'd give it some thought, and in fact Vinnie stopped coming to the game. The guys were surprised to learn, not long after that, that Janie and he had broken up, that she had moved out, and that she was already seeing someone else. Oh, and by the way, Wally had heard that Vinnie was in GA. Some five years and two therapists later, Vinnie was able to construct a chronological account of his story.

"I was about fourteen when I was introduced to gambling, by my grandfather, of all people. I'd spend some time with him and my grandmother at Buzzards Bay during the summer, and he took me to the dog races at Taunton. I enjoyed it, and he got a big kick out of my excitement. Then some kids my age introduced me to poker, and we'd gather on the beach for long summer evening sessions, dealing cards and betting quarters on a big old beach blanket.

"Through high school and into college, I kept playing cards fairly often, the stakes growing steadily but not too fast, and pretty soon trips to the racetrack and Atlantic City were part of my entertainment calendar. It wasn't till my junior year that I got into sports betting. A guy I knew told me how easy it was to win hundreds of dollars betting on baseball games, and since I thought of myself as a pretty knowledgeable sports fan, I figured I could do it, too. That fall, I was betting NFL games pretty regularly, twenty-five bucks a shot, sometimes fifty, winning some, losing some, holding my own pretty much, but enjoying it so much that the little I lost was worth it. Sunday afternoons were the best part of my week.

"I thought about the action a lot during the week, but not obsessively. I mean, it never got in the way of anything else. I kept up with my schoolwork—graduated on time—and I enjoyed an active social life. When Janie and I got together and then moved in together, she knew how involved I was, but she went along with it even though she said she wished I would stop or at least cut it back. I guess she was a kind of enabler.

"I was really enjoying my life, on top of the world, but I guess it wasn't all wine and roses for Janie. When it all unraveled it moved very quickly. Took about half the football season. By the first of November, I was putting everything I had into trying to save that relationship. Because Janie wanted me to, I started going to GA, though she didn't go to Gam-Anon. But I was the one who persuaded her to give couples counseling a try.

"It didn't work. The therapist didn't know much about my gambling, or maybe wasn't able to address that as a couples issue. Janie moved out. She had found someone who suited her better, and I was a big loser. In more ways than one. Because that's when my betting got out of control. From one week to the next, my play escalated from fifty dollars a game to five hundred. I didn't care. Nothing mattered.

"I continued to see the therapist on my own, trying to deal with my grief at losing Janie, but paying no attention to the gambling. I don't even know why I kept going to GA. I didn't think I belonged. There was one guy at my meeting who kept after me to be my sponsor, and I thought that was pretty weird. But it was also pretty weird that I was even going at all, because I was betting my lungs.

"And then I hit a streak of ten straight losers, lost five grand. That's about impossible to do if you tried. My arrangement with my bookie was settle on two dimes, two thousand dollars, and I was always prompt. This time I had to max out both my credit cards to make it good, and I was done. I went to my father and told him everything.

"My parents have always been understanding and indulgent with me, trusted me to act with the integrity that I've always considered my strongest point. I guess they've sort of been enablers, too. But my father isn't a gambler and he attached no strings to the loan. It took me almost three years to pay it back, several hundred dollars a month, without fail, but that's what I wanted to do.

"By the time I started working with another therapist, I had stopped going to GA, but I had come to the end of my grieving for Janie. The new therapist led me to an understanding of what had probably been going on with me. The gambling habit was well established before Janie, but when I experienced the first traumatic loss of my life, a blow to my ego, my sense of myself as blessed—a 'narcissistic wounding' she called it—I couldn't handle the deep depression or the anxiety of the grief. The plunge into severe gambling losses gave me something concrete to blame for my feelings. And it's true, I could calibrate my depression according to the amount of my loss, quantify the grief.

"I'm still a sports fan, but I don't enjoy watching games very much now that I'm not betting on them. I'll usually have something on the Super Bowl and maybe every other year on the World Series, but that's it. And I know, my fiancée knows, my parents know, and of course my therapist knows, that anything more than that is a warning signal. Things are going great now, but I know that there are sure to be some kinds of losses down the road—it's natural—and that if I ever start making bets to give myself a reason for feeling bad I could very easily get into serious trouble again."

Listening to Vinnie tell his story, one hears a persuasive argument against the monolithic notion of "compulsive gambling." Indeed, when his gambling habit turned pathological—with the sudden losses, the not-caring, the hopelessness, the helplessness—he was presenting florid symptoms of a major depressive episode. As Wally put it to the guys one night, "When Janie canceled all the wedding plans, Vinnie went out and impaled himself on his bookie."

Observations of Vinnie's behavior over time might well reveal certain bipolar tendencies. More clearly they would probably reveal symptoms of anxiety in the sensation of being "wired," the sweaty palms and palpitations in tense situations, even the incessant fidgeting and persistent chatter at those poker games. But there is no pretense at making a firm psychiatric diagnosis here. The point is that appropriate therapy in this case might well look at the gambling, not for a primary diagnosis, but as symptomatic of a treatable mood, anxiety, or adjustment disorder.

There is an abundance of clinical evidence to support the correlation between depression and pathological gambling,[3] but to give added weight in support of this part of my presentation I turn to, arguably, the three most important names in the literature of gambling: Feodor Mikhailovich Dostoevsky, Aleksey Ivanovich, and Sigismund Schlomo Freud. An old joke says that Freud's last name must have been "Himself" because you never see the surname "Freud" in print without the reflexive "himself" attached. But I think it best serves the purpose of this investigation to address the case of Dostoevsky himself first (with a brief but significant digression), then the analysis of that case by Freud himself (with two necessary digressions), before turning to the literary avatar of most contemporary gambling characters, Dostoevsky's misunderstood self-portrait in Aleksey (with an irresistible digression).

The two best-known characteristics of Dostoevsky are his epilepsy and his gambling. Both are amply documented. His friend Baron Wrangel, for example, wrote of the frequent recurrence of epileptic fits (though Wrangel "never, thank God, saw one of them" [299]). He also mentions Dostoevsky's "craze . . . for play" as "surprising" because "he had never touched a card" in Siberia (317). In 1865, Dostoevsky had written Wrangel "that he had gambled away all his money," and his friend had sent him something to help him out. A particularly appropriate observation should be repeated here: "Probably his passionate nature and shattered nerves needed the violent emotions which gambling afforded him" (317). Wrangel also notes that Dostoevsky's public readings could be marked by "his masterly art in delivery" or by a "voice [that] sounded dead, and was sometimes barely audible." Dostoevsky's swings among abject despair, passionate energy, and nervous irritability are frequently noted in Wrangel's recollections.

Ivan Turgenev frequently spoke of Dostoevsky as "mad." At first mutually admiring, Dostoevsky and Turgenev fell out at least in part as a consequence of gambling. Turgenev felt himself to be the aggrieved party, but it was Dostoevsky who exacted revenge by caricaturing Turgenev in the character of Karmazinov in *The Devils* (aka *The Possessed*). Their dispute had aesthetic, philosophical, theological, and political facets, but the personal antipathy was fueled by a debt. Dostoevsky had appealed to Turgenev for help when on a losing streak in Wiesbaden in 1863; Turgenev responded with fifty thalers; Dostoevsky couldn't repay it in a month as promised—and never did. Four years later in Baden-Baden, again having lost at the tables all the money he could manage to lay hands on, Dostoevsky met with Turgenev and the smoldering feud escalated into bitter argument, though the debt that nagged them both was never even mentioned.

Joseph Frank's magisterial biography details these matters with nonjudgmental thoroughness.[4] His citation of Turgenev's description of the gambling scene in *Smoke* is worth repeating here: "familiar figures, with the same dull, greedy, half-stupefied, half-exasperated expression, which the gambling fever lends to all, even the most aristocratic features" (212). Turgenev's distaste kept him aloof from the action; Dostoevsky was even more appalled at his own "gambling fever," but it drew him inexorably into action.

As early as 1863, Dostoevsky had conceived of a story focused on gambling, reporting to N.N. Strakhov in a September letter that the "greater part of it is already jotted down on scraps of paper" (*Letters*, 109). It is to be about a Russian living abroad who has "wasted all his substance, energies, and talents on roulette. . . . The whole story is concerned with his playing roulette for full three years" (109–10). Almost four years later, about ten months after completing *The Gambler*, a long letter to Apollon Maskov introduces a description of his own gambling with a confession of his "baseness and shame" (118).

Dostoevsky's narrative summary follows:

When I was travelling in the neighborhood of Baden-Baden, I decided to turn aside and visit the place. I was tortured by a seductive thought: 10 louis-d'or to risk, and perhaps 2,000 francs to win. . . . The vile part of it is that in earlier years I *had* occasionally won. But the *worst* is that I have an evil and exaggeratedly passionate nature. In all things I go to the uttermost extreme; my life long I have never been acquainted with moderation.

The devil played his games with me at the beginning; in three days I won, unusually easily, 4,000 francs. Now I'll show you how I worked matters out:

on the one hand, this easy gain . . . ; on the other, my debts, my summonses, my heartfelt anxiety and the impossibility of getting back to Russia; in the third place, and this is the principal point, the play itself. If you only knew how it draws one on! No—I swear to you it was not the love of winning alone, though I actually needed the money for the money's sake. . . . I risked again, and lost. I lost not only what I had won, but also my own money down to the last farthing; I got feverishly excited, and lost all the time. Then I began to pawn my garments. Anna Grigoryovna pawned her last, her very last possession. (That angel! How she consoled me, how she suffered in that cursed Baden, in our two tiny rooms above the blacksmith's forge, the only place we could afford!) At last I had had enough; everything was gone. (How base are these Germans! They are all usurers, rascals, and cheats! When our landlady saw that we could not leave, having no money, she raised our prices!) (*Letters*, 118–20)

What was Dostoevsky doing in the neighborhood of Baden-Baden if he did not intend to gamble? His financial needs are used to justify the action, his knowledge of gambling and observations of the success of others argue for the possibility of winning, and his confessions of his weakness to overcome the powerful lure of play explain (away) his inability to quit whether winning or losing. All this, plus the notion of "playing with their money" when ahead and the anguished rage misdirected toward others (displacement, again, as a defense), argues convincingly for a diagnosis of pathological gambling. A further or underlying diagnosis, however, is also strongly suggested, and to this I will return shortly.

The fourth volume of Frank's biography is called *The Miraculous Years, 1865–1871*. It explores the immediate context for the matters that concern us here. In earlier volumes, Frank lays to rest at least one piece of the prevailing Dostoevsky legend, in large part sustained by the writer's own self-romanticization, that is, that he experienced the severe trauma of being on the verge of execution in Siberia (1849–1954). About the period of his imprisonment in Siberia, the evidence is clear that Dostoevsky was never in imminent danger, that he never participated in gambling despite the prevalence of card games among prisoners, and that he suffered from seizures assumed to be epileptic although Dostoevsky claimed that the onset of his epilepsy postdated the Siberian sojourn.

The sequence of symptomatic behaviors is important. The seizures began long before the gambling. These miraculous years saw the production of no fewer than four literary masterpieces: *Crime and Punishment, The Gambler, The Idiot,* and *The Devils*. And this was accomplished despite frequent seizures, feverish activities of financial and romantic pursuits, and gambling junkets at every opportunity. Whenever Dostoevsky went abroad, Frank says, he "hurried to the roulette tables soon after crossing the frontier" (32). Whether or not he had begun by winning, he would persist until he had lost all available and accessible funds. Seizures would not typically accompany the gambling episodes but were likely to punctuate all other emotionally charged experiences—and there were many in his turbulent life. What had received little attention before Frank's exhaustive research is the fact that once widowed (1864) Dostoevsky proposed to no fewer than five women (in addition to renewing a pursuit of a former lover, Apollinaria Suslova) before finding willing acceptance in his "little diamond," Anna Grigoryevna Snitkina.

In *Summer in Baden-Baden*, a remarkable short novel by Leonid Tsypkin (first published in English translation in 1987), the narrator takes a train trip which becomes a journey back in time more than a century to Dostoevsky's sojourn in Baden-Baden in 1867. Virtually reliving or recreating the complex, chaotic, chimerical state of mind of a great writer afflicted with an uncontrollable urge to play roulette, Tsypkin, a physician, portrays Dostoevsky's experience of gambling as not only emotionally charged, but often dreamlike and *derealized*, almost a fugue state, and sometimes evocatively similar to experiences surrounding seizures. Moreover, describing Dostoevsky's agitated, anxious, panicky behavior during gambling, he says it "resembled the medical condition known as obsessive-compulsive neurosis, when every attempt leads to even greater failure and at the same time an even more persistent impulse to repeat the attempt" (78).

This brief digression into Tsypkin's work serves as transition into the work of another doctor, Freud himself. The historical importance of the 1928 essay "Dostoevsky and Parricide" cannot be overemphasized because it legitimized psychiatric examination of a case he characterized as having the "bewildering complexity" (222) of a great creative artist, a neurotic, a moralist, and a sinner. Freud selects "three factors from Dostoevsky's complex personality": "the extraordinary intensity of his emotional life, his perverse instinctual predisposition, which inevitably marked him out to be a sadomasochist or a criminal, and his unanalysable artistic endowment" (224).

Supporting his diagnosis of neurosis, Freud offered the following paragraph of argument:

> How then, strictly speaking, does his neurosis show itself? Dostoevsky called himself an epileptic, and was regarded as such by other people, on account of his severe seizures, which were accompanied by loss of consciousness, muscular convulsions and subsequent depression. Now it is highly probable that this so-called epilepsy was only a symptom of his neurosis and must

> accordingly be classified as hystero-epilepsy, that is, as severe hysteria. We
> cannot be completely certain on this point for two reasons, first, because the
> anamnestic data on Dostoevsky's alleged epilepsy are defective and untrust-
> worthy, and secondly, because our understanding of pathological states
> combined with epileptiform seizures is imperfect. (225)

Following pages of detailed discussion, he concludes that it "is extremely
probable" that Dostoevsky's alleged epilepsy was "an expression of his mental life" rather than "his mental life [being] subjected to an alien disturbance
from without . . ." (227). In other words, Freud diagnoses Dostoevsky's
epileptic seizures as symptomatic of hysteria, an "affective" epilepsy, rather
than an organic "disease of the brain."

The murder of Dostoevsky's father and his experiences in and surrounding his exile in Siberia could well have triggered seizures of either kind. At
the heart of Freud's argument is the former trauma, contributing to a sustained rehearsal of his theory of parricide, guilt, and the Oedipus complex.
Indeed, he evokes the *Oedipus Rex* of Sophocles, Shakespeare's *Hamlet*, and *The
Brothers Karamazov* by Dostoevsky himself—"three of the masterpieces of literature of all time" (235)—in support. Following the literary analysis, Freud
turns to the "episode . . . in Germany when he was obsessed with a mania for
gambling . . . , which no one could regard as anything but an unmistakable
fit of pathological passion" (237).

Dostoevsky's burden of neurotic and parricidal guilt, in Freud's reading,
"had taken a tangible shape as a burden of debt" (238). Rationalizations and
pretexts familiar to profiles of pathological gambling behavior were acknowledged by Dostoevsky when he wrote, "The main thing is the play itself . . .
greed for money has nothing to do with it. . . ." Freud goes on,

> For him gambling was another method of self-punishment. Time after time
> he gave his young wife his promise or his word of honour not to play any
> more on that particular day; and, as she says, he almost always broke it. When
> his losses had reduced himself and her to the direst need, he derived a second
> pathological satisfaction from that. He could then scold and humiliate himself
> before her, invite her to despise him and to feel sorry that she had married
> such an old sinner; and when he had thus unburdened his conscience, the
> whole business would begin again next day. (238)

At this point, Freud turns to a "little masterpiece" by Stefan Zweig, "Four-
and-Twenty Hours in a Woman's Life" (239). Indeed, Freud focuses in substantial detail on the Zweig story. He interprets the narrator's fascination
with a gambler's *hands* in the Casino at Monte Carlo as representing mastur-

bation, that is, that the "'vice' of masturbation" as expressing "a wishful phantasy belonging to the period of puberty" has been "replaced by the mania for gambling; and the emphasis laid upon the passionate activity of the hands betrays this derivation. The passion for play," he goes on, "is an equivalent of the old compulsion to masturbate; 'playing' is the actual word used in the nursery to describe the activity of the hands upon the genitals. The irresistible nature of the temptation, the solemn resolutions, which are nevertheless invariably broken, never to do it again, the numbing pleasure and the bad conscience which tells the subject that he is ruining himself (committing suicide)—all these elements remain unaltered in the process of substitution" (240–41).

And here the argument rests. The final paragraph (241–42), two sentences in length, generalizes from the Zweig story to include the Dostoevsky "case." Zweig's gambler literally commits suicide; Dostoevsky's gambling was self-destructive. The Zweig story, of course, has no effect on Freud's "highly probable" conclusion diagnosing Dostoevsky's "so-called epilepsy" as symptomatic of neurotic hystero-epilepsy.

Viewed in the larger context of all we know about Dostoevsky, however, from his own voluminous correspondence and the extensive observations of his contemporaries, we may reach another tentative conclusion, assessment, and diagnosis; namely, that he was afflicted with a severe case of manic depression. His career, his creative process, his affect as he and others described it, his public and private behavior, all are marked by wild fluctuations among extremes. He would be full of grandiose expectations, boundless energy, and unwarranted generosity; and then turn around into abject self-abasement, deep despair, and abandonment of hope. Moments of anxiety, irritability, angry outbursts, and panicky movements alternated with transcendent calm and blissful repose. Such a diagnosis would account for the gambling behavior, the bizarre pursuit of marital partners, and other erratic activities. The volatility of his interpersonal relationships, suggestive of personality disorders, is not inconsistent with bipolar conditions.

As for the seizures, it is impossible to know whether epilepsy was present; but if a pseudo-epilepsy was the case, even if associated with Posttraumatic Stress Disorder (as some of the episodes that seem to have triggered seizures suggest—and not, as Tsypkin suggests, OCD), manic-depressive illness remains an appropriate primary diagnosis. It is interesting to note, moreover, the absence of reported seizures associated with gambling traumas, though apparently seizures were triggered frequently by many other types of emotionally charged or traumatic events. This suggests that for Dostoevsky the gambling was an *alternative* to seizures, a way to express or discharge the conflictual, conflicted, inexplicable anguish of his interior experience.[5]

The guilt-driven transformation of masturbation anxiety into self-destructive gambling is another matter. Freud's interpretation is based not on observations of Dostoevsky's gambling, not even on a careful reading of *The Gambler* (which strangely is absent from his consideration, while *The Brothers Karamazov* is thoroughly mined), but on his reading of Zweig's story. In that story, a young widow apparently saves a man from suicide, only to have him break all vows and take her money to gamble yet again. From humility to grandiosity, from amorous bliss to angry rejection, with a face that can be "transfigured with gratitude" and hours later "possessed by the infernal tremors of the gambler's lusts" (94), this character betrays all the familiar characteristics of pathological gambling in extremis: the desperation, the rationalization, the irresistible urge to put at risk all possible redemption in order to continue gambling, and a self-destructive drive ending in suicide. But it is Zweig's focus on the young man's *hands at play* that supports Freud's association with masturbation, not Dostoevsky's hands, not even a glimpse by Dostoevsky of Aleksey's hands or by Aleksey of other gamblers' hands.

Unfortunately, Freud's argument has been misunderstood by later writers.[6] For example, Rosecrance (*Gambling without Guilt*, 1988, 54), in his otherwise excellent summary of gambling studies, cites Freud's theory as based on analysis of Dostoevsky's "published writings" (note plural and absence of Zweig) and on Dostoevsky's "fascination with masturbation" (again, the evidence for the fascination is in Zweig). Freud, Rosecrance acknowledges, "did not attempt to generalize beyond Dostoevsky"; but the fact is that Freud did generalize, from Zweig to Dostoevsky.

The best place to look for evidence and understanding of Dostoevsky is to what is substantially a self-portrait in *The Gambler*,[7] the first-person narrator and protagonist, Aleksey Ivanovich, a tutor (*outchitel*) in the household of an impoverished General who has staked his hopes for a happy future on the imminent demise of the still-wealthy Auntie (aka Granny). Aleksey is in love with Polina, the General's stepdaughter, who is admired from afar by the wealthy Englishman Mr. Astley, but is somehow involved with an unscrupulous Frenchman, de Grieux, who is in league with the courtesan Blanche, who herself is the object of the General's obsessive attentions and transparently foolish hopes.

Of these seven major characters in *The Gambler*, at least six present direct evidence that they suffer from some mental disorder, while the exception,

Mr. Astley, perhaps masks his neuroses behind the stereotypically English stiff upper lip and is arguably as unbalanced as any of the others, given his tendency to conduct nocturnal vigils while waiting for a sign or communication from Polina. (Aleksey calls him "strange" and "stupidly shy" [383]). In a sense his foolishness is a mirror of the General's, his infatuation with Polina no different in degree or kind from that of the General's with Blanche.

Of the seven, only Mr. Astley and the General are not directly involved in some form of gambling, although the General appears in the Casino in one scene as a model (the traditional stereotype) of noble diffidence with regard to the turn of the wheel. Of course staking your whole life on the long shot chance that you will be accepted by your inamorata is "gambling," but of a different order of submission to chance or fate. But alone in this cast of characters, the General's gambling behavior does not enact his mental state or disorder; it belies it.

All five of the others are gamblers per se. And for all of them their gambling behaviors are symptomatic of their conditions—neurotic, neurasthenic, personality-disordered, mood-disordered, and even psychotic. The villainous Frenchman le Compte, or the Marquis de Grieux, does not himself engage in games of chance at the Casino. What he does instead is provide stakes for others, taking a chance on substantial return should the General (or Polina) come into a substantial inheritance. He hopes and believes it will be all his because of his deal with Blanche, his holding of de facto mortgages on the General's properties and expectations, and his "agreement in principle" with Polina.

In other words, like an independent moneylender, a shylock (in gamblers' jargon), de Grieux has bet on a reasonable chance of profit from excessive interest and service charges on the loans. (It is not coincidental that the close association of shylocking and bookmaking is both an observable phenomenon of criminal behavior and also a basic assumption of American law enforcement operations.) In many ways perhaps the most rational of these characters, he is the least admirable. His Axis II diagnosis: Antisocial Personality Disorder, with his taste for criminal behavior an egosyntonic trait—and with the good sense to know when to cut his losses and move on to other victims.

Dostoevsky named this character de Grieux in an act of homage to Abbé Prévost, after des Grieux, the protagonist and primary narrator of *Manon Lescaut*. In that eighteenth-century French classic, bowdlerized of course in both Massenet's *Manon* and Puccini's *Manon Lescaut*, des Grieux details his own gambling as sometimes a tribute to his rational skills, sometimes a gift of good fortune (or providence), and sometimes a sign—when he practices the arts of a cardsharp—of his decadence, or, we might say, of an antisocial personality. Des Grieux also experiences extreme mood swings depending on whether Manon is with him or with someone else, a likely source of Dostoevsky's appreciation. Like Zweig's portrait of the suicidal gambler and Tsypkin's novelistic portrait of Dostoevsky in action at Baden-Baden, Prévost's portrait of des Grieux—even while it reverts to the stereotypical profile of the rascally cardsharp trickster—can support a diagnosis of manic-depressive disorder.

Returning to Dostoevsky's cast, we may understand the characters in action by charting their fortunes at their games of chance. For Blanche, arguably the least disturbed of the whole lot, gambling is not only a means to a variety of ends but enjoyable and exciting in itself. She may have base motives and is certainly willing to engage in fraudulent pretense in pursuit of her expensive pleasures, but she is honest in many ways, generous, affectionate, and sensitive to others in ways that balance her self-indulgence. Dostoevsky, in this character, depicts gambling as pleasure and not evil in and of itself.

Polina, whose name, allure, physical description, and volatility are all derived from Apollinaria Suslova (just as Aleksey's enchantment with the character seems to match Dostoevsky's with the woman), is driven to gambling by desperation, as her only hope for extrication from her financial obligation to de Grieux. She manipulates Aleksey into playing roulette for her, and she experiences elation and despair in the consequence of his successes and failures. Her eventual breakdown and hospitalization are never attributed to the gambling, but the symptoms of her deteriorating mental health are enacted thereby.

For most readers, the sudden appearance of Granny on the scene is a breath of fresh air in the turgid atmosphere of Roulettenberg. But it is a mistake to see her primarily, as Frank does, for example, as "fundamentally humane and kindhearted, represent[ing] the traditional down-to-earth virtues of the Russian gentry unspoiled by any truckling to foreign tastes and fashions" ("Study," 311). The central part of the book, the turning point of the action, is the episode of Granny's overnight plunge into addictive gambling. She enacts a cameo of conventional wisdom's profile of a compulsive gambler, yet seen in a context larger than the Casino, her delusions of grandeur, loss of memory, impulsivity, irascibility, tunnel vision, and reversals of attitude toward those around her seem symptomatic of senile dementia, the onset of "second childhood." As the clever de Grieux says, and repeats, "*Cette vieille est tombée en enfance*" (441, 445). Indeed, Aleksey himself accepts this diagnosis ("Granny's personality had shown itself so clearly . . . a refractory and imperious old lady, *et tombée en enfance*" [456]).

Examination of these characters reveals corollary points: that personalities, peculiarities, and varieties of mental conditions may be revealed dramatically by gambling action; and that traits of gambling behavior are reflections of more generalized states and conditions, rather than causes of them. Aleksey is the best example of these points. He is susceptible to the pathological gambling that overtakes him because his manic-depressive illness predisposes him to act out its symptoms at the tables. Indeed, he sketches his bipolar mood swings before he ever steps foot inside the Casino, and he begins there as an observer undecided as to whether to play.

He tells us repeatedly of his "strange" moods and his recurrent "excited state" (401). On the journey to Roulettenberg, he has been "completely absorbed in analyzing the essential nature of my feelings toward Polina" and has been "as melancholy and restless as a madman" (388). He is "simply mad," he tells her later, accusing her of "driving me into brain fever" (409). His explosive rage, his irrational rudeness, his offer to throw himself off the Schlangenberg for Polina, his provocative playacting as fool or devil's advocate or gadfly, even his running off to Paris with Mlle Blanche, all testify to the violence of his mood swings, where both the extreme melancholy and the frantic mania ("flecks of foam on my lips" [410], "state of frenzy" [413]) retain anxious features. Ultimately, the shifting fortunes, the hopes and despairs associated with gambling provide a more effective way of objectifying or justifying his bipolar condition than the affective vagaries of passional attachments. In this way, too, Dostoevsky's portrait of Aleksey expresses his own perceived (if undiagnosed) manic-depressive illness.[8]

The brief, intense period in which Dostoevsky wrote *The Gambler* occurred when much else was happening in his life. He had already caught the gambling fever and was putting his experience of it to profitable use in this book. He had met Anna when she came to work for him as stenographer, and it was to her he dictated *The Gambler*, which delayed his dictation of the final portions of *Crime and Punishment*. The period of composition thus coincided with the courtship of Anna, typically abrupt for Dostoevsky, and included episodes of panic attack and seizure. No sooner were the manuscripts completed, delivered, and paid for than the wedding took place, followed shortly by the trip back to Europe, to the spas of Germany, to the roulette tables. Having extrapolated his own experiences for *The Gambler*, Dostoevsky reenacted Aleksey's experience in his own. Life imitates art imitating life, the addictive gambling life of a manic-depressive.

I would venture to say that dysthymia and depression—perhaps mood disorders of every variety—are more common among gamblers than in the non-gambling population in general. Further, it may be possible to diagnose most pathological gamblers as depressed. The inordinately high rate of suicide among them seems to support this view. It would be easy, and perhaps comfortable, to assume that depression is the result of the gambling, the effect of the inevitable losing, the corollary of having hope turn to hopelessness and desperation, of having good fortune reversed, of feeling betrayed by luck, helplessly beset by destructive, implacable, unpropitiable forces.

That would be a simple and perhaps obvious conclusion. But in my view it would be wrong. In some cases such a conclusion would rely on the post hoc propter hoc fallacy that because the visible signs of depression came chronologically after the gambling it must have been caused by it. Depression might well precede the gambling losses but have lacked any outward manifestation. Certainly in many cases the gambling and depression feed on each other just as alcohol and depression do. Moreover, it is entirely likely that gambling may be used to mask or justify depression, that is, to account for those otherwise inexplicable feelings that make the inner life of a manic-depressive so wrenching in its inchoate anxiety and mysterious anguish.[9]

Even the mildest dysthymia may well be a precondition for the appeal of gambling to some people, perhaps even more than the more severe forms of depression. A vague malaise that is very nearly subclinical responds fairly readily to the pleasurable excitement inherent in the play of gambling action. On the other hand, the grandiose sense of omnipotence that accompanies some gambling experience may on rare occasions indicate a manic or hypomanic episode, though it is sometimes difficult to separate a manic episode from a psychotic condition that characterizes the cases in chapter 7.

Nevertheless, the evidence is convincing, perhaps even overwhelming, that pathological gambling in many—perhaps most—cases is a behavioral manifestation of underlying (typically, preexisting) conditions of mood disorder. And this being the case, when gambling behaviors even begin to suggest pathology, one should undertake a careful, thorough examination for the presence of depression.

He . . . would pass night after night sitting at card tables, and follow, with a feverish agitation, the various turns of the game. . . . "He's gone out of his mind."

Alexander Pushkin,
"The Queen of Spades"

Every trace of morality, religion, and humanity is effaced from the ruined gambler's mind. . . . the emotions which agitate a gambler's breast when he sees himself hurrying faster and faster to ruin [and] he is in a state of madness. . . . The more he loses the deeper does he feel disposed to play. He is for the time being completely under the influence of a spell. His reckless-ness grows upon him. You cannot move him from his seat. . . . His bosom is all the while the seat of a perfect tempest of passion. He curses in his own mind the moment he entered the pandemonium. . . . To utter ruin he will go, and the nearer he is to it the more furiously does he rush forward. The storm within is all the while visible without; you see it in his face. He is supremely wretched; as miserable as man can be in this world; he is in a hell, and has a hell in his bosom. . . . Such is the agony of his mind, that his legs will quiver beneath him, his whole body tremble, and the cold perspiration fall in drops from his brow. There is not a vestige of humanity left in his composition. . . . He has more of the nature of a demon than of a human being in him; the cards or the dice have wrought the awful transformation.

James Grant,
The Great Metropolis

Gambling and Psychosis

Before the Olympian troika of Tolstoy, Turgenev, and Dostoevsky towered over Russian letters, the preceding generation had its own mighty threesome of Pushkin, Gogol, and Lermontov. Necessarily beginning his writing career in their shadow, Dostoevsky had at least two influential models for treatments of gamblers. Gogol's contribution in his play *Gamblers* was a treatment of the familiar character type of the sharpster, the cheater, the amoral outsider or trickster. Examples of this tradition are to be found in Abbé Prévost's *Manon Lescaut*, Melville's *The Confidence Man*, and Poe's "William Wilson," as well as in the stereotypical denizen of the saloon in stock Westerns.

This type has maintained its currency, as may be seen by its appearance in such recent works as Thomas Pynchon's *Mason & Dixon*, Brendan Boyd's *Blue Ruin*, and the 1993 play *The Gamblers*, by Val Smith, which, like Gogol's seminal work, turns on the theme of the duper duped. (Another stereotypical gambling type is the sea captain ruined by his addiction, a character neatly epitomized in Hoeg's *Smilla's Sense of Snow*.[1])

At the other extreme from the cold calculation of the gambling cheater or swindler in Gogol, however, is the association of gambling and madness in Pushkin's even more influential "Queen of Spades." Dostoevsky's *The Gambler* may well have been undertaken in part as a response to Pushkin and the popularity of "The Queen of Spades,"[2] the point being to argue that his own gambling may at times have been impassioned, extravagant, and impulsive, but that didn't mean he was insane—a concern by no means paranoid. And it is interesting to observe that the character of Granny in *The Gambler* replicates the behavior of the old Countess in Pushkin, a quirky willfulness that suggests a "falling into second childhood." The difference is that the Countess's gambling habit prevailed in her youth, while Granny falls prey to the fever in her dotage.[3]

The first part of the epigraph from Pushkin at the head of this chapter describes his protagonist *before* he ever makes a bet. Though "a gambler at heart," Hermann has coldly calculated his resources as a young officer with a very small patrimony and concluded that he could not afford "*to sacrifice the essential in the hope of acquiring the superfluous*" (67). Yet hearing the story of how the Countess had been given a magical formula, a sequence of cards that would guarantee winning and that not only got her out of debt but later saved another gambler with whom she shared the secret, Hermann becomes obsessed with learning the identity of the three cards.

He conceives an elaborate scheme to court the Countess's protégée, the "martyr of the household" (66), in order to gain access to the Countess herself. He devotes his days to carrying on a secret courtship, while he dreams at night of unbroken streaks of winnings at cards. Succeeding in his deceitful suit, he surprises the Countess in her rooms, tries first to wheedle, then to frighten the secret from her. Only after she dies in front of him, presumably scared to death, does he follow the directions to the trusting Lizaveta's room— less to confess to her than to enlist her aid in getting out of the house.

The irrationality of the whole plan, from motivation and conception to execution, though carried out with almost diabolical precision, gives way to increasingly radical departures from reality. At the Countess's funeral, Hermann sees her winking at him from her coffin. That day, drinking excessively to silence his "inner disquietude," he manages only to "enfever his imagination still more" (79). Waking in the night, he conjures up a visit from the Countess, who gives him the sequence of cards—trey, seven, ace—and tells him the conditions under which their magic will work and he will be forgiven for her death: that he play them one at a time at twenty-four-hour intervals, that he never gamble thereafter, and that he marry Lizaveta.

It is at the point when he has placed his first bet, his entire inheritance of 47,000 roubles on the trey, that the second part of the epigraph appears, in the observation of a friend. It is indeed an act expressing madness, but the reader understands that Hermann had long since gone out of his mind. The added element of intense guilt only augments his inner conflicts; it does not deter him from the insanity of his course of action. He doubles his roubles, doubles them yet again on the seven after twenty-four hours, and returns for his final play at the appointed time. There, instead of playing the ace, he plays the queen of spades, the image of the Countess herself, who winks at him from the card face, and he loses all.

In the "Conclusion," Pushkin uses the same phrase (in at least one translation) to describe the outcome of this case: "Hermann went out of his mind." Confined to a hospital, he mutters "Trey, seven, ace! Trey, seven, queen!" over and over "with remarkable rapidity" (84). Lizaveta marries well, after all, thankfully extricated from the madness of her young officer. If the psychotic behavior is acted out in deranged gambling, and if the self-inflicted loss and terminal frustration of his wishes are what have pushed Hermann permanently round the bend, it should be clear that the seeds of the psychosis preceded any gambling. The intensity of the repression, denial, agitation, and anxiety indicates a "prodromal" stage of mental illness; Hermann and Pushkin have located the gambling as a powerful vehicle to carry it through to its florid, full-blown emergence.

Edgar Allan Poe was almost the exact contemporary of Gogol, but not surprisingly it is with Pushkin that Poe shares the gambler-as-madman motif. One of Poe's stories about M.C. Auguste Dupin ("Murders in the Rue Morgue") begins with a disquisition on calculation versus analysis, in which he says, "The analytical power should not be confounded with simple ingenuity; for while the analyst is necessarily ingenious the ingenious man is often remarkably incapable of analysis . . . the ingenious are always fanciful, and the truly imaginative never otherwise than analytic" (143). To exemplify his distinction he applies it to the game of whist, the precursor of bridge and a game of skill for intelligent gamblers, as more worthy of serious attention than chess, a game of skill and intelligence not customarily a gambling vehicle.

In "Never Bet the Devil Your Head," Poe presents a comic cautionary tale about a man who "could scarcely utter a sentence without interlarding it with a proposition to gamble" (483). In "The Man of the Crowd," on the other hand, he seems to have the Gogol-gambler motif in mind, when the narrator says,

> The gamblers [were] easily recognizable. They wore every variety of dress, from that of the desperate thimble-rig bully, with velvet waistcoat, fancy neckerchief, gilt chains, and filigreed buttons, to that of the scrupulously inornate clergyman, than which nothing could be less liable to suspicion. Still all were distinguished by a certain sodden swarthiness of complexion, a filmy dimness of eye, and pallor and compression of lip. There were two other traits, moreover, by which I could always detect them: a guarded lowness of tone in conversation, and a more than ordinary extension of the thumb in a direction at right angles with the fingers. (477)

But it is in "William Wilson" that Poe gives his fullest attention to the characterization of a gambler, and it is to a gambler gone mad. At Eton, William indulges in "miserable profligacy" and has his first confrontation with his ghostly double at a time when, "madly flushed with cards and intoxication," he "was in the act of insisting upon a toast of more than wonted profanity" (634). For Wilson, as for many, Eton is preparatory for higher education at Oxford. He tells us, "I had so utterly fallen from the gentlemanly estate, as to seek acquaintance with the vilest arts of the gambler by profession, and, having become an adept in his despicable science, to practice it habitually as a means of increasing my already enormous income at the expense of the weak-minded among my fellow-collegians" (636).

In particular it is Lord Glendinning, thought to be "immeasurably wealthy" (637), who is the target of William's hustling: "I frequently engaged him in play, and contrived, with the gambler's art, to let him win considerable sums, the more effectively to entangle him in my snares" (636). One night, Wilson and Glendinning are playing écarté and the trap is sprung. When the pigeon starts losing, the cardsharp allows him to double the stakes "with a well-feigned show of reluctance. . . . In less than an hour he had quadrupled his debt" (637). Wilson observes in his victim a "wild nervousness of manner for which his intoxication, I thought, might partially, but could not altogether account" (637). The hour's loss has in fact led to his "total ruin," his fortune being all too finite.

Now Poe changes Lord Glendinning's affect from the nonchalance of the typical courtly gambler to the anxiety of the pathological "chaser." And in Wilson he has the traditionally dissolute, immoral cheater, who not only deals from the deck with the skills of a "mechanic" but also is found to have cards up his sleeve and decks of marked cards in his possession.[4] But the point and whole effect of the story transcend these stereotypes in Poe's presentation of a man driven to distraction, given to schizophrenic delusions and hallucinations, rendered psychotic by a ghostly double who takes his shape and name and betrays his gambling criminality. It is remarkably akin to Pushkin's presentation after all.

Almost a century after Poe and Pushkin, Stefan Zweig used the motif to great effect, but with psychoanalytical implications that place "Four-and-Twenty Hours in a Woman's Life" at once closer to Dostoevsky and to latter-day notions of pathology. We have already seen Freud's association of this story with Dostoevsky, but we may also see in it a pair of examples of brief psychotic episodes.[5] The examples are so conjoined and mutually dependent, however, that we may refer to the twenty-four hours as a folie à deux, though the participants have entirely disparate perceptions of their shared experience.

A widow in her forties, not herself a gambler, idles away her time in the Casino at Monte Carlo observing the gambling behavior of others, especially the revelations she finds in observing their hands. She becomes fixated upon a particularly expressive pair of hands, convulsively writhing in spasmodic torment. From this point on, what she observes over the next twenty-four hours (reported for the first time, in the structure of Zweig's narrative, twenty-four years later) is a pair of psychotic episodes, one of the young man whose hands have mesmerized her, and the other her own.

When her gaze finally moves from hands to face, she anxiously beholds a beauty which expresses the same "unrestrained" and "fantastic and extravagant language as the hands" (37); and it exercises "a strange fascination" upon her. She watches the young man play for an hour, charting the ebb and flow of his action and reactions, until, having lost everything, he "sprang to his feet like one who rises when suddenly taken ill" (42) knocks over his chair, and staggers from the table.

The widow herself feels as if "turned to stone," gestures convulsively with her own hands as if mirroring his, and irresistibly follows him out from the Casino into the rainy night. The man who at the roulette table had seemed "instinct with a magical energy" now portrays "despair, self-abandonment, death-in-life" (49), and she is certain he is suicidal. She watches him for an hour, finally overcoming her modesty and inhibitions to approach him "to put an end to [his] mad and desperate inertia" (50).

In their ensuing dialogue, as she tries to get him to take shelter from the downpour and he mistakes her for a prostitute, their exchange three times echoes the closing passage of Dostoevsky's *The Gambler*, thrice sounding the repetition of the word "tomorrow" (57). Perceiving herself as "wrestling with a man for his life" (60), she rents a "sordid room" (61) in an inexpensive hotel, and spends with him a night that seems "to last a thousand years" (60). In the morning she awakens with horror at her situation, "overcome by a fresh and more terrible anxiety" (63). But the "most horrible moment of a lifetime" is followed by "a sister-moment which was full of sublimity" (65) as she takes in the transformed appearance of her companion, his expression once "monstrous" now "perfectly angelic" in its "paradisaical release from internal tensions.... He was saved, and I was his savior" (64–65).

As he awakens, she rushes off, arranging to meet him at noon, planning to pay for his return home. Over lunch, he tells her his story, in which the profile of a compulsive gambler is telescoped so severely it seems like a Classic Comics version of the course of the disease: instantaneous affliction, brief success, sudden decline into impoverishment, ruin, and crime. The widow reflects that "the actions he recounted seemed rather the outcome of illness than of crime" (73) and although told "with characteristic grace and charm" (72), the story alarms her by "the febrile glare in his eyes, the twitching of his features whenever he was speaking of his passion for play." She realizes, with a "nameless fear [that he] was poisoned through and through by his craze for gambling" (73).

She sees him as "hopelessly enslaved by a mad passion" (74) but offers to redeem him, to pay for the redemption of stolen family jewels and his return home, to escape from the temptation of Monte Carlo. He accepts with what seems to her "ecstatic and supraterrestrial happiness" (75), and after they stop at a church he blesses her as an angel sent him by God while she can "hardly bear to look at the miracle" (81) she had wrought in the transformed life and face of the young man.

They arrange to meet later, when she will see him off on the train home, but now she gives him money for his fare and to redeem the pawned jewels. He is reluctant even to touch the bank notes, but she prevails upon him to take them after writing an IOU. It is only after she is alone that she realizes how empty she feels without him, how his abject gratitude is not what she wants. She determines "in a frenzy of delight" that she must abandon everything and run off with him, and she laughs out loud at the "rapture" of her own thoughts (88).

Delayed by a well-intentioned relative, she narrowly misses the train. Suffering a "mingled sense of stupefaction and frenzied impotence," she is "drawn, as if by an irresistible force," to revisit all the scenes of their passionate attachment (91). She goes first to the Casino, where of course she sees the young man at play, not "the hallucination of a fever" but the "horrible" and "dreadful reality" of the "madman [sitting] at the roulette board" (93). On a winning streak, in his "obsession" and "ecstasy," he is oblivious of her, but when she finally makes him aware of her he looks at her as if they "shared a mysterious secret" (95).

She tries to get him to leave. He starts to obey, makes one more bet, then another, loses both, accuses her of bringing him bad luck, pushes her away, tosses bank notes at her in payment of his debt, and dismisses her forever with a shout of "leave me in peace" (99). In her eyes he is behaving "like a maniac" and she rushes out of the Casino to collapse on the very bench where he had sat in despair the night before.

Zweig's novella, collected with two other "tales" under the title *Conflicts*, compresses a case of severe pathological gambling into a twenty-four-hour sequence of abandonment, redemption, and false recovery. That the widow learns years later of the young man's eventual suicide supplies closure for her but is unnecessary for the reader. The extreme degree of suddenness and violence in the swings of his emotional pendulum moves his condition beyond typical bipolar disorder into the range of psychosis.

More important, the widow's experiences, which reflect a kind of symbiotic involvement in his mania and despair, directly mirror the obsessiveness, the fantasies, the uncontrollable impulsiveness, and the utter failures of reality testing that mark his condition. The story served Freud well in his interpretation of Dostoevsky. It serves even better to illustrate a pairing of characters in a folie à deux. Their concurrent psychotic episodes are triggered, directly and indirectly, by a morbid fascination with the spinning of the roulette wheel.

The young man may have already lost touch with reality when they meet, but it is only when the widow projects her own psychic disturbances onto him that she suffers her own brief but profound descent into madness. And their encounter plunges him more profoundly and inescapably into his derangement. It is the ultimate relapse.

Bolen and Boyd, in their 1968 historical review of gambling studies from a psychiatric perspective, rejected the nearly universal assignment of pathological gambling to categories of neurosis: "Our experience has shown a significant proportion of psychiatric patients afflicted with problematical gambling to have been schizophrenic" (627). As supportive as their general remarks are for the argument being presented in this book, their specific examples are neither convincing nor comforting: "Only two reports appear in the literature which indicate that psychotic individuals were afflicted with pathological gambling. One individual was probably manic depressive, and Israeli reported the case of a likely schizophrenic individual who designed elaborate wagering systems involving complex probability schema which were of a grandiose and delusional nature" (627).

A careful examination of the case reported by Israeli in 1935, however, fails to support that likelihood. The presentation of the forty-seven-year-old mental patient he calls Q (uncannily anticipating his pseudo-namesake in the James Bond series who matches his single-minded obsessiveness) focuses on his depressive episodes, including repeated suicide attempts, gestures, and plans. The grandiosity noted by Bolen and Boyd is readily attributable to a bipolar patient's experience of manic phases, during which

Q confidently predicts a month-by-month pyramid of gambling successes, a book on gambling that will instruct people how to win and will undermine casinos and other gambling establishments, and successful courtship of the widow he had once planned to marry.

It is the "elaborate wagering systems involving complex probability schema" that I would focus on here. While there is clearly a paranoid element in Q's thinking, his delusions do not appear to rise to the level of symptomatic schizophrenia. His schemes and systems, rather, are all based on applications of "the law of averages," an irrational translation of *probabilities into predictions*. This is not madness; it is common garden-variety vulgar error.

That Q was obsessive-compulsive is demonstrated in Israeli's description of his behavior, which includes elements of other personality disorders as well. But to the extent that he experienced psychotic episodes, they seem to me to have been the extremes of his manic-depressive range of mood swings. Rather than assuming that the suicide attempts were *caused* by losses in gambling (and stock market speculation as well, by the way), I would tentatively suggest the possibility that Q's intermittent feelings of total despair on the one hand and triumphant promise on the other were incomprehensible to himself except by relating them to the objectified experience of his gambling losses and his gambling prospects.

Q's madness must have been maddening to him. His gambling ventures were foolish, self-defeating, doomed. His charting of probabilities over thousands of tests was extraordinarily obsessive but served several ego-sustaining functions—as void-filling behavior, as justifications of the time spent institutionalized, and as providing data to support his grandiose wish-fulfillment plans. Q's hospitalization occurred in 1932. Had appropriate medication been available, his bipolar disorder might have been manageable, while the diagnosis of schizophrenia might well have been ruled out. What would also have been useful in this case would have been a therapy informed by an understanding of gambling behaviors and how they function, what they indicate, and how patients may be led to appreciation and modification thereof.

Could gambling behaviors be syptomatic of some forms of schizophrenia? At least one survey suggests that some problem gamblers have also suffered from schizophrenia,[6] though I have found no documented cases where individuals gambled as they did because they were responding to voices instructing them to do so. Admittedly, that absence renders this aspect of my argument rather tenuous. However tentatively, I may yet offer convincing examples in other (than clinical) kinds of literature, starting with Jack Richardson's *Memoir of a Gambler.*[7]

Once a prodigy of the American theater who weaved preoccupations with drugs, jails, and hookers through a sequence of plays, Richardson turned to reportage and subsequently fashioned an autobiography from his magazine pieces, structured around an extended gambling odyssey from which he flashes back to earlier periods, episodes, and people in his life. Aspects and symptoms of pathology mark all of Richardson's gambling experiences, whether as motivation, context, or behavior.

What stands out most clearly are the moderate to severe depressions that mark all his resorts to gambling, though episodes of depersonalization are also vividly described. In Las Vegas, he attributes the distortions of time to the deliberate use of power by casino owners, who "forbid clocks or windows in their gambling rooms so that day and night pass by uncharted by anything more precise than vague degrees of desperation or euphoria, and time becomes something privately carried in the mind of each gambler, a quiet or needling companion creating its own idiosyncratic clock." (85).

Richardson's obsessive record-keeping includes the amounts of tips to waitresses as well as dealers. His generalized speculations on gambling and gamblers tend toward the bizarre or at least colorful. An episode in a Vegas sports book includes the idea that "all sensitive gamblers have known witches and believed in their powers" (99–100) but rather than move away from the woman he identifies with that role he stays next to her because "the gambler's tenet of not abandoning a winning seat took precedence" (102). Speaking words of rationalistic rejection of superstition to her, he nevertheless feels "sunk in superstition," struggling to "slip back, without misgivings, into enlightenment" (104). Later, playing high-stakes baccarat, he describes "a gambler's instinct [which] comprehends relations between events that are perhaps too subtle for ordinary modes of observations. It is this instinct on which his survival is based, for if he ignores it and, while feeling disconnected from propitious flows and patterns, continues stubbornly to force a return of the good feeling he had about himself, he becomes nothing but an item of desperation, someone doomed to be unloved by fortune and destroyed by mathematics" (127).

It is not, however, these excursions into magical thinking, nor other outré flights of fancy pervading the text, that suggest psychotic episodes or schizophrenia. It is not even the aftermath of his biggest losing night in Las Vegas, when he experienced a series of visual, auditory, and tactile hallucinations that sound very much like delirium tremens. In fact, it is not even

Richardson himself but Peter, his guide to the gambling haunts of Hong Kong, the penultimate island on his odyssey.

Hired as a guide specifically to lead Richardson to where the action was, Peter took him everywhere but gambling dens until the tourist demanded to know why. Peter explained his aversion, stemming from the fact that as a boy he had been lost to gambling—literally. His father's increasing unpayable debts to a syndicate had caused the man to turn over first his wife, then his daughter, finally his only son Peter in payment to his creditors. It is the story of a high school science teacher who, as Richardson records Peter's account, "had begun gambling, and how he had one day covered the walls of the apartment they lived in with charts of lunar phases, horoscopic signs, and other perversions of the discipline he earned his living from. Shortly after, voices began to speak to him, and he to them. Hunches were whispered, and secret rituals worked out which, if rigorously performed, would bring success at fantan, poker, and the race track" (226).

In other words, the man's addictive gambling had triggered—or occurred contemporaneously with—the onset of his full-blown schizophrenia. Peter, at eleven, had become an item of gambling currency, passed from losers to winners, until the Hong Kong police cracked down, not on gambling itself, but on the use of human beings for stakes. Nevertheless, Richardson's spectacular successes at the tables and other betting venues to which Peter reluctantly led him drew Peter into action himself.

In the book's final scene, on a hilltop overlooking Macao's harbor at the base of an unfinished church building, Richardson has a "visitation" with the devil. Dressed as a tourist and speaking in cultured if archaic diction, this conjured figure speaks to him of the "excitation, the energy, the joy, despair, manias and moping—in short the high fevering of life that gambling gave you." But that is no longer "the devil's element," he says, nor is he "just a symptom of a worn-out mind" (251–53). Readers of the context, with its juxtaposition of gambling and psychotic behaviors, may not be convinced of the latter assertion, nor readers of this selected redaction of the former—at least by way of cautionary metaphor.

Another case in point might be Mickey Sabbath, the narrator/protagonist of *Sabbath's Theater*, the 1995 novel with which Philip Roth broke through the limitations of the Zuckerman books that had bound him for so many years. Symptoms of bipolar and several personality disorders are prominent in Sabbath's story, and though it is not clear that he is actually psychotic, he is certainly polymorphously perverse. He demonstrates inappropriate affect, inappropriate language with occasional loosening of associations, and bizarre behavior. All of this suggests severe mental illness and the possibility of some form of schizophrenia.

The bizarre behavior includes gambling, which he had learned as a boy on the Jersey shore: "We used to play blackjack . . . under the boards. I was introduced to blackjack by the Weequahic guys,[8] then developed my skills further at sea. Those blackjack games were legendary in our little backwater. Down for double! Up the shoot! Bai-ja!" (199). From what might be considered a normal introduction to gambling, Mickey has come to the point where he is likely to bet on anything and at the unlikeliest times. At his most bizarre, his most inappropriate, for example, he challenges a hospitalized mental patient to bet on blood pressures: "Wanna bet the spread? . . . A buck on the spread, another buck if you hit the diastolic or the systolic, three if you nail 'em both" (279). What takes this episode beyond a gambit of black humor is the fact that actual betting ensues.

For a more explicit representation of psychotic gambling, we travel far south of the Jersey shore. Rosario Ferré's brilliant novel *The House on the Lagoon* (1995) chronicles several generations of life in Puerto Rico while at the same enacting issues of family, faith, loyalty, love, class, mythology, epistemology, aesthetics, the nature of reality, and—above all—narratology. Along the way she provides a striking portrait of a woman whose gambling is labeled (by her daughter Isabel, one of the primary narrators of the saga) a "confounded hobby" (143) that brings about the dissolution of her family.

Isabel's version of family history, however, suggests other factors contributing to the mounting dysfunction. Her memory of her father, for example, only calls up "a faded photograph; sadness has washed away the sharp contours of his face," but the sadness may as well be the daughter's as the father's. She says, "I loved Father deeply, but he was a weak man. . . . He could never say no to Mother—no matter how harebrained her requests. If Carmita wanted to spend a fortune on beauty creams, Danish chocolates, or French perfumes, it was fine with him. He was always eager to please her, as if she were a child, and at first he thought it amusing when she started to sneak out of the house to gamble in San Juan's elegant casinos" (143).

Carmita's gambling, apparently, has been preceded by other indulgences, in a pattern of childlike tastes for simple sensual pleasures. But after the traumatic loss of a child, the gambling becomes the salient feature of her symptomatic behavior, in an apparent attempt to escape from or avoid grief or any concern with time, mortality, the stasis of death.

> At four o'clock every afternoon she would begin to feel restless, as if Poe's "Imp of the Perverse" had taken hold of her. She would hurry to the corner,

> hail a taxi, and have it take her to the Continental Club, the only casino in San
> Juan that was open during the day. She enjoyed the Lady Luck Afternoons,
> when until eight in the evening a lady got six chips for every dollar, instead
> of three. She met all kinds of women there, housewives running away from
> unhappy marriages, widows bored with their lives and afraid to travel by
> themselves, prostitutes looking for an early customer. Carmita was running
> away, too, though none of us could ever figure out what she was running
> away from. She lived in a fantasy world; reality was the roulette table.
> Between the *"faitez vos jeux"* and the *"rien ne va plus,"* everything was possible:
> trips to Europe, Dior's latest fashions, Tiffany jewels—all the privileges she
> had had to give up when she married Carlos. . . . (143–44)

Isabel may be projecting her own fantasies, a kind of nostalgia for a life
she had not experienced because her mother had "married down" for love.
But her inability to identify the roots of Carmita's escapist behavior is probably due to her focus on the gambling itself, which soon progresses from
"hobby" to "addiction" in her view: "she didn't just gamble at the casino;
the minute she went out on the street, she was looking for the lottery vendor,
or she would go to the racing agency to bet on next day's favorite horse. If she
didn't have any money, she would simply take whatever jewelry she was wearing to the pawnshop. She was hardly ever home, but spent the greater part of
the day wandering the streets, asking people for money" (144).

There are suggestions here, in her wandering, her being out of touch
with reality, her dissociation in what approximates a fugue state, of a dementia that could be Alzheimer's-related, or premature senility, or a pseudo-de-
mentia associated with trauma. For that matter, it could indicate a full-blown
schizophrenia. That it is not specifically a case of disordered impulse-control
is shown by what happens when Carmita comes into an inheritance. The
money is not used for gambling at all, but allows the family to move to
Ponce, where she is "almost cured of her habit: there were no casinos in
Ponce, and she had nowhere to gamble" (200). But when "a luxurious casino" opens at the Ponce Intercontinental Hotel and replicates the Lady Luck
Afternoons of San Juan,

> Carmita was delighted. She began to go to the casino with her friends, and
> soon she had a competition going as to who would win the slot machine's
> pot. When she lost, she asked her friends to lend her some money. If they
> refused, she just walked out into the street and asked anyone she met for a
> loan. Pedestrians couldn't understand why a well-dressed woman . . . was
> begging for money, and some began to take advantage of her. They would
> lend her ten dollars, then knock on our door and tell Carlos they had lent her
> a hundred. It might very well have been true, but Carmita would never admit

it, and Carlos didn't dare refuse. Months went by and the situation grew worse. Every time Carlos went out of the house, there would be someone waiting on the sidewalk, asking him to pay a couple of hundred which Carmita owed. (200–201)

Carmita's mental condition deteriorates from disorientation to derangement, which Isabel assumes is the reason for Carlos's suicide. Implicitly, Carlos's despondency over the wreck of his love object, his frustration over his inability to sustain her, and his shame over the public spectacle of her behavior, not to mention the embarrassment and impoverishment caused by it, are all attributed to her gambling. "Carmita's gambling finally did him in" (200), Isabel says simply, and she perpetuates this projected notion, thus diverting attention from her own trauma, the "nightmare" of Carlos "hanging himself from the rafters in the attic" (201).

The focus remains on Carmita, though the florid symptom of pathological gambling is eclipsed by a sinking into a near-catatonic or autistic or vegetative state:

Carmita got worse, and we had to get a nurse for her; she couldn't be left alone, because she'd wander out into the street and start asking people for money. . . . I knew I had to put Carmita in an asylum, but I wanted to postpone that as long as possible. During the day the nurse and I had to feed and dress her, carry her to the bathroom, and get her on and off the toilet; but at night she did everything on the bed. Every morning we had to give her a bath and change the sheets, because she woke up covered with excrement. [For some time she] refused to talk. She just sat in her rocking chair, combing her long, gray hair all day. (202–4)

Carmita dies in an asylum, without regaining her faculties, and without benefiting from a diagnosis of whatever disease may have been signaled by the sympomatic gambling behaviors.

We are dealing here with a character and a scenario inside a novel's character's scenario—several removes from a case-study of a particular patient's disorder. But clearly this material demonstrates both the capacity of a florid symptom to either signal or mask an underlying (and, in this case, undiagnosed) condition and also its capacity to serve as the identified focus of the family's "explanation" of its dysfunction. The symptom is a scapegoat for the dysfunction that radiates from the mental illness and is the center of the family's life. Such a person (character) could be treated for pathological gambling with every good intention, but neither individual nor family stability would be restored thereby.

There prevails often in such families a condition known as "pathological equilibrium," where it is threatening to the marginal functioning of the system to have the overt dysfunction it contains actually treated or perhaps even accurately diagnosed. As long as the rest of the family can operate *around* the perceived, accepted, tolerated "bad habit" of the one identified as troubled, they do not have to deal with their own separate and cumulative contributions to the dysfunction. Nowhere is this phenomenon more vividly demonstrated than in studies of what have often been called "schizophrenic families," that is, families that revolve around acknowledged cases of severely mentally ill members.

Again, I hope for the emergence in the clinical literature of pathological gambling behaviors in such families to support the picture painted so vividly in the creative literature. But at this point I can only echo Bolen and Boyd's caveat concerning facile categorization of all pathological gamblers as compulsive and severely neurotic. Psychotics who gamble are not likely to be healthy, rational, successful gamblers.

Life for me is a fast horse, five lengths in front at
the eighth pole, with my money on his nose.

Arnie Wolfenden,
a philosophical horse player,
in William Murray's
Now You See Her, Now You Don't

Filling the Void

The epigraph above is a variation of the universal tribute to "action." It is what makes a gambler feel truly alive. When the poker-playing hero of *Rounders*, trying to explain his return to action after months of abstention, tells his girlfriend, "I felt truly alive for the first time in . . . ," she knows their relationship is doomed.[1] It is useful—perhaps necessary—to be philosophical about such perceptions, however limited their approach to understanding or wisdom. The same William Murray, in *Tip on a Dead Crab*, says, "Trying to pick winners is an act of faith in the human condition" (73), and again, "we are dealing here with one of the great, enduring mysteries of existence—the isolation of winners from the great snarl of often conflicting statistics that shroud the average horse race" (72).

These reflections suggest that Murray would have us see horse racing as emblematic of more general paradigms for living, as he makes explicit in *The Hard Knocker's Luck* when, through his narrative persona Shifty Lou Anderson, he says, "all racetracks . . . are like great ships embarking on a new voyage every day and in which we strive for the only forms of immortality I believe in—the achievement of ecstasy, the blinding flash of revelation, the dream made true—each day containing all the seeds and hope and risk needed to make life a renewable adventure" (18–19). Almost half a millennium ago, Erasmus, as my colleague Bob Coogan pointed out to me, made similar observations about our inclinations to embrace any behavior that seems to fill the perceived emptiness inside human awareness. It is to considerations of this existential awareness that we turn in this chapter, specifically to its relevance for psychopathology.

Irvin D. Yalom has long been considered one of the great gurus of group therapy. Practitioners have leaned heavily on his seminal work, *The Theory and Practice of Group Psychotherapy* (first published in 1975), with additional helpful reference to his three subsequent books relating to groups and group practice. In his most recent incarnation as a novelist, Yalom has presented material valuable for this study of pathological gambling (see the following chapter) in *Lying on the Couch* (1997). I continue this chapter, however, with reference to another of Yalom's valuable contributions, an approach to treatment which he has called "Existential Psychotherapy" in a persuasive 1980 book by that name.

On his way from professional/theoretical scholarship to novel writing, Yalom composed a book called *Love's Executioner* (1989), which told the stories of ten case histories in such compelling narrative form that one may treat them (as I have for classroom purposes) as models of short story structure and technique. It is from the prologue to this book that I take Yalom's short-form explication of what he means by "existence pain": pain "that is always there, whirring continuously just beneath the membrane of life" and "all too easily accessible" (3).

Yalom believes that existence pain is always "the primal stuff of psychotherapy," and his clinical work is based on the assumption that "basic anxiety emerges from a person's endeavors . . . to cope with the harsh facts of life, the 'givens' of existence" (4). He finds four such givens that are "particularly relevant to psychotherapy: the inevitability of death for each of us and for those we love; the freedom to make our lives as we will; our ultimate aloneness; and, finally, the absence of any obvious meaning or sense to life" (4–5).

To acknowledge death intellectually, according to Yalom, is one thing, but we must also be dissociated from the terror of death, protected by the unconscious from overwhelming anxiety. The sense of freedom, on the other hand, evokes anxiety because it implies that "we do not enter into, and ultimately leave, a well-structured universe with an eternal grand design" (8). Existential isolation reflects the perceived truth "that we are born alone and must die alone" (11–12)—a perception that may break through "with chilling clarity" at almost any time during our lives. The cumulative effect of these concerns, along with an awareness that "the world is contingent," produces the "existential dilemma" for human beings, a species searching individually as well as collectively "for meaning and certainty in a world that has neither" (12).

This is as neat a parsing of what has been generally and vaguely labeled "existential angst" as any I have seen. Oscar Hammerstein's song-lyric version of the existential questions ("Why was I born? / Why am I living?") may be sung with a wide variety of intonations. But while the awareness of it may be experienced as anxiety, boredom, resignation, solipsism, or despair, among others, it seems to me that a common sensation is of inner emptiness. Something is missing. There is a hole in the self and concomitantly an unbridgeable gap between self and other/others/world.

What is called "the void" in metaphorical attempts to characterize what is "out there" is a projection of the perceived void within. In *The Tennis Partner*, Abraham Verghese quotes his drug-addicted friend about the first time he was offered a needle: "'from the very first shot, I was hooked, it just seemed to fill the hole' he said, putting his fist over his chest. 'Right here'" (126). Filling the void is my way of describing many behaviors, some of them addictive, by means of which people combat the forces of Yalom's givens.[2] For some, gambling is an exemplary choice, seeming to attack those givens head-on.

Specific application of existential theory to gambling has been made by psychologist Igor Kusyszyn: "through the free, independent self-regulation of action . . . gamblers confirm their existence. They prove to themselves over and over again that they are alive by speeding up their heart rate and increasing their muscle tension and by becoming emotionally aroused either positively—with hope, for example—or negatively—perhaps with anxiety" (137). The gamblers discussed in this chapter exemplify ways in which gambling serves in the struggle against "internal chaos" or existential angst.

For several chapters now I have followed the DSM taxonomy, which I find here—as I do in clinical practice—to be a useful way of organizing material, putting things into classifiable order, defining by genus and species (rather than arbitrary labels). But such taxonomy has its limitations, acknowledged to a degree in its concept of "multiaxiality." Individuals may as often as not be found resistant to single categories of classification; the lines of demarcation get fuzzy; conditions and symptoms overlap and contradict one another. Moreover, it seems at times preferable to abandon the system, to cut across the lines of disorder, classes of disorder, and even axes of diagnosis. The cases of pathological gambling examined in this chapter seem to me to be best approached in the context and grouped under the rubric of void-filling behaviors rather than via DSM classifications.

I begin with an adolescent who could be a poster boy for the idea that informs this chapter. Tony was referred for treatment by one of his teachers and his school counselor because his gambling behaviors at school were disruptive. When he had been confronted by those concerned educators at his school, Tony had acknowledged to them that it was a problem and "out of control." He accepted the referral immediately and made an appointment for the earliest possible opening.

A bright, articulate, personable, attractive eighteen-year-old, Tony was completing his final two years of high school in a special program for troubled youth. Alcoholic at fifteen, addicted to a variety of drugs by seventeen ("garbage-mouth druggie" in the local parlance), Tony was considered a leader at the school, a model of the potential for success in a highly structured program that included a heavy dosage of support groups, peer counseling, and outdoor activities along with academic rigor.

Now all the gains were being undermined by a new preoccupation. Every day, at every opportunity, whether at lunch or between classes and activities, Tony and two other boys would match dollar bills. Money-matching is a venerable form of gambling with and for money: matching coins, heads or tails (odds or evens). With three players, the unmatched surface gives the winner a two-for-one payoff; with paper currency, the last digit of the serial number, odd or even, determines which of the three gets to keep the money; if all three are the same, the next coins or bills double the stakes.

"I'm powerless to control it," Tony said at his first session, and the therapist thought, "Uh-oh." The young man talked the talk so well, it would be hard to know whether and for how long he would walk the walk.

Tony's parents were affluent property owners whose enterprises included an upscale suburban liquor store. Married but going separate ways, both were alcoholic: the father still drinking in a maintenance mode (though Tony remembered past binges for both parents), an indulgent, generous, "good-time Charlie" without the capacity to sustain closeness in any relationship; the mother in recovery, sober five years, a cold, angry, withholding woman intensely focused on seeing her only son straighten out, at times stern and punitive with him, at other times sorrowfully, guiltily forgiving. Tony spent most of his home time with his maternal grandmother, a sensible but somewhat overwhelmed woman who provided at least a dependable consistency for Tony. She found it difficult to say no to him, while the parents and paternal grandparents found it impossible—he was too charming.

Three evenings during the week and three or four times during the weekend Tony went to meetings—AA, NA, CA, sometimes ACA; some of them were twelve-step meetings, but not all. He often spoke at length at the meetings, sometimes led them, and all the friends he socialized with were in one program or another. He derived great satisfaction from being a well-liked, admired leader of this subculture. Tony claimed, convincingly, that he'd been straight and sober for fourteen months after his last slip.

After two sessions, the therapist hadn't made up his mind whether to add GA to Tony's routine. The gambling behavior, though persisting, showed no sign of escalating. Tony's observant ego monitored the gambling even while, as he said, he was unable to stop the game once begun.

It was inappropriate, in the therapist's view, to treat a client for pathological gambling without requiring him to attend GA meetings and without asking for a commitment to stop the gambling while treatment proceeded. In this case, however, he had decided, perhaps more intuitively than rationally, to postpone the imposition of those terms. And in the third week there was a kind of breakthrough in absentia.

Tony called to cancel his appointment, leaving the message that he had to appear in court. At the rescheduled session, two days later, he revealed that he had had to face traffic charges. For the second time he had been arrested driving at high speed on the interstate highway that ran along the border of the county. It was his frequent habit, late at night, to get on that road and drive out and back ("yo-yoing," as Thomas Pynchon calls it in *V.*) as fast as he could get his Olds to go (it was his own, not his father's Oldsmobile). When the arresting officer could not appear, the case had been continued to the following week. The court, which ordinarily would drop charges under such circumstances, took this matter seriously enough to grant the state's request for a continuance.

"What do you expect to happen?"

"My license will be suspended."

"Will that stop you?"

"Yes. I won't drive illegally. And of course, I'll have to go to traffic school." He said this with a contented smile. "I guess I'll have to give up my other late-night diversion as well."

"What's that?"

"I like to drive past the drug markets I know, the playgrounds and parking lots where people go to score, and see if I can get close to a bust." This was something he did alone, like the speeding. No one at the school or in any of his meetings knew anything about either of these behaviors.

At this point, the therapist instructed Tony to begin attending a weekly GA meeting and to agree to quit matching dollar bills, without substituting any other game of chance. These were imposed as conditions of continuing treatment, and Tony readily accepted them.

The focus of treatment then shifted to the common denominators in all the addictive and risk-taking or thrill-seeking behaviors, including a taste for the more dangerous forms of the rock climbing and rappelling which were actually part of the school's programmed activities. Tony began to talk about the emptiness he felt whenever he wasn't "into" something. He felt dead inside, and the buzz from booze or drugs, the kick of gambling or speeding or flirting with imminent danger, made him "feel alive." He saw his inner emptiness as a reflection of the randomness and meaninglessness of a world in which inevitable death was the only reality.

Where the risk-taking behavior filled the inner void, the imposed structure of the meetings to treat the addictive behavior gave a sense of meaning, even of value, that was a bulwark against both the void inside and the meaninglessness outside, an embraceable defense. Moreover, the membership at the meetings provided a stable, solid, extensive, and nourishing society.

Tony's relationships with girls did not manifest the same sort of risk-taking, thrill-seeking, void-filling behaviors. During his active drinking and drug-using days, he had had a lot of casual sex but even then had preferred exclusive connections. They had rarely lasted more than a couple of months, but he thought of his practice as "serial monogamy." As soon as he began "the program," however, he had bought into the idea of abstaining from sex while relationships developed—with a rule-of-thumb time period of six months. He thought this was important because the only girls he was interested in were themselves in recovery and he didn't want to threaten their program.

He had had one long-term (almost a year) relationship, and was now a few months into the (nonsexual) development of another. Rejection was not a problem. He had been turned down on occasion, but it didn't bother him because he had found that he could have almost anyone he wanted. This remark was offered without braggadoccio or grandiosity, but matter-of-factly with a slightly bemused smile, and the therapist accepted it as accurate.

For the next months, as Tony's crowded schedule added traffic school and GA to his program, he seemed to have all his addictive behaviors under managed control. The "drug-store" scene, too, was avoided when he identified the attraction as another "feeling of being alive" when close to the action—and life-threatening action at that. The quicker Tony could acknowledge that anything he was doing could be something he was powerless to control, the quicker he could accept the imposition of strictures against doing it.

The cognitive aspect of treatment, then, focused on Tony's awareness of being clearly a member of a highly at-risk population, and on a growing understanding that for such a person any risk-taking is likely to become addictive. If this was a loss in the ways that life could be enjoyed, there was at least some compensatory gain in knowing that safe, controlled, defensive, unthreatening, structured activities could themselves be "addictive" (in the sense of a strong dependency).

A considerable portion of the therapy in those months dealt with Tony's gradual appreciation that his feelings of inner emptiness and outer meaninglessness defined a common experience of existential angst. The therapist introduced him to the four issues of Yalom's approach to such problems, which Tony found to fit his own experience "like a glove." The therapist joked about a friend of his who complained of "terminal solipsism," but in all seriousness offered the paradoxical insight that solipsists were never really alone because at some level every person shared the common experience of his own solipsistic hints, perceptions, or misgivings about life. In other words, solipsism was part of the universal human condition of consciousness.

The client's insightfulness might well have led in time to an understanding of the psychodynamic processes and etiology of his condition (preferably while keeping in mind the likely genetic, biochemical, and environmental factors). But therapy was terminated when Tony graduated (with honors) from his high school, went away to work for the summer, and decided to pursue an "outdoors vocation, at least for a time," in the West. He assured the therapist at termination that he knew the warning signs of relapse, that he'd be able to recognize further or recurring problems, and that he knew exactly how to deal with them. The one letter the therapist received from Tony that summer spoke glowingly of the mountain country and his job there, but also described in positive terms the new groups he had found and the people in "the program" there.

As defense against the many factors that made potentially destructive void-filling behaviors appealing to Tony, he had developed ego-strength in an identity as leader of each and every recovery group. The therapist was concerned that Tony might have to discover other pretexts for being assigned to new groups that would honor and cherish him, but he hoped that Tony's developing understanding of such needs would obviate the necessity for doing it over and over again. Unfortunately, no follow-up was available.

Tony's gambling behavior was clearly not in and of itself pathological. Rather, it paralleled many other exhibitions of common symptoms. The therapist, to whom he had been referred because of a reputation for treating pathological gamblers, resisted treating him for that *specific* impulse-control disorder. Only after he interpreted the behaviors as signs of a global need for impulsive, dangerous activity did he impose standard procedure for addressing the gambling per se. Ironically, when this was done and it served as a model for Tony's whole range of pathological loss-of-control, then the underlying condition could be addressed. Treated as an addiction (see chapter 11), the gambling provided a vehicle to get through to the underlying pathology.

If gambling may be identified as a void-filling behavior, it is always a good idea to look for other manifestations of such behavior. It may be that all impulse-control issues bear some relationship to this complex of symptoms and the "existence pain" that underlies the behaviors. Conversely, any addictive or void-filling behavior identified in treatment should suggest to a therapist the need to inquire about gambling. All too frequently this (additional? peripheral? essentially interrelated? potentially life-threatening?) symptom or habitual behavior or pathology goes unremarked, unidentified, and untreated. In the next two examples of void-filling behavior, one literary and the other clinical, there is in the first only a general or philosophical connection with existential angst and in the second a cluster of behaviors identified as void-filling in the interests of effective treatment.

Irwin Sherman is a character in Cynthia Ozick's short story, "The Doctor's Wife," which appeared first in *Midstream* in 1971 and then in her collection *The Pagan Rabbi* in 1983. Ozick's profound understanding of the existence problems that underlie gambling and other pathological behaviors is revealed here (and in many other parts of her work as well), as the character struggles to apprehend and articulate them himself.

Irwin is a middle-aged dentist with a number of problematic behaviors. One observer describes him as puffy-necked and mostly bald, a dentist who often lifts his own intact teeth "up to the light in perpetual melancholy glinting laughter" and with "the sort of fat-lidded marble eyes that make anyone look prosperous" (175) (his brother-in-law the photographer calls him "Ice-Eyes"). He has been known to announce himself at the office of his brother-in-law the doctor by throwing pebbles against the clinical windows, to be found "weeping under the elm, holding a fistful of stones" (182).

The misdiagnosing doctor asks him if he wants money, to which he responds by saying, "Please, don't shame me. Listen, what's money to me? I want happiness, happiness," and insists that they drive around in his car ("crackly with candy wrappers") to talk.

At one time, Irwin's impulsive behavior was focused on his wife Sophie— before they were married. "She used to be a gorgeous woman," he tells her brother the doctor, and "we used to go on in a certain way for hours. Right after your grandmother's funeral we did it, even then. It was a fantastic attraction, I'm telling you. Between me and Sophie it was something special, fantastic. . . . Then, afterward, we got married, nothing" (184). The "existential" nature of his pathology is suggested in the way his memory of premarital sexual activity with Sophie alludes to Camus's Meursault's behavior on the day of his mother's death.

Now, unsurprisingly, he chases other women, but channels much of that impulsive energy into dancing. His sister-in-law Olga calls him "Saint Vitus." During the winter he shuts up his practice for weeks at a time to perform in dance contests, marathons, and exhibitions. Then in the summer, alone, he goes to resort hotels famous for their dance bands. An observer describes him as "short, still blond at the back of his head, [with] a lewd tongue, but . . . as scholarly as any adolescent about the newest steps." A recent acquaintance calls him "a clown, thinks he's still a kid," and at a birthday party tells the doctor, "The bald one doh-see-dohing with the kids . . . gave my girlfriend the runaround last year in the mountains. Said he wasn't married, then she looks in his pocket where he keeps his keys and finds a wedding ring" (201).

It is not surprising that Irwin also gambles frequently. He is a regular at the harness tracks. Despite his disclaimers but in part because of his profligate ways, money is an issue for him. With his two older sons in expensive colleges, he sometimes has to owe his own assistant her salary for a week or two. When, in one of those confessional dialogues with the doctor, he attempts to account for his gambling, he puts his financial status into the context of his existential angst:

> Listen, you know why I go to the track, say? I don't go for distraction. . . . Just the opposite, I go because it scares me there. I'm scared stiff of losing, I get these dunning letters from the kids' bursars. I get so damn scared. But when I'm scared it's like I feel myself, you know what I mean? It's like dancing. God, I'm forty-six, I start doing some of those bits I'm so out of breath I think I'm getting a heart attack. But I start feeling my heart beat, I know it's there, and I figure well, if I have a heart I have a body, if I have a body I'm alive. I figure if I'm alive there's something to be alive for. (185)

In another passage, he reflects on how his sons' attitude toward him ("boys think they're smarter than me") is a challenge to his very existence: "I said something and they laughed in my face and started talking biochemistry like I didn't exist" (184).

At the heart of Irwin's despair, the feeling that underlies all his void-filling behaviors—the gambling, the dancing, the womanizing (all "chasing" in one sense or another)—is the constant awareness of the emptiness within. Ozick gives him deep awareness, though it offers him less consolation than a kind of rationalizing justification for the behaviors: "I don't think I can live with it any more. I want something, I have this hollow feeling in me all the time, no, I mean it's more like a full feeling, there's something I want to get rid of inside me and I don't know what. Like if I could suddenly vomit it up I'd feel better, you know?" (184–85).

Work, he says, helps, but only as a distraction, and then insists, "That's my trouble . . . I don't *want* distraction. I want to pull the rotten core out of me and look at it. I want to be happy, that's all" (185).

Ozick has given Irwin his own metaphor for Kierkegaard's "sickness unto death." And then he responds to the doctor's cold insistence that nobody can answer the question of what he's alive for with his own paraphrase of the essential question: "You mean nobody can *ask* it. Who asks such a thing? Go on, tell me, you know somebody else who asks a question like that, what he's alive for?" (185). Irwin has probably danced to the tune of "Why Was I Born, Why Am I Living?"

His brother-in-law the doctor has no answer, but Irwin's self-absorption cannot obscure for Ozick's readers the obvious rejoinder that many people, perhaps at some level at some point everyone, must ask the unanswerable questions. Existence pain is felt in the asking, and certain behavioral responses to the impossibility of knowing answers are our concerns here.

The perception of the void leads not only to vain attempts to "fill" it but also to rationalizations of the "why not?" variety. In the absence of meaning or even value in existence, anything that provides the sense of being alive or the semblance of life-affirming value is justifiable. What is paradoxical in such thinking, however, is the presence of "justification" in response to a sense of the human condition that implies the absence of the very concept of justification, never mind any rational need for it.

Though presenting herself in a much less philosophical context, the woman I call Monty seems to exemplify the practical effect of the existential issues as clearly as Irwin. A patient who had never presented any dreams during several months of treatment, Monty came to her session one day with a beauty, which she reported with some delight, as if pleased to be giving a kind of gift to her therapist.

"This morning, after I hit the snooze button on my alarm, I dreamed that I was in a warehouse, and my father was coming toward me when he slipped onto the concrete floor. Then I saw a pile of stuff start to topple over, and I thought it was going to fall on him. I didn't know what to do or how to stop him from being hit, and then I saw that it was styrofoam and it wasn't going to hurt him anyway. That's when the alarm went off again."

"What do you make of it?"

"I don't know."

"How old are you in the dream?"

"My present age."

"Were you watching yourself in the dream or were you seeing things from where you were located in the dream?"

"I wasn't watching. I was just there."

"On one level, this is an archetypal rescue dream, where there is often ambivalence and anxiety about whether to act or whether the action will be timely. But let's look at some other aspects of the dream. What are your associations to styrofoam?"

"Nothing I can think of. It's light and harmless."

"What are your associations to slip?"

"Nothing. It's just kind of an embarrassing accidental fall."

"Well, maybe your dreaming self was punning, as dreamers often do, playing with words and names and the like. What are the other meanings of slip?"

At this point, let me provide some background from this sudden dreamer's case. Monty was a fifty-year-old professional woman who had been referred for treatment because her gambling had gotten out of control. She was spending so much money buying lottery tickets that she couldn't pay her rent and was being threatened with eviction. A good-natured and attractive woman, though substantially overweight, Monty entered cooperatively into every aspect of the treatment process. She stopped buying tickets, she agreed to attend meetings, she was observant about the immediate contexts of her impulses to play the numbers, and she willingly explored the backgrounds of her gambling, her family, and her emotional life. Everything, that is, but dreams, until this particular session.

"Well, in program jargon, a slip is a relapse."

"So this dream is about fear of relapse?"

"Yes, except that it's my father's slip, not mine."

"You're projecting your fear onto him—naturally enough since the gambling habit can be traced back to him?"

"OK, but doesn't the dream say that the slip is light and harmless? And that there's no weight—importance—to what is going to fall onto him as a result?"

"So you think it's OK now to buy a ticket every once in a while?"

"Yes, I guess I do believe that."

"Anything else?"

"Well, a slip is a little piece of paper that the numbers runners used to write the bets on. Betting slips in general, I suppose, are the bookies' records of bets."

"And this is the way you remember your father betting?"

"I never actually saw him do it, but yes, that's the way I pictured it."

"Do you suppose the dream is suggesting that your father should allow the weight of the gambling to fall on him?"

"It's me putting him in that position, isn't it? But I understand that it starts with him, for me and my sister, too. Still, I've learned that most of the burden, the weight, is my own."

Oddly enough, this dream marked a turning point in Monty's treatment, a turn back to gambling issues. Monty had a number of behaviors classified under impulse-control issues. She was a binge eater. And she was a binge spender. Required to attend meetings regularly, Monty chose Overeaters Anonymous as her venue, and this was acceptable to her therapist.

He believed in the value and necessity of "the program" as an adjunct to therapy. Even for patients who failed to identify with the program, or who could not swallow the "spiritual" component of AA and its spin-offs, he felt that the regular attendance provided a structured support for the conjoint processes of recovery and therapy. He suggested that "higher power" could mean the group itself or even the collaborative entity of the therapeutic relationship, as long as the patient acknowledged that she was powerless to deal with the impulsive or addictive behaviors on her own.[3]

Less directly or explicitly than Tony, the high school student described earlier, Monty's struggle was to fill the perceived void within. Her own search for meanings often had a numerological component. She played numbers that "came to her" as in a hunch (but not a dream—she had looked at dream interpretation books and dismissed them as superstitious crutches for the gullible) or that she saw repeated in store windows or on license plates or addresses or phone numbers. She bought things she didn't need when she could justify it by attractive sales prices—and when the opportunity was one she "couldn't afford to miss," she might buy several of the item she didn't need in the first place. The eating behavior, however, was an escape from the tyranny of numbers—calories, weight.

The common denominator among Monty's three areas of impulse-control problems was the trigger for the behaviors. It was consistently associated with a perception of an emptiness, a missing element at her core, specifically an inability to express anger. This, too, like her gambling, she had learned from her father, the powerful figure of her childhood, made more powerful by his frequent absence and then premature death. Petty peeve or mammoth rage, Monty found her anger inexpressible, and this void of feeling would be filled by binges of eating, spending, and lottery gambling.

The selection of OA as her group of choice signaled the primacy of the binge eating among her symptoms, serving as it did to reveal significant issues that are not relevant to this discussion. But it was the gambling that created the financial crisis that led to treatment. To begin a recovery of financial stability, Monty had to get the gambling (as well as the impulse spending) under control. More important, though, the gambling symptom led to a recovery of emotional stability as treatment focused on the void-filling significance of the binge eating.

The most extreme case of pathological gambling as void-filling behavior that I have encountered is the one depicted by James Caan's portrayal of Axel Freed in Karel Reisz's 1975 movie *The Gambler*, from a screenplay by James Toback. A case, however, could be made for the character of "Fitz" in the British television series *Cracker* as the most complex example. Yet I reserve both of these cases for discussion in a later chapter, on personality disorders.

For the purposes of the bulk of this project, as I have said, I have chosen to follow the taxonomy of the DSM, the APA's "multiaxial" guide to diagnoses of mental disorders. It is in many ways a useful system of classification. Aside from serving the practical purposes of managed-care coverage (while often disserving both practitioners and patients who are required to have such labels imposed), it certainly serves the therapeutically valuable function of anticipating treatment dilemmas in clearly diagnosable cases. In my own practice and in consulting with other therapists on their cases, I have found it most useful as a way of systematically focusing attention on coherent patterns of symptoms. More often than not, however, I cannot comfortably pigeonhole a subject exclusively in one category of classification, and I am careful when providing documentation for insurance companies to use the words "preliminary" or "tentative" with every diagnosis. The Medicare forms, for an example of acknowledgment of the limits of the DSM taxonomy, allow one to list several code numbers for multiple diagnosis—but then they require an indication of which condition is being treated in a particular session, as if any single session could ever be devoted to any single condition of a person with multiple diagnoses.

The limitations of this system of classification are acknowledged in its own articulation. The concept of multiaxiality explicitly accommodates the need in many, if not most, cases to assign separate, disparate elements of symptoms to more than one category. Implicitly, the insistence on "differential diagnosis" accepts that the proverbial "thin line"—rather than what legal scholars call a "bright line"—is what typically separates the divisions and compartments of the classifications.

As a matter of convenience, the DSM's taxonomy has served my organizational purposes in forming groups of (superficially?) similar cases, though my theoretical purpose has been to show that the *particular* diagnosis of pathological gambling is more often than not misleading and potentially counterproductive (in treatment terms, "contraindicated"). Moreover, in this chapter I have strayed beyond the DSM guidelines to describe a relatively inchoate category that in a sense adds a new "philosophical" axis to the system.

All this underscores one of Freud's most valuable and still viable concepts, that much of what we attempt to explain by cause and effect or narrative order or insight is by nature "overdetermined." To reduce any symptomatic behavior to a single cause-effect explanation is to flout much of what we have learned about the complexity of human experience and behavior. And, at the other end of such linear analysis, to reduce a set of such symptoms and behaviors to clearly defined categories of diagnosis is to impose rigid, static, generalized abstractions on concretely individual, demonstrably dynamic subjects. It is an enactment of what is called "entropy" in communications theory, where the more organized the information becomes, the less meaning it can impart.

Axel and Fitz, then, who might appropriately have been grouped with Dostoevsky and his Aleksey (themselves both diagnosable under other rubrics) as manic-depressives, could have been among my clearest illustrations of void-filling behavior. Yet I have chosen to hold them until chapter 10, where I discuss what may be the most problematical area for the DSM taxonomy: the personality disorders.[4]

Jorge, however, the narrator/protagonist of Cristina Peri Rossi's *Dostoevsky's Last Night* (1992), enacts the "existence givens" so precisely I actually looked for an acknowledgment of Yalom in the text. A fortyish Barcelona bachelor who writes for a slick magazine, Jorge is being treated by a psychoanalyst (Lucia), ostensibly for his gambling addiction. But he displays a generic addictive personality in his cigarette smoking and his pursuit of sexual pleasure.

The context of therapy allows for interesting interchanges about gambling. In one session, for example, Lucia observes that the gambler "dreams of winning *all* the money, *every* game, to quench his desire for playing once and for all" (37).

But they both know that it is not really about money for Jorge, and part of his response is an anthropological observation that in primitive times numbers were essential elements of religion.[5] So maybe gambling, he rationalizes, "is a displaced manifestation of this religious sentiment" (42).

In another session, she suggests that if "people only lost, they wouldn't get hooked on gambling" because the "illusory fantasy of winning reinforces the habit" (53).

Jorge's response seems to support her view, but he is really saying that it is the specific *experience* of winning that does it, not fantasy (suggesting that she can't know this without having had the experience). He cites Norman Mailer speaking of "the magnificent elation of the winning gambler, who feels touched by the gods" (53).

The religion/gambling metaphors occur with some frequency. Early on, Jorge observes that "a real gambler," who is "[s]ensitive to luck's obscure maneuvers," must understand "that bingo boards and playing cards contain a sacred code granted by the gods, a unique and individual gift" (3). As his ruminations continue, he comments that gambling houses, in certain places and times, have been called "Temples of Chance" and "Temples of Pleasure." The latter alludes to a far more prevalent metaphor, Jorge's speaking of gambling in terms of sex, and vice versa, and then acting out the intimate connection between the two activities.[6]

In one passage, Jorge develops a fanciful notion about "The Sex of Numbers" in which he personifies various integers with sexual characteristics. In another, he describes a session with a slot machine in elaborate sexual terms. More to the point, he punctuates his own sexual activities with gambling sessions. He goes to San Sebastian on assignment for his magazine to interview a Basque separatist leader, and he is determined not to gamble on this trip. But at his hotel he meets a young woman named Magda, and they have casual sex. As soon as she leaves his room he goes straight to the Kursal casino. This replicates his experience with his former lover, Claudia. He would gamble before and after their sexual encounters, often while she was still sleeping in his bed. He pursues and seduces Marta, a married woman he meets playing bingo, in part because he appreciates her style of play (and has contempt for her husband's). Finally, when he inadvertently meets Claudia in the street one day and they have a drink together, the sexual tension has turned to bitterness, but Jorge rushes off to Billares (the bingo palace)—although that meeting comes the day after he has sworn off gambling.

This is a major motif, but it is hardly all that is going on in this short but profound novel. Indeed, Jorge himself consciously puts this metaphor in its place: "If casinos are like brothels," he says, "so are psychoanalysts' offices and so is the magazine's editorial room" (25). The explicit comparison between sex and gambling, however, is made in a conversation in a bar after a losing session at roulette. "You don't play for money, pal," he says to a stranger who has scoffed at the way Jorge has gone about losing; then, in answer to the question of what, then, he says pointedly, "For pleasure" (32).

On one level, as the title suggests, the book chronicles Jorge's fascination with Dostoevsky. (The conversation referred to in the last paragraph takes place at Baden-Baden. Jorge has gone there ostensibly for a magazine piece, but really to enact his identification with the greatest of the gamblers-as-writers—though he doesn't have his picture taken in front of the daguerreotype of the Russian, like many tourists at the casino.) He quotes passages from Dostoevsky, interprets the great Russian's views on and experience of gambling, and finally places his own life-altering decisions in context with the closing sentence of *The Gambler*.

Jorge cites Dostoevsky's "Tomorrow, tomorrow everything will be over" as expressing "the futile hope of the hardened gambler who, after a disastrous night, promises himself to give up the vice" (134). Never mind that for Dostoevsky's Aleksey the line probably means no such thing. For Jorge, however, it allows him to scribble, "Last night, last night I quit gambling" (180). And for Jorge, as he says in his last line, that "seems like a good beginning."

For he has not only given up gambling (having, for the first time, the night before, walked away from the tables a winner), but he has terminated his therapy, abandoned his nostalgic longing for Claudia, given up his dangerous pursuit of Marta, and quit his job (on the pretext of the magazine's refusal to print his exposé of Marta's husband). He has determined to write seriously, and his echo of *The Gambler*'s last line is presumably to become the first line of his own post-Dostoevskyan novel.

Beneath these surfaces, and frequently rising to conscious, explicit levels, however, is the subject and substance of Yalom's "existence pain," a concrete dramatization of my notion of gambling as void-filling behavior. As an introspective analysand, as well as existential "philosopher," Jorge supplies many insights about his pathology. He acknowledges his addictive nature, for example, when he experiences the physical symptoms of a hangover and says that alcohol is "not the only thing that breeds hangovers; obsessive gambling does too" (137); when he calls attention more than once to his own narcissism; and when he and Lucia both allude to a strain of sadomasochism in his behavior, both in his gambling (where he expresses the wish to dominate others and also acts out patterns of self-infliction of pain) and in his courting of Marta (where he is threatened, is injured, and still persists to the point of receiving a severe beating).

Yet it is his existential angst that is at the empty heart of his condition. While the inevitability of death lurks tacitly in the shadows of his psyche, rising to consciousness only in ruminations about the possible death of his absent father, the other three "givens" of Yalom's "existence pain" are articulated and examined by himself and his therapist.

That Jorge associates his gambling with freedom is implied by the novel's epigraph from Dostoevsky's Notes from the Underground: "Gambling is the first experience of freedom in the physical world." Jorge often ruminates about the anxieties attendant upon freedom, while Lucia labors to lead him to choices that affirm value in life in the face of apparent ultimate meaninglessness. The reader appreciates, though perhaps Jorge does not (yet), that it is she and their work together, at least as much as his identification with Dostoevsky, that have brought him to the life-affirming decisions to forsake gambling and devote himself to serious writing.

Most of all, it is Jorge's sense of profound isolation that dominates his pervasive feeling of "malaise" and his experience of gambling as well. He asserts that the "true gambler" must be a "loner who hates company or crowds of any kind, who reserves all his concentration for his encounters with luck" (2), that is, he focuses on his solitary experience of randomness, maintaining all the while a fondness for meaningless rituals and empty forms. Jorge's intense abandonment issues are inextricably bound up with his sense of aloneness.

His father had abandoned him and his mother, going off perhaps to the jungles of South America, perhaps to write a book, never to be heard from again. His mother Michelle, herself withdrawn and isolated, became more of a distant friend and sometime companion than a parent. So traumatized, Jorge has avoided close relationships, fearing replication of abandonment, preferring transient connections and escaping commitment by being the one to abandon Claudia (and Lucia). At the same time, he romanticizes his father as an existential hero who has gone off alone on high adventure, with possibly artistic aspirations, to embrace the randomness of experience. Abandonment thus becomes a virtue, and Jorge can fantasize, in the desperate financial situation his losses have brought on, about existential crimes like robbing banks or dealing in counterfeit currency.

Aloneness or isolation is the product of abandonment. The void is the emptiness experienced by one who is alone and abandoned. In Dostoevsky's Last Night, Cristina Peri Rossi has depicted a "fanatical" and "obsessed" pathological gambler whose behaviors are manifestly attempts to fill that void. In Bob the Gambler, Frederick Barthelme presents a similar process, though he achieves his effects in a wholly different, less direct, complementary, but no less satisfying way. That novel, for reasons that become clear, begins the following chapter rather than concluding this one.

I've made some killings in my time the gang still gab about. I've been in the big bucks. More'n once, and I will be again. I've had tough breaks too, but what the hell, I always get by. When the horses won't run for me, there's draw or stud. When they're bad, there's a crap game. . . . What I fed Hughie wasn't all lies. The tales about gambling wasn't. They was stories of big games and killings that really happened since I've been hangin' around. Only I wasn't in on 'em like I made out—except one or two from way back when I had a run of big luck and was in the bucks for a while until I was took to the cleaners.

Erie Smith
in Eugene O'Neill's *Hughie*

Gambling and the Brothers Barthelme

For Ray Kaiser, the narrator/protagonist of Frederick Barthelme's novel *Bob the Gambler*, the void is externalized, rendered in a landscape of objects: "What I'd always liked about Biloxi was the decay, the things falling apart, the crap along the beach, the skeletons of abandoned hotels, the trashy warehouses and the rundown piers jutting out into the dirty water" (1).

As an architect, Ray is particularly sensitive to the structures of emptiness among which he lives, and as he details the civilization's detritus within which the action takes place he presents a substantive portrait of empty lives, dead-ended jobs, meaningless behaviors, and idle existence.[1] It is "the void" objectified in an architect's blueprint. He shares a day in his mother's life which is dominated by her notion that the tall stranger at a neighbor's barbecue across the street is none other than John Larroquette; after his father's death in Houston, Ray moves the remaining furniture into a "corrugated metal storage unit" (111) in Biloxi, where he arranges it so that he can sit in its midst: two enacted symbols of the emptiness in their lives.

Into the externalized void and dying economy of Biloxi and the whole Gulf Coast of impoverished Mississippi come the casinos. Jobs! Action! Color! Investment! Entertainment! The whole Mississippi Sound reverberates as it comes alive with money. And after years of ignoring it, as they channel-surf and eat take-out Chinese, Ray and his wife Jewel venture forth into the Paradise Casino to fill a few hours of their own personal emptiness, in part to divert themselves from the toxic prospects of their daughter RV's incipient adolescence.

To Ray, the Paradise is an "eyesore," "a joke on itself, the kind of joke you got used to" where inside "everything binged and wizzled, everything was fast, especially sound . . . like a monster video arcade souped up with time-lapse photography and on Fast Forward with a thousand chrome machines cheek by jowl" (5).

Jewel wins big playing the slots and is excited; Ray loses a little, is unimpressed. No big deal, one would think, except they keep going back. They lose more than they win, and it becomes a routine part of their lives. They take up blackjack, read books about it, stay longer, lose bigger. They acknowledge their common dissatisfaction with the dullness of their lives, see that the gambling is fun—but not much. Except that it has become a "jones" (60) that intrudes on Jewel's thinking while she is at work.

"It's not an addiction," Jewel insists, wondering if maybe they are just "bored" (62). Ray responds with an explicit reference to the void in his professional life ("I'm doing nothing") and they both agree that they may indeed be bored. When she insists she likes the gambling, though she doesn't want to "lose everything," Ray for the first time mentions that it wouldn't be so bad. When they stop off to try their luck at the Copa in Gulfport, he increases his betting, insults Jewel when she tries to distract him from his preoccupation with the action, loses more, and then behaves remorsefully with her—for his anger, not the gambling behavior that evoked it. All these are signs of accelerating pathology.

There are obligatory references to Dostoevsky and The Gambler in the text, but Barthelme's title is explicitly drawn from Jean-Pierre Melville's 1955 film noir classic (which Ray and RV rent on video but do not watch). There is a resemblance between Barthelme's depiction of the Gulf Coast and Melville's ambience of decay, world-weariness, staleness, anomie, and cynical sameness on the Left Bank. The dreary repetition of dark scenes, trashiness, and tawdriness, all shot as if they represent a mundane ordinariness, is intercut with flashes of the sleazy, phony, and garish glitter that serve ironically to reinforce that dreariness. The sense of existential angst, of an inner void unfilled by action and unfulfilled by material trappings, is the essence of Ray's world, as it is of Bob's.

Bob is totally engrossed in the action of gambling as a way of life, but he never betrays any emotional response to the results of action, in manner, facial expression, language, or behavior. Nevertheless, the climax of the movie occurs when Bob, on an incredible winning streak at the tables of Deauville, loses track of the time and fails to give a timely signal to his cronies, leading into a disastrous attempt to rob the casino.

The overall effect of all the gambling action in the movie, however, from the poker games to the racetrack to the roulette wheel to the baccarat tables, is of boredom. This is an aspect of the gambling life that is rarely depicted in the frenzied excitement and glittering action of most dramatized or fictionalized treatments.[2]

After Ray observes that he is tired of trying to understand the attraction of gambling, he records his emotional responses to winning and losing. While it was "riveting" to hit his first jackpot, and he "sat in front of the machine and touched the symbols . . . in a blissful state," he has already realized that there were "many pleasures" in gambling, and that "it didn't seem to matter that much whether you won or lost. I sort of felt it was more exhilarating to lose a lot than win a little. Losing meant you had to play more, try harder. Losing burned intensely; winning became tepid fast" (76).

Increasingly, Ray experiences an impulsive pressure to boost the action. Their losses and indebtedness rise from about two thousand to ten thousand dollars. Ray goes table hopping, from blackjack to craps, and winds up back at the slots. Here, Barthelme's description of the hypnotic appeal of the one-armed bandits is perceptive. Ray is

> transfixed by their peculiar beauty, the noise, the garishness, the roll of the spots past the windows, the payline, the extraordinary feeling I got each time the wheels came to a stop, one after another, left to right, click, click, click. The excitement stuffed into fractions of seconds between the first wheel stopping and the second, between the second and the third. When I got a double diamond on the payline on the first reel, time seemed to slow way down while I waited for the second reel. And if that landed on something good, a double or triple bar, or a red seven, then I was instantly focused on the final window, and I waited, heat in the back of my neck. The whole process took maybe a full second, but it felt like an hour. (114)

The only mesmerizing element omitted from this description is that of the repeated movement of hand and arm, in rhythm with the eye movements and the wheel movements. These ritualized, repetitive movements have a kind of hypnotic effect that induces a low-level trance state including an inhibition of muscular fatigue, or catalepsy. Players of certain video games, pinball machines, and computer solitaire, for example, may continue their trancing play for hours, unaware of time or of physical discomfort, impervious to sets of distracting signals. This element in slot-machine addiction has not been sufficiently recognized or satisfactorily addressed.

About three months into their flirtation with casino gambling, their folie à deux, Ray and Jewel have learned that they are unable to quit an evening's play even when they are ahead by as much as five thousand—and an evening can become an eighteen-hour session. The action is interrupted by Ray's father's death and its immediate aftermath, but a week before Thanksgiving Ray decides he'd rather go to the Paradise than watch ER because he "was feeling kind of lucky": "I felt guilty leaving the house, but then I was out and driving, and it was great to be alive—I felt free and young, the way I used to feel when I was eighteen, going on a date in my father's car" (117–18). Whether this is an adrenaline rush, an endorphin high, a manic episode, or the reaction formation of his unresolved grief over his father's death, it portends big trouble in Paradise.

Ray plays blackjack for a couple of hours, wins about two thousand, cashes in, and walks outside. His manic good feeling is suffused with a mellow appreciation of his manifold blessings. He is in love with his life. But he is also overflowing with confidence, with the magical feeling that it is his night and his casino. When he goes back in to play it is with the exhilaration of giving in to an impulse he has had before but never followed: to take his winnings, borrow all he can to provide a substantial stake, and play the big-time gambler.

What follows is the most extraordinarily gripping presentation of a gambling episode I have ever read. The cards run in his favor, almost to his command, and his play escalates, hot and fast. He wins as much as ten thousand in a single hand, his stack of chips grows and multiplies, until he is playing three hands at ten thousand each. Three good hands, too, but the dealer hits blackjack and he has lost thirty thousand. He comes back in at five thousand a hand, loses again, finds he can scrape together fifteen thousand more, goes for broke, and is beaten. It is only then that he realizes he had been ahead fifty thousand dollars.

The sequence covers just twenty-five minutes of play, fills five pages (130–35), and captures both the external rhythm and the internal excitement of the action. The reader is breathless with immersion in the gestalt of it. Numbers and colors and cards are reported but the details are lost in the emotive effects of the play, just as Ray himself is playing on a kind of automatic pilot to destruction.

Ray is down but not out. He exhausts all his credit cards and plays on, another eight pages' worth. Broke before dawn, he waits till his bank opens to cash in all assets and borrow more. In "worse shape now than ever," he finds himself in "liquidation country" where "another five thousand didn't make any difference" and he "had to try" (135–36). And he loves it, is carried away by it, intoxicated past caring:

> I was excited, filled with a sense of abandon I hadn't felt in so long that I couldn't remember when I *had* felt it. . . . The way I played was a kind of probable suicide. . . . It was a joy to see the money move at a sedate pace back and forth across the table, as if it had a life of its own, or was reacting to my will, or the dealer's, or even the magic in the cards. It was thrilling to see stacks of blacks [hundred-dollar chips] coming at me, to see purples [five hundred-dollar chips] in play, to watch my hands and the cards, and to be at the table when the cards turned perfect for a few hands. . . . (135–36)

Only in Faust's "Bar Bar Bar," and not even in *Oscar and Lucinda,* will we find a couple so compatible in their gambling. Jewel not only condones Ray's behavior, she embraces it. And it is Jewel who announces to RV that she wants "to lose everything," to which Ray responds, in admiration, "Start over?" (160). And so they do, selling the house, both Explorers, most of everything else in a terminal garage sale; and moving in with Ray's mother in Bay St. Louis. Ray takes a job as assistant manager at a Jitney Jungle grocery store, then puts his elementary drafting skills to work detailing toilet enclosures. It is as fitting a representation of the externalized void as his one fit of anger, where he dumps his fast-food trash out the car window and shouts "Fuck you" at the empty environment of his world (158).

That this novel is a comedy, with a happy ending for its characters, is testimony to the essential irony of its enactment of Yalom's ideas of "existence pain." The regression into his mother's home is in the service of a healing process. RV's rebelliousness is contained; the family reintegrates as a functional whole; the permeable boundaries nurture the several interrelationships; they all love one another (including Frank the dog). They have nothing; therefore, they have everything.

Still, Ray wants to gamble, to build up another stake and risk it on one play. Before the end, Jewel comes up with a stake, and they do risk it and—happily—lose. At the end, they are contemplating buying a used pickup truck and moving into a trailer park. I was reminded of a minor-key Annie Hopkins lyric ("For two checks down and the rest of your life / You could live in a trailer park / See your family after dark"). From the Paradise Casino to Lake Forgetful, where RV and Ray in their (step)father-daughter affirmation scene have heard two trailer-parkers piss in the pond, is not all that far. But the Kaisers have had to piss all their holdings away to get there.

It should be clear from this summary that Ray and Jewel Kaiser both exhibit traits of various forms of pathological gambling. But the tone and texture of the narration, as well as the nonjudgmental representations of

themes in action dealing with death, freedom, aloneness, and meaninglessness, seem to me to demand that Bob the Gambler be placed in a discussion of
void-filling behavior.

Barthelme has depicted the void of a decaying culture in a desolate landscape of abandoned values. His characters have striven to balance their existence
in such a time and place by matching the externalized void with a personal
emptying-out of what passes for value in that world. It is a high-wire act fraught
with peril. Their divestiture has achieved for them a kind of peace, a full acceptance of themselves, that renders them as existential heroes.

But if it is their successive, successful losses at gambling that have won
them their triumph, it must be understood that their story's comic resolution is achieved—ironically—not because they are bitten by the gambling
bug but in spite of their infection with it. It was Conrad near the opening of
Heart of Darkness who spoke of the "fascination of the abomination"; Barthelme
here speaks of the immersion in the unspeakable void.

I had originally intended this discussion of Bob the Gambler as the conclusion of chapter 8 on the void, but the publication (as "Personal History") in
the March 8, 1999, New Yorker of "Good Losers" by Frederick and Steven
Barthelme, followed shortly by their book Double Down, suggested separate
treatment. These accounts reveal the origins of much of the material in the
novel. Rather than husband and wife, the partners in folie à deux are brothers Rick and Steve; the course of the gambling escalation is the same; the
death of their father and subsequent fitting out of a storage shed is the same;
and so on. Ray's style of play, his emotional responses, his psychological
processes, all mirror Rick's. But oddly enough, for so perceptive a writer,
Rick apparently shares Ray's capacity for denial and rationalization.

It seemed at the time that the New Yorker piece was timed to preempt a
New York Times Magazine article by D.T. Max which reported (not for the first
time—the story had made the wire services) the strange case of the criminal
indictments brought against the brothers and a casino blackjack dealer for
felonious collusion. The charges have since been dismissed—they seemed
absurd on their face—and Rick and Steve are free to gamble again in the
Mississippi Gulf Coast casinos. The notoriety made their memoir the more
marketable and their Kafkaesque experience provided rich material for their
narrative, but it is Double Down's full account of their gambling itself that is
particularly useful for the present discussion.

I kept wondering if Rick and Steve had read Bill Barich's Laughing in the
Hills, where an odyssey into gambling is explicitly a reaction to the death of
the writer's mother, or Jack Richardson's Memoir of a Gambler, where the

gambler's odyssey is explicitly both an escape from a life worn down by bipolar symptoms and an acting-out of apposite self-discovery. In the Barthelmes' case, they are reacting to serial traumatic losses, beginning with the death of their older brother Donald in 1989, followed by the death of their beloved mother (the "architect" or creative spirit behind the family that was the center of all of their lives) in 1995, and then the death of their architect father in 1996, from which they benefit with a considerable inheritance.

They plunge into a desperate escalation of their gambling pastime. They thus divest themselves of their inheritance, with accompanying "chasing," where "getting even" becomes the explicit goal, a punning rationalization of vengeful rage. And their preoccupation with gambling reaches the point of interfering with their professional and private lives. They refer to "craziness," but they appear to be in denial of the actual pathology, failing to recognize its clinical symptoms or its possible etiology.

The "case" of Frederick Barthelme's character Ray Kaiser, which I have discussed as an example of void-filling behavior, may have originated in the author's own experience of undiagnosed major depression masked by his desperate dive into gambling. The profound unacknowledged grief, the inadequate mourning, the intolerable financial consequences of the deaths, all may have been experienced as a kind of inchoate void that the gambling escapades sought to fill. The Barthelme brothers were bailing a sinking boat with a fishnet.

A. Alvarez astutely described *Double Down* as "a wonderfully seductive performance—witty, self-aware, at once full of subtle feeling and implacably knowing—a triumph of style over temporary insanity" ("High Rollers," 26). That very stylishness in conjunction with high intelligence can be a self-destructive formula, and the jury must still be out regarding "temporary." The capacity for erecting elegant, insurmountable defenses of intellectualization, rationalization, and denial seems limitless. And they know this; that's the most frightening aspect of this kind of self-deception: "As card-carrying Barthelmes we believed two things, though neither provided adequate emotional cover: first that we could 'understand' things and thus tame them, and second, that words, adroitly deployed, were a bullfighter's cape—they allowed you to step aside and avoid the horns of a threatening experience" (27).

"Understanding things" in this context means that they acknowledge their tendency to addiction: "We didn't deny we were addicted, just as we had never denied addictions to cigarettes or alcohol years before. There seemed no point in denial. But both of us thought that an addiction was just an addiction, a set of circumstances, a habit that could be undone, rebuilt, fixed"

(62). To accept a condition intellectually while believing you can think your way out of it is to deny its emotional grip. It is "copping a plea"—and so is the "clear" acknowledgment "that there were connections between our gambling and the deaths of our parents" (61). In fact, it seems that their inability to mourn, to express their grief, to deal on a feeling level with the "existence pain" of death in the family, goes back to the shocking premature death of their older brother Donald.

They are still enraged at that loss, but have displaced their rage in the direction of all the non-Barthelmes who made much of the death of a literary eminence, co-opting the occasion so that it was about them (Donald's friends, colleagues, admirers) and not about the surviving Barthelmes: "everybody wanted a piece of him. And took it, too, one after another" (15). They were deprived of the privilege of making the public mourning their own. In a sense, their arrest and the book it has occasioned mark their own emergence as public figures, out from under the shadow of their more prominent brother—or his shade, as it were.

It is in the nature of memoirs to accomplish this sort of thing. One of the issues raised is the relative value of an autobiographical account and its transmutation into a work of fictional art. In contemporary marketplace terms, the memoir has greater currency, particularly where scandal may be involved. The Barthelmes acknowledge that they have taken certain liberties with factual details in the interest of narrative coherence, but that strategy is to be expected whenever memory is employed in explanation or even exoneration.

Double Down would be considered by some to have more to offer an examination of pathological gambling than *Bob the Gambler*. Though both have their value, I disagree: in the novel the author has been able to reach deeper into the emotional lives of his characters than he allows himself in the intellectual exercise of the memoir. (Rick Barthelme has claimed that this was not a case of art imitating life, but of life imitating art imitating life. Answering a question by Terry Gross on *Fresh Air* regarding his depiction of Ray in the novel, he said, "It turned out to be me, something I was not prepared for," and laughed. But it was already him, I might have said, as he was creating Ray.[3]) Besides, the gambling scenes themselves are more exciting, the gambling experience more "real" in the novel for this reader/gambler.

Double Down takes a sophisticated approach to analyzing the authors' pathology, phrased often with self-deprecating humor. For example, they say,

> The psychiatrist who works at the bus stop would have a field day with
> us—guilt, depression, loss, loneliness, destroying the inheritance. But that

doesn't take into account the seductiveness of gambling itself. The excitement. The giddy foolish mindlessness. To go there and lose felt strangely heroic. How crazy we were being, how bad, how stupid. It's easy to diminish the magic in hindsight, but at the time we were deeply in its thrall. It was a remarkably powerful and seductive bit of theater, with real and bitter consequences, consequences that we wanted. We would have been willing to win, but we were content to lose. (196)

Yet there are serious attempts to do the Barthelme thing of "understanding things," to assess "what, if anything, it meant" that they'd "gone from workaday English teachers to gambling junkies in a matter of a couple of years" (107). Among the tentative answers are "grief and relief and release" and "newly visible aggression" at what had made them "hostage for a lifetime" to their family. "Or perhaps the gambling fever was only a desperate and pathetic gesture of pampered children who had to face the absence of their beloved and devoted parents, their only family, the only group or community tie of substance that either of them had known" (108).

Then again, they try "still another explanation. Something simpler, something that has to do with gambling, that has to do with money." Unprepared for using their inheritance to make a lot of money in any strategic investment, "did we perhaps imagine that we could use our (always highly regarded) intelligence to beat the casino at its own game? Is it possible we thought we could win in spite of how we knew the casino operated . . . ? Is it possible that we imagined we could win?" This seems now to be "a terrifying thought. That we could have been so stunningly arrogant, so unspeakably naive as to imagine that we might actually come out ahead" (108).

But there is no felt, no experienced terror in the thought as it is communicated in this book. The focus on cognitive process and prowess (think, know, thought, idea, imagine, intelligence) is what comes through most clearly in this revealing passage. One wonders why, given the superior intellect doing the examining and reexamining, they would choose to joke about their condition rather than take steps to address it: "We two brothers . . . depended on each other, enabled each other, even while we laughed at the word 'enabled.' Taking that seventy-mile drive from Hattiesburg to Gulfport, sometimes more than once a week, we talked with an easy friendliness and warmth we often could not quite achieve otherwise, without gambling as the common card between us. Even when we were losing, we knew our conversations were something of value, a feature of the addiction, and that in any system of values this one could clearly be marked as priceless" (61). What they also must have known was that effective help was close at hand.

Diagonally across the street from their university's campus in Hattiesburg is Forrest General Hospital, which houses a forty-eight-bed facility called Next Step, a residential treatment facility for addictions. Virtually always filled to capacity, Next Step's population includes about 10 percent whose primary addiction is gambling, but about 60 percent for whom gambling is one of the problems being addressed. Moreover, approximately 50 percent of its clientele consists of addiction-impaired health professionals, with another 30 percent being professionals from other fields. Conceivably, some of the conversations at Next Step might be up to the Barthelmes' intellectual level. And best of all, under the aegis of Vicki Pevsner, a vice president of the hospital in the area of behavioral health, the cost of treatment has been kept to a moderate $3,800 a month.

Those conversations the Barthelmes do value have now expanded to a conversation with the reading public. Clearly they have enjoyed telling about their gambling exploits in *Double Down*. Indeed it was the exultant tale-telling that put me in mind of Eugene O'Neill's 1942 one-act play *Hughie*, a kind of chronological entr'acte between *Long Day's Journey into Night* and *Moon for the Misbegotten*. In the passages that serve as epigraph for this chapter, Erie Smith is addressing the Night Clerk who has replaced Hughie in a seedy Manhattan hotel. O'Neill describes Erie as "In manner . . . consciously a Broadway sport and a Wise Guy—the type of small fry gambler and horse player, living hand to mouth on the fringe of the rackets" (832).

What Erie lives for, perhaps more than the action itself, is the opportunity to tell stories about it. When Hughie dies, what Erie mourns is his audience for those stories, perhaps the only one he had left. "He thought gambling was romantic" (844), he says in what amounts to a dirge, and "He thought gangsters was romantic" (845). As long as someone else buys into the fantasy, Erie can believe in its validity. Ironically the play achieves the final purpose of elegies—consolation for the survivors, a degree of acceptance of death in the belief that the deceased lives on in some way—when Erie discovers a new audience for his tales. The inattentive Night Clerk, virtually ignoring Erie's lament, indulges in a reverie in which he romanticizes the gangster/gambler Arnold Rothstein, and he invites Erie to tell some new lies about that legendary figure, with whom he claims to have rubbed shoulders.

Alongside those of the brothers Barthelme, Erie's stories are pathetic and trivial. What is comparable is the delight, the relish, the self-satisfaction in the telling. Even more clearly than in the text of the memoir, this attitude may be experienced by listening to Terry Gross's interview with the Barthelmes on the December 6, 1999, *Fresh Air* program. Joking with one another, sharing laughs with the host, sophisticatedly amused at the spectacle of themselves losing more than a quarter of a million dollars in the casinos—and then being arrested for cheating—they both demonstrate a canny acknowledgment of their pathology and at the same time evoke an uncanny, uneasy feeling that they still don't get it.

One of the standard clichés of evasion, rationalization, and denial among pathological gamblers is the notion of "playing with their money." Here is Rick: "It wasn't even our own money," and "We only stopped doing it eventually when legal troubles happened and we ran out of money, ran out of the inherited money." Now that the legal troubles have been expunged, are they gambling with their own money? Might whatever advances and royalties accrue from *Double Down* be rationalized away as not really their own money?

Terry Gross's clever questioning evoked responses in which the Barthelmes displayed their intellectual grasp of what happened to them but also their intellectualization of it all as laughable material for a pseudo-confessional memoir. A few excerpts should give a sense of both the illuminating and the frightening dimensions of their narrative and its sophisticated mingling of tones:

TG: As novelists you understand motivation and self-delusion. . . .

STEVE: Understanding self-delusion doesn't cure you of it. [laugh]

RICK: [Gambling] took us away from ourselves. [It was] sort of a way to be bad without hurting anyone. [We'd] feel quite extraordinary . . . shot through with adrenaline . . . there's something quite magical, almost religious, about it.

TG: How about a little psychoanalysis? . . . You say that you've read enough to know that you were both acting as enablers and codependents when it came to your gambling obsessions, so what's it like to understand that, to know about it, to know the language about it, and still do it anyways?

STEVE: The language proves remarkably unsufferable on the one hand and really not accomplishing what it promises. It made little difference to have jargon to apply to it.

RICK: Knowing that we were doing that didn't have any effect in terms of helping us to stop doing it.

STEVE: We tend to operate at a very high level of consciousness anyway so that psychiatric terminology and so forth just was a fancier language for what happens every day.

RICK: [laugh] Also it's sort of like a joke, when we say to each other we're enabling each other we're actually making fun of this language, this jargon. Because often that stuff is used and you think that by naming it, you help it or you solve it or you resolve it or you heal it. And I don't think that's the case at all. By naming it you don't do any of that at all, you're just naming it. . . . Eventually we ended up calling ourselves——

STEVE: Lyle and Eric.

RICK: Lyle and Eric—after the Menendez brothers. [big laugh]

Such a black humor riff portrays their ironic sense of being "bad" though the idea that they were not hurting anyone may be called in question, even if only in regard to one another.

The tone of *Double Down*'s text is sometimes droll, sometimes sardonic, but the reader would have to be more clairvoyant than careful to detect the genuinely gleeful charge the brothers are heard to project together in this interview. It is almost as if, in their memoir-writing and -promoting personas, they continue to act as codependent enablers. If they can laugh at one another and at it all, then they would still not have to deal with their losses in a profoundly emotional way.

Nevertheless, the book offers certain intellectual profundity regarding pathological gambling. For example, "The money was not real either," they say in one of the most powerful passages,

> but an idea, an abstraction, more so when it was in Treasury bonds in the computer of some brokerage house in Boston than when it was chips on the blackjack table. It got closer to being real when it was hundred-dollar bills in your pocket. . . . Part of the lure of gambling was its promise to make the money real, and it even did that, briefly, before snapping it away.
>
> We wanted to win, we went and played and tried to win, we felt great when we did win, we felt lousy when we didn't. Of course, that's not the whole truth.
>
> The second thing often said about chronic gamblers is that they love to lose. It assuages guilt, they say. What sort of guilt? The usual. See Freud on Dostoyevsky. Did we love to lose? That would overstate it. One would not want to place the weight of the losses on this small proposition, but certainly there is something about losing that is not entirely unpalatable. It satisfies the need for excitement, thrills. It's dangerous and it truly burns in a way not so readily available these days. So if not love to lose, then something else; we were at least willing to lose. (109–10)

In *Bob the Gambler*, Frederick Barthelme has given us a brilliant portrait of pathological gambling in a cultural context that outwardly mirrors the perceived inner void. With his brother Steven, now, he has given us a personal account of addiction, intelligently analyzing a wide range of contributing factors. One message of *Double Down* is its clear warning that even the best and brightest among us, once a gambling habit is in place, can be tilted over into pathology by the accumulated weight of events, histories, family mythology, and personalities. That is a worthy service the brothers Barthelme have performed (besides writing an artful, stylish book), but there is also the enormous disservice (not to mention its cost to themselves) of dismissing, denying, and denigrating the remedial powers of psychotherapy for that very pathology.

I yam what I yam.

Popeye the Sailor Man

Gambling and Personality Disorders

All that we know of "CJ" comes from "Total Loss Weekend" by Don DeLillo, which appeared in *Sports Illustrated* in 1972. I don't know whether to call it reportage, short story, memoir, character sketch, or cautionary tale—perhaps it is all of these, and more. Regardless of genre, it provides ample testimony to the acuity of DeLillo's observation, the artfulness of his selection and arrangement of material, and the intelligence with which his nuanced language captures and enacts the marginal crannies of contemporary American culture. Moreover, it gives us (marginally) enough material on which to base (tentatively) a diagnosis of CJ's pathological gambling.

As DeLillo creates a context for the particular weekend he spends with his "cousin," he describes a person in an environment in a way that suggests a diagnosis of clinical depression. DeLillo has gotten off a train in a station that says "Mount Vernon," but he knows it to be somewhere in Yonkers, with its "mortal sadness," a place with "fatigue and defeat in the air" (114), and has walked five minutes to CJ's apartment building. He walks down "the long dim hall" (99) of the fourth floor to where CJ seems "the least animate thing" in the dismal living room, its blinds drawn and "his very flesh reflect[ing] a pale stain of trepidation and doubt" as he sits, wearing dark glasses, in front of two TV sets, "T-shirted and unshaven, nearing 40": "CJ is a gambler. He likes to bet on sporting events, almost any kind, and the dark crawling horror of Total Loss Weekend is never very distant. Misgivings and dread. Panic, remorse and deep trauma" (100).

The cousins exchange perfunctory remarks on "disease, poverty and madness" in the family, and then the marathon of sporting events begins to run across the TV screens and radio bands. Language of powerlessness, hopelessness, helplessness, "Transylvanian dread" (104), despair, and—especially—death dominates the narration. Yet, as depressing as the whole experience may be, there is no evidence that CJ is seriously impaired in his "normal" functioning, or that this language is anything but metaphorical. However negatively the losses may be totaled, CJ likes what he's doing (and what is happening to him), thrives on it: it is his life and it is what he is.

In utter innocence and simplicity, flying in the face of appearances and contexts, CJ says, "I gamble because when I don't gamble I feel sick" (101). What is the nature of such sickness? Are we talking about symptoms of withdrawal in addiction? The symptoms seem rather to suggest an "existential" ailment of the kind discussed in chapter 8. Indeed, a long segment of the piece develops an extended metaphor of void-filling behavior, under the heading, *"What does CJ have in his pockets?"*

The emptiness of his pockets is cluttered with scraps of paper listing his bets for the day and five other items related directly or indirectly to his gambling: an old horse-racing tout sheet, a football parlay ticket, a box score from an old baseball game detailing a traumatic loss, an OTB account card showing he has nothing left in his telephone account, and a form letter from his finance company giving him a high credit rating for his "splendid payment record" (101).

As with other categories, and perhaps even more so with the two in question, it is often difficult to distinguish between personality disorders and the potentially pathological condition I've labeled void-filling behavior. In CJ's case, however, as will become clear, DeLillo's presentation makes the choice relatively easy. Yet before turning to the behavior I find decisive in this case, I think it is useful to examine other symptomatic hints, suggestions of paranoia, masochism, and phobia.

That saved box score is CJ's "reminder of death, hatred, plague and all those bloodsucking ills which keep people up after their bedtime" (104). But the generalized message of such writings-on-the-wall typically gives way, in CJ's experience of "the true contest, the interior contest" (100), to messages delivered to, at, and for him alone. Why does a sudden reversal in a game make CJ a loser over and over again? "Who is aiming this sorrowful arrow at CJ's heart? Who is behind this wanton event? Whims are supposed to be things flitting suddenly to mind, but this one has been engineered by a deterministic intelligence" (109). Because it "is destined to happen. God will make it happen" (108).

Not only does the result of a sporting event played thousands of miles away have special meaning for him and him alone ("ideas of reference," in DSM terminology), but it is "with a feeling of total happiness and despair" (109) that he suffers its impact ("betting on college football is a form of Armenian water torture"). Yet most of all, "in this life and in the life to come" (111), what CJ fears is "the weather." That fear may feed both the paranoid and the masochistic aspects of his experience, as sudden turns of weather—the very natural embodiment of whimsical fate—will turn his best handicapping efforts or sports forecasts into futile nightmares of freakish results.

Yet, with all the symptoms of pathology, CJ has managed to retain a hold on reality. DeLillo "normalizes" these gamblers' symptoms and recounts CJ's avoidance of pathology, of psychosis:

> The gambler's life is a rhythmic tale of numbers, premonitions, symbols and dreams. He worships magic, and is magic's willing victim. He wins and loses in seasons. But within all these cycles and prismatic mysteries, he must fight to maintain a fingerhold on ordinary reality. In the past, when CJ gambled much more heavily than he does now, when it was getting away from him and threatening to lead to a form of nondrinker's delirium tremens, when he was afraid of seeing the pterodactyls come flying out of his TV set—yes, in those days of superstition and bad acid magic, it finally came to him that he was traveling beyond action and into the realm of the unreal. He came out of it like a diver surviving a rapture of the deep, and since then he has lived in a state of carefully controlled enchantment. (109–10)

We may infer that the "careful control" involves a nine-to-five five-day-a-week job (most of his action is limited to weekends, though he walks the thirteen minutes to Yonkers Raceway on Monday evenings). We may even guess at some marketable skills from his ability to assemble a color TV set, "working his way through a 187-page" technical manual "night after night for well over a month" (114). But the key to his habitual behavior, the dangerous element that threatens to push him over or back into nonordinary reality, is found in another of DeLillo's extended metaphors.

What I find strongly suggestive of obsessive-compulsive personality disorder in CJ is revealed in a decade-old behavior. He had discovered ten years ago "a way to prolong the glorious agony of checking results in the newspaper" (109). He covers the results in the paper, using a matchbook, paper napkin, or his hand, slowly moving it across the page. Basketball and football line scores are revealed quarter by quarter, baseball inning by inning; horse races best of all because you can move vertically up the chart to expose the names of finishers in reverse order, the "sense of action ... almost dizzying" if your choice's name fails to appear among the also-rans.

Sipping his coffee in the morning before going to work, CJ experiences his "greatest moments in gambling" as he moves "a matchbook across an inch of small print," sometimes pausing before the final result "to draw it out of real time into some secret hour-glass of gambler's sand," before "slowly and lovingly and with a feeling of total happiness and despair" bringing the "splendid scrap of action to its end." This is also an aspect of "careful control," and if CJ is aware of the potential danger of his ways, he finds their ego satisfactions worth the risk. The ritual itself is regular, prolonged, pleasurable (irrespective of wins and losses), and sure to annoy anyone but the person performing it. No wonder CJ lives alone (visited occasionally by his younger brother Kool, also a habitual gambler/loser, who lives in "the Jersey swamps" [111]). But he likes it this way, likes what he does, who he is.

In the Folger Library, at the reception following a rare DeLillo public reading (from Underworld), I surprised him by asking how CJ was. He had just exchanged pleasant comments with my wife about Mario's on Arthur Avenue, a venerable restaurant in the heart of the Bronx's Little Italy, and I don't know whether he was reacting to the sudden incongruous shift, to the personal nature of the question, or simply to the fact of someone (someone who is on record as revering him for writing at least half a dozen masterpieces of fiction) actually remembering a twenty-five-year-old magazine piece; but somehow he was caught off guard and answered the question.

CJ wasn't in Yonkers any more, DeLillo didn't know where he was, and if he knew he couldn't tell because CJ was being looked for—presumably as a result of unpaid gambling debts. The life of the "character" had been projected long past the story that delimited his existence to a single weekend, and the habitual behavior (leading to a tentative diagnosis of his condition described above) had over time, one might reasonably infer, deteriorated into pathology with serious consequences.[1]

The personality disorders, on the other hand (and this is the essential distinction that requires a separate axis for classifying and coding them), refer to the structures of personalities. Here the characteristic behaviors may be unconscious signs of off-putting personalities (often defined as deviations from the ways of the culture at large), but even when brought to the conscious attention of the person are likely to be affirmed by the notions, "That's me, that's who I am, take it or leave it, love it or get lost" (or in the case of Popeye, learn to live with the corncob pipe permanently fixed in the mouth, the muttering coarseness, the grotesquerie of the physique, the squinty eye, and the addiction to canned spinach). Notoriously resistant to any therapeutic "change-agency," the behaviors of personality-disordered people are comfortable for them because they are ego-affirming.

The DSM observes that symptoms of Antisocial Personality Disorder and Pathological Gambling may overlap and that dual diagnosis is appropriate.[2] We are also warned, under a discussion of "differential diagnosis," to distinguish between Manic Episode and Pathological Gambling, where the latter would be chosen if the "manic-like features dissipate" away from the gambling or if "maladaptive gambling behavior" occurs at times other than during an apparently Manic Episode (617).

These two caveats are the only ones among the standard guidelines, but Julian Taber et al. persuasively discuss the prevalence of narcissism in pathological gamblers. "It is most likely narcissism, rather than ego, that permits an otherwise intelligent person to embark on a course of gambling that eventually leads to addiction," in their judgment. And they conclude: "Anyone familiar with gamblers cannot help but relate certain narcissistic criteria to the personalities of many gamblers: grandiosity, exaggeration, fantasies of unlimited success, exhibitionism, cool indifference or rage in response to criticism, and feelings of emptiness to name just a few. . . . We have the impression that many pathological gamblers could carry a collateral diagnosis of NPD. Many would probably demonstrate other disorders of the self or ego development colored, perhaps, with narcissistic features" ("Ego Strength," 78–79). In the same volume, Richard Rosenthal's article supports their observations (with suggestions for treatment to be addressed in chapter 12).

The DSM is also careful and explicit in its distinctions among specific personality disorders and "clusters" into which they may be grouped. But in practical applications, it is often difficult to distinguish among them, so commonly do symptoms overlap. Gambling, when it can be identified as part of the behavior pattern, can be useful in arriving at a precise diagnosis. But that does not render it more accessible to treatment except for this factor: a personality disorder that involves habitual gambling behaviors is likely to escalate to a degree of pathology demanding remediation.

It is difficult to hold on to the ego-enhancing, self-affirming value of a behavior that has led one to willful infliction of self-injury, to the brink of suicide, to the loss of job and family, or to jail. Learning the likelihood of such progression may lead to recognition of the value of change (suggesting a cognitive-learning component to therapy). As in other areas, where education plays a vital role in public health issues, early detection and diagnosis are significant keys. In their absence, a scenario like that of Axel Freed may be played out. He is the gambler, the eponymous protagonist of Karel Reisz's 1975 movie, written by James Toback.[3]

Axel Freed (James Caan) teaches classes in literature at a New York City college. Early on we catch a glimpse of him giving a lecture—on Dostoevsky. This takes place after an all-night session of gambling at a private (illegal) casino run by his "friend" Hips (Paul Sorvino). During the night he has run his debt up to "44 dimes" ($44,000), and on his drive uptown to the school (intercut with flashbacks of the night's action) he stops his convertible at a schoolyard basketball court to challenge the best player to a game, one-on-one, at odds of twenty dollars to ten cents. In Axel's distorted perspective, there is no distinction of value between a figurative dime (a thousand dollars in gambling jargon) and a literal dime. It's a close game, but Axel loses.

Axel's mother (Jacqueline Brooks) is a pediatrician at a clinic. Her affluence is made apparent when Axel takes her from the hospital to a rooftop court at her private Manhattan tennis club—where he plays aggressively to beat her thoroughly. This scene follows one with his girlfriend Billie (Lauren Hutton) in which sex is mixed with playful boxing. Later we see him dancing with his mother after giving a toast to his wealthy grandfather (Morris Carnovsky) during the latter's birthday celebration at his luxurious estate. When Axel subsequently takes his mother to the beach for a swim, he confesses his indebtedness and insistently asks for her help.

It is apparently not the first time. Dr. Freed suggests that this is a relapse in a condition that she had thought under control. But her outrage is moralistic, based on her belief that her son's gambling losses support the "monsters" who deal drugs to children. "Have I been such a failure?" she laments in the perennial cry of the mother-as-enabler. "Have I raised a son who has the morals of a snake?"

After arranging for the bank withdrawals to cover his debt (for the last time, she insists), she adopts a more professional stance and says to him, "Unless you come to terms with why you're doing this, no money's going to get you out."

Another classroom lecture scene follows, with Axel giving historical examples of people he denigrates because they hated to lose so much that they only undertook ventures when they had seemed to eliminate risk. But in a scene with Billie, when she confronts him not only about his gambling but about his choices of lifestyle ("You're just throwin' it away, not just the money"), he says, "It's just something I like to do. I like the uncertainty of it. I like the threat of losing, the idea that I could lose but somehow I won't because I don't want to. And I *love* winning even though it never lasts."

Approaching the plot's climax there is a verbal exchange between Axel and Hips. The professional gambler calls other gamblers "degenerates" and says, "I never made a bet in my life. You know why? I've observed firsthand the different kinds of people who are addicted to gambling. I've noticed there's one thing that makes all of them the same."

Axel, naturally, knows what the point is and interrupts in a bored tone: "Yes, they're all looking to lose." But he is different. Insisting that he not only wants to win but actually would win if he stuck to bets that he knew were winners, he says in final justification of his behavior, "If all my bets were safe there just wouldn't be any juice."

On the surface the movie is cliché ridden and formula driven. It has the obligatory trip to Vegas, the loan-shark encounter, the object-lesson destruction of a deadbeat gambler's property, the connection of gambling to organized crime, and the inevitable fixing of a sporting event. But beneath its glitzy-squalid and melodramatic surface it presents enough elements of a sophisticated case study to warrant more careful attention here.

Superficially, this gambler seems to sketch a dramatic profile of the "compulsive" character of conventional wisdom or modern mythology. But if we look more attentively, we may see a comprehensive portrait of a personality-disordered individual. We've already seen some hints of his diagnostic classification in the dialogue quoted above, in his conscious awareness of the value to him of the "juice" and doing what he likes to do, regardless of negative consequences and totally exclusive of what anyone else might think of him. Many other symptoms are shown, including some clues to the etiology of his condition.

Throughout the movie Axel is seen looking at himself in mirrors. No matter what else is going on in his life, however great the issues or possible consequences, he is meticulous about his hair (requiring a lock to descend over his forehead in the proper position) and his clothes (requiring his shirt to be opened far enough to reveal a perfect triangle of torso and chest hair). Gambling is what he likes to do best, but he derives narcissistic satisfaction in sex, athletic "prowess," and classroom performance as well, seeming always to be watching himself, with approval, in his mind's mirroring eye.

This is almost a caricature of narcissism, but there are other indications of the movie's profound psychological understanding of the condition. One is his displaced anger, directed at a low-level bank executive (James Woods in an early cameo role) in presumed defense of his mother's dignity, but enacting his inability to be angry at himself or to acknowledge that he is the one who has offended his mother's very sense of self. This scene is one of several in which Axel explodes in irrational and misdirected rage, while in several other incidents where anger might be expected he displays unusual self-control. In all these scenes, it is the distorted, self-contained, internalized self-image that evokes the emotional or unemotional expression.

The narcissist's scenarios of abandonment and betrayal are drawn from his sense that others are mere extensions of himself, existing only in relation to himself. Implicitly, we learn that his father had "betrayed" Axel by dying young. As for his mother, Axel assumes that she exists only to serve his needs—he doesn't ask for her money so much as demand it, and he can also demand that she take time out from her practice for him to beat her up on the tennis court. To him her function is to be his personal whipping boy, not a career caregiver for other children.

He extols his grandfather in the celebratory toast as a self-made man, risen from shtetl youth who defied "Cossack" authority with his bare hands in Lithuania to entrepreneurial eminence as owner of a chain of stores. He is Axel's ace in the hole. Axel assumes that he will be the heir to his grandfather's fortune, just as he is the heir to his existential heroism, because he had projected his self-image onto him. When he discovers that his grandfather has already been approached by the racketeers to pay off his debts, that the very same mobsters had in fact done business with him years ago, Axel responds with predictable rage.

But when he confronts his grandfather, it is not about the dishonorable connections but about dishonoring the connection with his grandson by failing to buy off his debts. He expresses disdain for that but fails to recognize the essential connection between his grandfather's behavior ("I did what I had to do, I used them when necessary") and his own tacit justification for using others when he has to. And he is able to tell his grandfather that he doesn't need him, because he knows he can use someone else to save himself—his student, the star basketball player on the college team.

Two scenes with Billie most clearly demonstrate the narcissistic nature of this character. In one, the discovery that she might have *any* kind of relationship with someone other than him provokes an outburst of violent rage. In the other, she literally walks out on him, leaving his car which he has carelessly parked at the side of a road in order to place bets with a bookie over a public phone. He cannot tolerate such a loss of an extension or part of himself, the pain of a narcissistic wounding, and he chases her, cuts her off, woos her back.[4]

Another pair of scenes enacts the primitive defense mechanism of splitting, a defense typically associated with the class of personality disorders to which the Borderline and the Narcissistic belong. In his toast to his grandfather, he salutes an all-good, all-worthy ideal (with whom he strongly identifies). But when Axel confronts the same man who has "betrayed" him (as the old man listens to a scratched recording of Caruso singing "Una furtiva lagrima" from Donizetti's L'elisir d'amore), he vilifies him as all-evil, valueless, unworthy of his "love." The irony that it is himself he loves and that what he is raging against is his own betrayal of self is lost on Axel. All that has changed is the way his grandfather has treated him; for the narcissist, the same object can be split into all-good and all-evil embodiments.

In the climactic sequence of the movie, Axel appears to be arranging his own punishment, perhaps death, for having acceded to the organized-crime insistence that he corrupt a star student-athlete in a point-shaving scheme to satisfy his own gambling debts. He provokes a dispute with a whore and her pimp in a rented room above a bar in Harlem, strikes out violently, and is severely cut with a razor. The final scene shows him once again before a mirror, this time smiling in grim satisfaction at the bloody reflection of a wound that will surely leave a permanent scar. The narcissistic wounding, the injury to his image of himself that his sellout entails (loss of existential freedom, corruption of his gambling behavior and values themselves), has become a literal disfigurement. In the closing shot, his frozen smile says that he beholds what he has wrought. And it is good.

One of the most notorious gamblers of mid-twentieth-century America was clearly a personality-disordered character. If Jack Molinas, who was often thought to be "crazy," could have been diagnosed with any Axis I disorder, I have not been able to ascertain what it might have been, even though it is reasonable to say that from time to time he was so out of touch with reality that he could disregard threats to his personal safety, willfully swear to what he knew was false (and he was a lawyer), believe that he could manipulate people and events to his own satisfaction when his projected scenarios seemed implausible if not impossible to others, perform mental juggling acts and tightrope-walkings that had no basis in concrete numbers or events, appear unable to distinguish between fantasy and fact, and deny discrepancies between his own contradictory versions of events.

Amoral he certainly was, but amorality is not classified as a mental disorder on Axis I in the DSM. I have gone so far as to invent a diagnosis, "The Icarus Syndrome,"[5] to account for his wild career and ultimate plunge. Having devoted a substantial portion of a book (The Great Molinas) to his life story, I find it a daunting task to reduce that tale to a case study. But I will try to summarize the behaviors that are revealingly symptomatic for the purposes of this chapter.

Young Jacob Molinas was a prodigy both intellectually and athletically. Doted on by his parents and the whole Bronx neighborhood where he grew up, he was amply rewarded for what he learned and performed by celebrity, adulation, and—when he learned how to make his wit and skill pay off—money. Through junior high school in the Bronx, high school at Manhattan's prestigious Stuyvesant, and summers at Coney Island in Brooklyn (where his father owned a successful hot-dog-and-beer place), Jackie literally and figuratively towered over his peers. His early life was a kind of triumphant "Tale of Three Boroughs."

Early on, gambling became a significant part of his aggressive competitiveness. When I say that he would bet on anything, I mean that his action included games of skill in which he played, games of skill played by others (he developed a reputation for that quality essential to a sports bettor or handicapper called "a good opinion"), and games of chance—where he also had an edge because he had far more money in his pocket than his peers and so could ride out any streak of bad luck until he would be able to recoup losses. He had no compunctions about winning bets from his friends when he knew results in advance, no scruples about cheating when he could get away with it, and no sense of obligation to pay off losing bets.

In the Coney Island playground where he honed his basketball skills, one of the resident bullies ("bogards"), called Cozzi (because he bore a perceived resemblance to Quasimodo), was a runner for a local bookie. Molinas would bet on sporting events through Cozzi, brag about and show off his winnings, and instead of paying off losing bets would get even by playing Cozzi one-on-one.

In his senior year, Jack led his Stuyvesant team to the 1949 PSAL basketball finals in Madison Square Garden against perennial powerhouse Lincoln High. He was clearly the best player on the floor, but he seemed to disappear in the decisive fourth quarter, when Lincoln pulled ahead. Molinas won by losing. He had taken a few hundred dollars (which he didn't need) up front to lose the game, and then, confident of his own ability to control the event, bet against his own team.

He went on to play for Columbia, a highly ranked team in 1951. It was the big time, and Molinas's gambling got bigger and bigger. When the college basketball scandals broke in 1951, Columbia along with the metropolitan Catholic schools evaded the politically driven, selective prosecution of

District Attorney Hogan's office, but from 1951 to 1953 Molinas was taking money to shave points, betting on those games and controlling them, and becoming directly involved in Joey Hacken's bookmaking business. None of this prevented him from being drafted by the Fort Wayne Zollner–Pistons of the NBA.

When the second major college basketball scandal erupted in 1961, Jack Molinas was identified, indicted, tried, convicted, and sentenced as the "Master Fixer." In the intervening decade he had (1) made the NBA All-Star team as a rookie; (2) been banned for life from the league for betting on games, before he even got to play in that 1954 All-Star Game; (3) earned a law degree at Brooklyn Law School; (4) played, starred, and coached in the Eastern Basketball League, where Chet Forte was one of his players; (5) cultivated basketball contacts all over the greater metropolitan area with his flamboyant, free-spending ways; and (6) become a full and, to all intents and purposes, managing partner in Hacken's bookmaking and sports-fixing operation.

What did it mean to "buy a game" in the jargon of the period? Molinas would act as a broker, "selling" a game, say for $25,000, typically to an organized crime entity or individual. He would then use some of that money to bribe players and sometimes referees to control the score of a game in order to produce a desired result over or under the betting line or point spread. And the buyer would bet as much as possible on the "sure thing" to make many times the investment. Molinas would bet as well, and Hacken would accept bets only on the losing side of the proposition.

But that wasn't enough for Jack Molinas. Sometimes he would simply pocket the money, relying on his good opinion to predict the outcome of a game without bribing anyone. Sometimes he would sell a game to more than one party, thus reducing the opportunities for the buyers to spread their action around. And in at least one case, where the line shifted by enough points to make the dumping team a likely winner anyway, he sold the game to two parties on *opposite sides* of the action.

Leonard Kaplan was Molinas's star player on the Alabama team. A Pittsburgh mobster had paid to have Alabama fail to cover a four-point spread against Tulane. Molinas then sold the game to a St. Louis "investor" who was betting Alabama to win at the tipoff-time line of minus one point. Kaplan became a Molinas hero, scoring twenty-seven in the game, sinking the last-second basket to win by two for Alabama (and "St. Louis") but staying under the spread of four for Tulane (and "Pittsburgh"). Molinas rewarded Kaplan with a promise that he could play for his Eastern League team any time, when he had finished his business at Alabama.

While this was going on, Molinas took on a bigger gamble. He became aware of the D.A.'s investigation of sports fixes, that he was a target, and that his phones were tapped. His response was to increase his activity. He assured Hacken that they would never be stopped because the cops had known for a long time what they were doing and were themselves cashing bets on sure things. Why would they kill the goose laying all those golden eggs in their laps? He found proof for this assumption in the fact that as soon as he arranged to fix a particular game, the point spread would immediately start to move; whoever was tapping his phone was betting on the basis of the information overheard. Molinas then indulged a rare fit of anger, punishing the cops for causing those unfavorable shifts of betting lines, and consequently endangering his own lucrative business.

He set up a game in Philadelphia, announcing over the phone that it was the surest thing ever, that he had "three and two and the tooters," that is, that he had bribed three players on one team, two on the other, and both officials. But he gave out the wrong team, knowing that whoever was listening would mortgage their homes to get down on this one. Then he went to Philadelphia, not to watch a game with its outcome in no doubt at all, but to watch the faces of the plainclothes cops from New York as they realized gradually what was going on—slow torture because Molinas had instructed his agents to keep it close until well into the second half.

This venture was costly, because his arrest followed shortly thereafter, but Molinas was already backing another bet. When all others involved either turned state's evidence or plea-bargained their sentences (including Hacken, who served a long term rather than testify against his associates), Jack went to trial, believing his charisma would be more persuasive to a jury than the weighty evidence against him. It was not a good opinion. When the jury found against him, he was confident of a light sentence. When he received the maximum sentence allowed, he bragged that conviction and sentencing did not mean he would ever serve that time.

In fact, Molinas was sent away, serving his hard time in Sing Sing, Attica, and the Tombs, but always plunging into whatever action he could find. He broke the bank of a bookmaking operation (cigarettes, food gifts, and "futures" as the primary currency), then took it over himself. He played wide receiver on the football team (whose exploits were memorialized in Jimmy Breslin's newspaper columns and in Robert Aldrich's movie *The Longest Yard*). He shortened his time by providing information on other, ongoing, scandalous—and mob-related—cases. And he applied his good opinion to the stock market, earning furloughs and other favors from powerful clients.

After his parole, he engineered a transfer to California on the pretext of a movie deal that never materialized. But once established there, he wheeled and dealed in every imaginable way: bookmaking, loan-sharking, pornographic films, hijacked goods. He gambled in Las Vegas, on credit, and ran up unpaid debts. No risk was too great—in fact the bigger the better—in a spiraling ascent of action in which he moved ever larger figures around (numbers on accounts rather than money). And he enjoyed every minute of it, including the frustration of his creditors, the complexity of his transactions and transgressions, and the prospect of an infinite progession of numbers.

This period of flying ever higher is what brought Icarus to mind. Molinas and his partner in a fur business had a life insurance policy on one another, with the survivor as beneficiary; just before it was about to expire, Molinas had his partner killed. He collected the half million but neglected to pay the hired killer. At this point a gathering of organized crime gray eminences determined that Jack Molinas was too disorganized, disorderly, and anarchic to be allowed to continue. They ordered his wings clipped (or, in what may be the more appropriate metaphor, that the wax on his wings be melted—with hot lead). He was dead at forty-three.

Flagrant symptoms of personality disorders are boldly drawn all over this portrait. Of the ten types delineated in the DSM, symptoms of only two, the Dependent and the Avoidant Personality, are absent from his profile. For the Histrionic, we have his need to be not only at the epicenter of action but to be the cynosure of attention as well, plus his egregiously provocative or seductive behavior. For the Obsessive-Compulsive, we have his need to exercise control and incessantly, indefatigably, to pursue his preoccupations. For the Paranoid, the Schizoid, the Schizotypal, and the Borderline, we have a lifetime of failure or unwillingness to engage in stable, enduring interpersonal relationships, whether out of distrust, restricted emotional expression, distorted perceptions of both self and others, or impulsive responses such as inexplicable rage immediately succeeding affectionate gestures (along with hints at some of the other symptoms of these conditions).

It is into the categories of the Antisocial and the Narcissistic Personality Disorders, however, that Jack Molinas seems most comfortably to fit. He could hardly be called antisocial in the general sense of the word. Always the center of attention in groups, convivial in parties and at large dinners in both of which he seemed to take great delight, always the quickest and loudest to laugh at jokes—often his own—he appeared to thrive on surrounding himself with acquaintances, cultivating a sense of intimacy with men and women.

But this was all show. The telling points of his personality were his amoral disregard for the laws of the land, the norms of social behavior, prudent consideration of the physical safety of himself and others (people often spoke of the thrilling danger of riding in a car driven by Molinas), obligations financial and other, and perhaps especially the truth. Add the fact that remorse and guilt were totally alien to his nature and you have as good a profile of Antisocial Personality Disorder as you are likely to find in the clinical literature.

The criteria for Narcissistic Personality Disorder are met equally well in this complex character. There is one perhaps apocryphal story (attested to by several sources, but all secondhand) that is pertinent here. When Molinas had taken money from certain parties to fix a game and the result had been the opposite of what had been paid for, he was visited by some associates of the aggrieved parties. They held him upside down outside an upper-story hotel window to let him know what would happen if the offense were repeated. Of course, he said it would never happen again and that he would make restitution, but that was after he had shouted out the crux of his response with the indignant line, "You can't hurt me—I'm Jack Molinas."

Grandiosity, arrogance, a sense of entitlement, and belief in the limitless powers of one's own brilliance, prowess, charm, and abilities are hallmarks of this disorder. A sense of one's own physical beauty almost goes without saying, but it is incidental. Charismatic and gifted, Molinas used every aspect of his attractiveness and talent that allowed him to manipulate the many people drawn to him. He did so without a bit of empathy, without ever acknowledging the needs or feelings of others. It was as if other people existed only as extensions of himself, as if the worth of others was entirely measured by the degree of admiration they paid to Jack Molinas. His need for adulation was what drove him to center stage of whatever arena of action he could find.

Was Molinas's gambling pathological? Terminally so. His aggressiveness was boundless if often disguised, his need for action insatiable and self-compounding, his risk-taking incessant and ever-growing as if an addiction were producing higher and higher levels of tolerance, his grandiose confidence in his own limitless abilities delusionally arrogant, his acceptance of the authority of others or norms or systems as nonexistent as his sense of morality, and his hunger for the attention and adulation of others outdone only by a need to be in solitary, secret splendor above and beyond what those others could know. All of this was expressed in his gambling behavior. All this was symptomatic of his diseased self. And the course of his illness was deathward.

Clearly, Jack Molinas's pathology stands outside the model of a diagnostic manual that includes Pathological Gambling. Yet it should be equally clear that his gambling behaviors, if recognized soon enough as symptomatic of serious mental (not to mention social) impairment, might have led to useful diagnosis and treatment. Perhaps not. It is the daunting and self-defeating aspect of the personality disorders, after all, that people with these constellations of characteristics are satisfied to be what they are.

Molinas would probably have scoffed at the idea that he needed treatment, resisted the suggestion that he receive it, and—had it been forced upon him—enjoyed the possibilities for game playing in therapy and the prospect of manipulating his therapists. Wherever he was, whatever he was doing, whatever games within games he was playing, whatever gambles he was taking, whatever troubles were mounting for him because of his behaviors, however much he was in debt or danger, Molinas, like Robert Coover's character John, "loved the days of his life" (John's Wife, 141). Amidst a dizzying array of wins and losses, chances and debts, a myriad of juggled numbers, he was enjoying the last day of his life when a .38 long shell from an assassin's weapon ended it. That end was the logical, rational, inevitable termination. This was a case of pathological gambling in extremis.

If Molinas was blissfully unconcerned with the pathological nature of his personality structure, Dr. Fitzgerald, the forensic psychologist who is the protagonist of the TV series Cracker, is painfully, insightfully, articulately aware of his. The florid displays of that pathology and the consequences they provoke are a substantial element in the serial complexity of the character and the individual scenarios in which he is involved. To be sure, part of that complexity may be the result of the collaborative effort that involved several writers, the directors of the separate shows, and the projected persona of Robbie Coltrane, the lead actor (who played a comic cameo of a racetrack teller in the movie Let It Ride and reemerged on the big screen as an outlaw Russian intelligence veteran in the James Bond film Golden Eye).

This is not a case for easy categorizing. At best, dual diagnosis is in order. Fitz exhibits too many manic-depressive characteristics to ignore his mood disorder. His mood swings take him into prolonged episodes of helpless wallowing in self-pity and hopeless despair which he articulates in language of existential angst. As a professional practitioner, he should be a ready candidate for medication, but he is rigidly resistant to treatment of any kind, preferring to self-medicate with tobacco, booze, and gambling. In his hypomanic phases he is a spellbinding marathon speaker and an indefatigable pursuer of solutions to the intransigent mysteries of puzzling crimes, with an uncanny, almost clairvoyant knack for cutting through the plausible stories that mask deceit and apprehending the unlikely details and the aberrant behaviors that account for the "truth."

And yet he *enjoys* the painful extremes of his affective range. He takes pride in his eccentricities, like an artist (Kate Millett comes to mind, as revealed in her *Loony-Bin Trip*, or Sean Connery's poet character in the Irvin Kershner movie *A Fine Madness*) who is aware of his need for those biochemical imbalances to fuel his genius in the service of his art. Fitz is incorrigible and damned pleased with himself for it, self-destructive though his manner and behaviors may be. He knows how difficult he is for others to bear, not only professional superiors and peers and inferiors but wife and children as well, yet he relishes that difficulty as his "charm" and their problem. Knowing that all three of his vices are bad for him, his answers to the explicit questions of why he drinks, smokes, and gambles so much are all the same: "because I like it" (from the initial episode, "The Mad Woman in the Attic").[6]

The first four episodes, regardless of the vicious crime cases which Fitz solves, are essentially devoted to developing the picture of a man with an overwhelming gambling problem. Diagnostic clues of all sorts are to be found in these scripts. They suggest every variety of pathological gambling I have sampled in the previous chapters, from the impulse-control problems to the void-filling behaviors, the anxiety and mood disorders to the distorted reality-perceptions of psychosis. But all those seem to me to be overwhelmed by the histrionic/narcissistic/borderline/paranoid/schizotypal/antisocial symptoms not only in Fitz's behavior but in his "clever" self-analysis as well.[7] And he takes perverse delight in playing up the provocative, trying, testing aspects of his character. It is his stock-in-trade, his acting out of his own love/hate relationship with his self. His wife is intelligent, too, but she has yet to understand that the last thing that would get her husband to stop gambling would be a rational loss of hope (like the statistician who proved that your chances of winning the giant multistate lotto grand prize were just as good if you didn't buy a ticket).

In short, the makers of *Cracker* have drawn a complex rather than simplistic portrait of pathological gambling (unlike most popular media treatments) and made it work in the context of sophisticated if improbable detective scenarios. The complexity may be seen in gambling behavior that is "overdetermined" (in Freud's useful phrase). For example, having promised his wife never to gamble again ("Brotherly Love," seventh episode), he takes his share of his inheritance from his mother (herself a devoted gambler) and heads for the casino:

FITZ: I'm going to make my mother a millionaire.

WIFE: You promised you'd never gamble again.

FITZ: This doesn't count.

"Cheap sentimentality," she calls it. But it is clearly something more, something other than that. The very presence of the money could be too much for Fitz to bear, the urge to play with it absolutely irresistible. Or he could compulsively wish to divest himself of the money he feels guilty about having. Or he could be enacting a final laying to rest of the mother in him that is the seat and seed of his gambling. Or, as a profoundly insightful self-psychologist, he could recognize all these determinants and accept the inevitability of playing. Or, as the personality-disordered character I have diagnosed—and this would be my choice if I had to fix on just one—he could be using these factors as pretexts for doing what he wants to do: he has an overabundance of excuses to gamble and can happily rationalize/intellectualize his way to the casino.

Gambling is the salient feature of Fitz's (personality-disordered) identity. It is also the distinguishing feature of the character, the thing that makes the improbable solving of bizarre crimes palatable if not plausible. In "White Ghost" (episode ten), Fitz is offered a contract to work in Hong Kong. "They'll pay you good money," he is told, "which is better news for your wife than it is for you, if your gambling is anything to go by."

The point is that it is everything to go by, the centerpiece of the personality. Because the quirks and behaviors are so strongly defended, Fitz will go on gambling (as long as the series may run) because unlike the other diagnoses which are characterized by pathological gambling, the personality disorder is highly resistant to and defended against change, that is, both consciously and unconsciously. Fitz may be anguished, torn, and tempest-tossed, but he functions at his job (and in his role as the centerpiece of the artifact that is the series) because of what he is. Even at cancellation or termination, such characters can never be thought of as entering treatment. It is the very solidity of the defenses that make the personality-disordered gambler so difficult to treat.

My next example is not a character from fiction, television, or the movies. When Patrick came into treatment he was already attending GA meetings, said he was not getting much out of them, but readily acknowledged that his gambling had become pathological. His debts had gotten out of hand and he was seeking counseling because if he did not he stood to lose his wife and children.

Patrick had done some reading about compulsive gambling and presented himself as reasonable, quick, and knowledgeable. He readily divulged a detailed history, not only of his gambling but also of his marriage, his career, and his family of origin. He was so primed for psychotherapy that it seemed to his therapist that he frequently anticipated the next question, commencing an answer before it had been asked for.

Like his therapist, Patrick knew the ins and outs of all forms of gambling, knew what he liked and didn't like, knew the angles and the odds and the procedures and the mechanisms. Unlike most gamblers, he was straightforward and accurate about his numbers, neither minimizing the extent of his action and losses nor exaggerating his wins and net results. And also unlike the vast majority of sports bettors among gamblers, his brand of cleverness and canniness came from genuine inside knowledge. He was a college basketball coach who had played big-time college football and basketball himself. In other words, Patrick was risking more than his money or even his family when he gambled; he was putting his career and his future on the line every time he placed a bet with a bookie.

The family history provided some significant material for insight. He was the sixth of seven brothers born to a Catholic military family, but by the time of most of his school years his family had settled into a single home in the town where his father taught at a military academy. One grandparent on each side, he believed, was alcoholic, and he knew that one of his older brothers also had a serious gambling problem, had been abstinent since attending GA, but was not in treatment. The household was a veritable minefield of competition, cheered on by Mom and Dad, in every area—academics, church and scouting activities, rewards for "service" at home, board games, dinner-table quizzes, and especially sports.

The brothers played at every sport, played against one another with intense aggressiveness, and even vied to amass the most comprehensive knowledge of sports. Patrick was so successful in this competitive environment, both in the athletic arena and his encyclopedic knowledge of sports pages and magazines, that he earned the family soubriquet of "Mister Sports"—which is what he was called by siblings, parents, friends at school, and eventually even teachers and coaches.

And Mister Sports was a winner. Star athlete and trivia champion, he thrived on every win and sought new fields for action and higher levels of competition. What he lacked in size he made up for in aggressive determination and the intelligence of his play. But if professional sports remained an ambition, a knee injury at the end of his junior year hastened a rational reassessment of his chances. The injury and dashed hopes for a pro career, however, were not the trigger for his gambling. By then Mister Sports had already been betting for two football and two basketball seasons, though mostly on NFL and NBA games, using his "good opinion" to show a modest profit, but being listened to attentively by others in the locker room.

So far in this scenario we have some correlation with familiar characteristics and patterns: the bright mind, the multiple rewards of winning, the alcoholism in prior generations, the aggressiveness in competition. But to this point we see neither the excitement of the action itself nor the addictive dose of a big initial win. In fact, Patrick lost his first bet, "getting even" with the second the following week—though he explicitly dismissed the suggestion that there was any revenge or anger in the experience, despite the use of that ambiguous phrase.

After graduation, however, and before his teaching/coaching career began, two changes occurred in his gambling behavior. Besides betting on games, he began spending more and more idle afternoons and evenings at racetracks. In addition, he realized that the larger the bets, the more enjoyment he got out of them. The onset of void-filling behaviors, then, was correlated with the direct "positive" benefits of the gambling action. But Mister Sports was still on top of his sporting world, keeping careful records that showed steady if small net profits.

In the next phase, three significant events/changes took place in his life. One was the beginning of his professional career as basketball coach and math teacher. The second was the accidental drowning of his oldest brother—the first overt trauma in a hitherto blessed family life. And the third was his marriage (preceded by a bachelor-party junket to Las Vegas: Patrick was neither intrigued nor tempted by casino gambling—his math background may have precluded that—but the sports book at Caesars Palace was a glimpse of heaven to him).

His bride did not aspire to be Missus Sports. Prudence enjoyed outdoor activities, was fairly athletic herself but apparently not particularly competitive, was also dedicated to a teaching career (unlike Patrick's mother, ever the devoted full-time "soccer mom"), and most important had a touch of puritanical attitudes so that she was "more than mildly" disapproving of his gambling, in Patrick's words.

His gambling, accordingly and not surprisingly, took new directions. First, a habit of concealment took firm hold. Prudence could not know about it, nor could his employers. Yet the public image and the personality identity of Mister Sports had to be maintained somehow. Another source of new tensions in his inner life had to do with Tim's death. He became painfully aware of feelings of inadequacy in his relationship with his sister-in-law and nieces. He simply couldn't face them, avoided contact with them, and instead of any adequate grieving process would sneak off to a racetrack where the mourning and guilt or shame or embarrassment were buried in intense study of the form sheets and the abandoned distraction of heavier betting. His bets on sporting events were also increasing, along with some preoccupation about keeping the activity hidden from Prudence while maintaining his reputation at school as authority on all things athletic. So both strengths and weaknesses of Patrick's evolved ego were reflected in his gambling behaviors as external events impinged on his sense of himself.

One other thing (which may remind us of the examples of "compulsion" reported in chapter 4): Prudence, as the only child of an only child, would soon come into a six-figure inheritance when her grandmother died. This factor would play a powerful role in the next phase of a pathology that was already overdetermined for the disasters yet—but sure—to come.

The next phase, an escalation of gambling up to a new plateau, coincided with the three-year period that saw the birth of two children and the acquisition of that inheritance. Patrick and Prudence made a careful decision to set the money aside, creating a trust for the purposes of educating their daughter and son. Still, there was the sense of having a financial safety net. Patrick, however, believed he was hiding from Prudence his own inner conflict: he resented having to adhere to a budget, and he longed for the kind of personal financial freedom that would afford him the pleasure of having a "slush fund" to play with as and when he wished.

Patrick refers to this as a period of "controlled chaos." He was a "bigshot" player now, at the track more often, betting all sports and almost every day (often several games a day, getting heavily into baseball for the first time). He had his own bookie and account number, with the understanding that they "settled on a dime" (that is, when winnings or losses totaled $1,000). Not surprisingly, the marital relationship cooled, to the point where it was devoid of sex, lacking affection, unmindful of love.

In his professional life, however, Patrick was experiencing great success. His prep school math classes were spirited and appreciated (he often used sports models and problems to the delight of his students), and he was given tenure and steady salary increments. As a coach, he had moved on to an assistantship at a local college, and already moved up the bench to the second chair alongside the head coach. But by now his gambling had "crossed over the line."

Mister Sports had become a loser: reckless, impulsive, and absorbed. In his own word, he was a "skywalker" (faint echo of Icarus) about to crash in mounting losses, debts, and threat of exposure. Having taken out a loan without Prudence's knowledge, he found himself at one point with more than enough cash in the slush fund to pay it off; but he gambled that money away. When he had run out of credit with his bookie as well, he had no recourse but to reveal the whole story to Prudence—because only with her support could he find a way to discharge his debts.

He pledged to seek help for his addiction, started attending GA, and found a therapist who would treat him on a once-a-week basis. He wondered whether a separation would be appropriate, since, as he put it, Prudence had no reason to trust him enough to continue a marriage so threatened by his gambling. He did not move out of the house, however, though for several months he slept in a separate room. Open, articulate, thoughtful, introspective, and—despite the therapist's tendency to view with suspicion the words of a pathological gambler—apparently honest, Patrick seemed an exemplary client, well suited to a cognitive-learning approach.

The therapy sessions proceeded smoothly and productively, largely because Patrick had already pursued the issues at hand to their logical and psychological implications, conclusions, and consequences. He understood certain causes, realized the risks—personal, familial, professional—that he was unwilling to take any more, and was alert to the warning signals. The one serious misgiving that occurred to the therapist was that it seemed to be *too easy* to accomplish the goals of treatment. Yet as they continued their work together, Patrick maintained his abstinence through what had been three prime betting seasons for him: the pro football season, the NCAA basketball tournament, and the period following his own basketball coaching season when he had more time on his hands and the major league baseball season was swinging into action.

Patrick seemed pleased with his progress in reestablishing his marriage, his recommitment to wife and children. He appeared to understand what had happened to him, at least intellectually, and the hope was that this understanding would support an internalized maturity, a new sense of identity residing not in the need to excel in competition or to win with wits but rather in committed accomplishments as mentor and provider—as husband, father, teacher, coach. The debts would be paid off over time; life could go sensibly on.

This is hardly a textbook case of pathological gambling, either as defined in the DSM or as profiled by Custer and others, though it shares common symptoms. What it shows, instead, is a personality disorder "not elsewhere classified" which seems to me a milder form of the narcissistic, a kind of adolescence arrested in an ego focused on aggressiveness in competition. Patrick is a man who was not only nurtured and trained in a variety of competitive contexts—in all of which he was unusually successful—but who associated his essential identity with that success in competition.

"Mister Sports" was most fully himself (full of himself) when he was a *player*, in two senses of the word, as winning athlete and coach and as winning bettor through superior comprehension. A sense of self that contains both skill and wisdom makes for a heady combination of identified gifts and accomplishments that "should" account for and insure a (narcissistically) charmed life.

But with age and the coming of experience, changes in lifestyle, mature responsibilities, and family trauma, Patrick's identity itself was threatened in ways that the habitual behaviors could not withstand. The anxiety caused by those threats could not be *relieved* but only *masked* by ever-increasing resorts to those behaviors. Marriage, a brother's death, the birth of two children, his wife's inheritance (not to be his, directly, and so a source of resentment rather than a resource), and the increasingly monstrous burden of the secrecy in which the gambling had to take place all served to build up the once rewarding, satisfying, egosyntonic habits past the point at which they became self-defeating, depressing, egodystonic.

A once-canny bettor and rational analyst began to lose judgment, to act impulsively, to feel some desperate need to get even, and to lose control. This is the inevitable process of a pathological condition that is helped along, of course, by the *numbers*, because in all forms of gambling the "house" odds against the player always make losing more likely, even under the best of conditions, and in sports betting the 11–10 proposition must wear the player down over time. The math teacher knew all this, but the gambler rationalized that knowledge away.

Forcing this case into a monolithic model of a single diagnostic category could only have been counterproductive. The progress that was made, both in terms of Patrick's self-knowledge and his continued abstinence (for as long as it lasted: see chapter 12 for discussion of relapse), were built on recognition of how the individual characteristics transcended the common symptomatology.

Unlike Patrick, for a character named Shelly the primary gambling venue is the poker table. Unlike Patrick, Shelly attributes his gambling problem to bad luck, though he comes to acknowledge such other problems as insufficient capital, an angry wife, the lack of gainful employment, and—his only recognition of personal responsibility or weakness—unconscious mannerisms that give away his hands to his opponents. His two courses of psychotherapeutic treatment are taken only to preserve his marriage, and at no time does he arrive at psychological self-knowledge or even diagnosis. Yet Shelly is a character in Irvin Yalom's *Lying on the Couch*, a novel that has as its main subjects and processes and sources of material psychotherapy and its manifold issues, scenarios, characters, settings, and dynamics.

Unlike Neil Simon's *The Odd Couple*, where the poker game serves as a convenient backdrop for the comic mirror-images of the title characters and as an opportunity for the one-liners that Simonize the script; and unlike Tennessee Williams's *A Streetcar Named Desire*, where the poker game is a mere contrivance for presenting a garish caricature of masculinity and a launching pad for the obligatory confrontations that rudely terminate the game, so that the dramatic complications may mount—unlike those devices, the poker game in *Lying on the Couch* is the pivotal element in a major subplot of the novel. That centrality should come as no surprise to the careful reader, however, since in the acknowledgments Yalom expresses his "deepest gratitude" to "the guys of my poker game."

In the novel, the poker game is a regular "friendly" gathering, a high-stakes dealer's-choice game rotating among the homes of the eight players, of whom only Shelly cannot afford to lose. But Shelly has been losing steadily for several months when we are introduced to the play at the table. Handsome and athletic (he has been a touring tennis pro), affable Shelly has never been able to cash in on his friendships among the poker group. Every touted business venture has gone bad, every employment opportunity has folded, and now even his cards have turned against him—his rare good hands winning only small pots, his good-odds possibilities failing to come through—and it looks like this will be his last game because he has run through his available gambling money and could not possibly borrow from anyone in the game.

Among Shelly's few remaining assets are his sexual prowess, his good looks, his senior tennis skills, and his marriage to a lawyer in a high-stakes firm. But most precious to him is his seat in this poker game, his only surviving gambling venue. At one time, as we have heard his wife Norma tell her friends, he "used to bet his whole salary on anything that moved: horses, greyhounds, football. Now he's satisfied with a small social poker game" (54).

Not surprisingly, Shelly has deceived her about the stakes, just as he has kept hidden from her a separate bank account that funds his gambling. Norma is not insensitive to the problematic nature of her husband's gambling, especially since she knows that it had cost him his first marriage. To show how much Norma meant to him, he had agreed to attend GA meetings, to turn over his paychecks to her and let her handle the finances, and to see a psychiatrist (Dr. Seth Pande, Shelly's contempt for whom he concealed from Norma). And now she observes that it "wasn't until he got laid off from his job that some of the old stuff's come back" (55).

Norma's perception suggests that Shelly's gambling behavior could be a way to mask the depression or anxiety he suffers when external stressors overwhelm him. But this interpretation is belied by the sequence of Shelly's affective shifts after his loss of $14,000 in the game:

> Shelly drove home in deep grief. Losing fourteen thou. Dammit—takes talent to lose fourteen grand. But it wasn't the money. Shelly didn't care about the fourteen thou. What he cared about was the guys and the game. But there was no way he could continue playing. Absolutely no way! The arithmetic was simple: there was no more money. I have to get a job. If not in software sales, then I'm going to have to go into another field—maybe back to selling yachts in Monterey. Yuck. Can I do that? Sitting around for weeks waiting for my one sale every month or two would be enough to send me back to the horses. Shelly needed action. (150)

The "deep grief" is ironic, not a euphemism for a diagnosis of a major depressive episode. Taking Shelly's shallowness, his superficiality, into account, we translate this feeling into self-pity for the narcissistic wounding caused by what he thinks is the loss of his seat in the game. But within minutes he thinks of a way to hang on to it, to defend his ego against the anxiety of such loss. There are some stock holdings he can sell, and he can cover the check for last night's losses, have a stake for the next game, and buy the stock back before Norma knows the difference—in about two weeks, after he breaks the losing streak in the next game. He calls his broker, with explicit instructions about the transaction, and goes to sleep happy.

This is where the intricate connections among the several plotlines of the book take hold. In what amounts to a good cop/bad cop paradigm, the two major players are Ernest Lash, a young psychoanalyst who is trying to be more honest and personal in therapy, less (hide)bound by traditional technique, and Marshal Streider, an arrogant, money-conscious, exercise-obsessed status seeker who happens to be Ernest's supervising training analyst and is positioning himself to be the next president of the Golden Gate Psychoanalytic Institute by leading an attack on Seth Pande (who was his training analyst).[8]

When Seth's bizarre techniques and interpretations are used to oust him, Marshal accepts a challenge for the Institute to issue a "recall" (on the model of automotive malfunctions) to any male patients (defective products) of Dr. Pande who may have experienced "deleterious effects" from his treatment—free of charge. The "recall notice" and the accompanying press coverage are the first winning hand Shelly has held in months. Norma has found out about his losses and the secret fund, hired her colleague Carol as attorney, and initiated the process to end the marriage.

But Shelly claims it's all Dr. Pande's fault. He blames his own behavior on Pande's faulty therapeutic technique, and he persuades Norma to hold off on proceedings while he goes back for recall treatment. Of course, it is Marshal who takes him on. Through other weavings of the narrative threads, Carol has become a patient of Ernest.

Briefly to tie up the threads (without doing justice either to the story or to Yalom's delightful dramatizations of psychotherapeutic sessions), the good cop is severely—deliberately—tempted to cross ethical lines for sex, but triumphs over his own baser inclinations. The bad cop is tempted to cross ethical lines, too—for money and prestige—and rationalizes his way into becoming a victim of a scam. Empathic sincerity is rewarded; exultant cleverness and self-absorption are punished. The point of summarizing the stories of the other characters in action is to contrast the outcomes. Poetic justice is served in these cases, but not in Shelly's outcome.

In the final chapter, Shelly is sitting on top of his world and his game: he has saved his marriage, won a senior doubles title, landed a cushy job with a fringe benefit of a secret slush fund, and—best of all—retained his seat in the poker game, not only catching a run of hot cards but having acquired new playing skills. The resolution of this subplot carries the ironic strain in the novel's composition, as a character who is characterologically flawed, and who receives faulty and inappropriate treatment, is made happy and whole, sublimely ensconced in his reinforced, defended, funded, rewarding, personality-disordered ways.

In this novel about psychotherapy where patients lie to their analysts and themselves, where practitioners delude patients and betray colleagues, where the best waver in conviction and the worst passionately pursue intense self-gratification, this one character charts a course that is almost simple-mindedly determined. Among Yalom's cast of serious, complex characters, Shelly thus provides a comic element. He comes by his gambling behavior honestly—from his father. As a boy, his greatest enjoyment came from trips to the track with his dad, watching sporting events with his dad when he had made bets on them, and watching Dad play various card games with his cronies. The strong identification with his father functions in Shelly's adult life as an excuse to lose, a justification for his failures in business (and tennis), which replicate his father's experience. And yet there is also the wish to outdo his father, crystalized in the memory of sitting in his dad's pinochle game at age sixteen and immediately suggesting that the stakes be raised. The competitive instinct having been honed, Shelly's aggressive behavior is translated into skillful salesmanship.

Shelly began his gambling career at fourteen, running a small bookmaking operation all through high school, paying stingy house odds against suckers who would pick three baseball players to get a total of six hits on any given day. Over the years, the sheer volume of his gambling activities assured occasional and heavy losses, but for fifteen years he has held his own in the poker game. His need for "action" has been acknowledged, but in the absence of serious impairment of functions, how could his behavior be labeled pathological? It is not clear whether his first wife left him because of the "marathon poker" or because it ended in a big loss (shades of Trotter in Let It Ride). There is clearly no compulsion to lose. Has the loss of his job made him anxious to the point where he has lost all judgment? Has it occasioned a depression that he fuels, masks, self-medicates, or justifies by losing at poker? Has his accumulated guilt for the mounting deceptions of Norma triggered a wish to get caught (by her finding out, by players calling his bluffs)?

Apparently, from what Yalom shows us, the answers are all negative. Shelly wants to play, wants to win, wants to keep Norma—and keep her in the dark. Moreover, there's a component of cleverness in this glad-handing, shallow guy and a genuine feeling for the group of poker players (as for his wife) beneath the superficiality. His quest for profitable angles is what leads him back to an analyst's couch, as much as the wish to remain in Norma's bed. If he can hold Seth Pande accountable for his poker losses and employment setbacks, he might be able to sue him and the Institute.

But Shelly hasn't an antisocial bone in his well-preserved body. He plays whatever angles he can, he practices deceptions when he has to, entirely in the service of maintaining his ability to play in the game. That is where his identity really resides—not in bed, not on the tennis court, not in a sales pitch—and the group of men, in a sense, represents the circle that is an extension of himself, spokes from his hub. Keep in mind that his "pride" precludes the possibility of borrowing from anyone in the game or acknowledging that he does not belong, financially, in their company. If personality disorders were fevers, Shelly would be diagnosed with a low-grade, subclinical narcissism.

How does Shelly get his groove back? By an unconventional psychiatric intervention that he imposes on Marshal. He teaches his analyst about "tells," players' unconscious mannerisms that give away their hands to other players.[9] His recent losses tell him that he has acquired certain tells, and he prevails on Marshal to watch him play Texas Hold 'Em at Avocado Joe's so that the analyst can identify the specific symptoms of his losing condition. Dr. Streider, for all his faults, is a good observer. He tells Shelly his tells, "cures" his patient, and redeems the Institute (grateful Shelly drops all claims).

And Shelly plays happily, winningly, ever after. This is the way the book ends, not with a bust but a winner. But if this were a living person in a case study, what would be indicated, given the absence of a diagnosis of serious pathology? Shelly might well maintain his place in the game, his identity, indefinitely. On the other hand, out on the road that lies ahead, as Willie Nelson says, there may be turns that will send him into a spin. His tennis game could deteriorate, his sexual performance falter, his job be exhausted, his wife . . . whatever. Is there any place other than the poker game where he could act out, react to, abreact from, the emotional effects of such stressors?

More to the point, his cards could turn cold again and the other players could—indeed are very likely to—adjust to his new moves, which simply invert the old ones, anyway: a new set of tells. Given his needs, his habits, and his personality construct, would there be any limits to what he would do to stay in action, to cling to his identity? Like Patrick, wouldn't he be likely to resume or elaborate the old pattern of deception? Might it lead to forgery or embezzlement? Would armed robbery become a possibility? Suicide? Then would diagnosis and treatment be appropriate? Only then, when it is too late?

What Marshal has done for Shelly is the opposite of effective therapy. He has entered into the pathology and empowered it, a process similar to "paradoxical" treatment.[10] Its effect is to fix Shelly into his pathological mode of behavior because the personality disorder (admittedly in a "prodromal" or preclinical phase) remains undiagnosed. But the warning signals are very clear to this reader, if not to the patient or his analyst. Perhaps this is Yalom's point in a book that is in many ways a send-up of psychotherapy. If Shelly were a living person, he would be a time bomb, playing, gambling his way toward detonation. If you were a betting person, would you bet against it?

I have suggested the difficulty of finding a clear distinction between personality-disordered gamblers and void-filling gamblers. The fine lines get even fuzzier when a separate category of "addiction" is added to the mix. Addicts of every stripe may well exhibit both personality disorders and void-filling behaviors, indeed often do. Multiple diagnoses are often appropriate for such cases. But if it is important to look carefully for personality disorders when pathological behaviors are observed, it may be even more important to look for concurrent addictions. It is, after all, in the nature of void-fillers, as it is in the personality-disordered gamblers, to be drawn into more than one addictive behavior. The next chapter begins with the story of a multiple-addicted personality, a story that argues convincingly that pathological gambling may sometimes be identified clearly as an addiction.

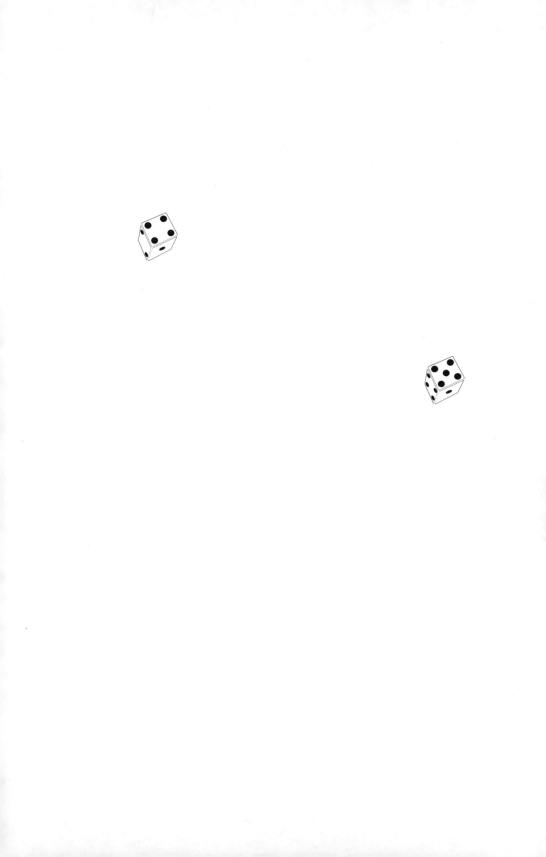

Down and down I go
Round and round I go
Like a leaf that's caught in the tide.
I should stay away
But what can I do?

Johnny Mercer
and Harold Arlen,
"That Old Black Magic"

I re-entered the chaos of addiction. I opened
myself up again to all the allure of the addict's
many escapes—drinking, drugging, stealing,
lying, gambling or anything else that takes us away
from the mundane, away from ourselves. So
gradually I came to accept the hard fact that I also
had to let go of my passion for gambling.

Rick Whitaker, "One Last Chance"

Gambling and Addiction

Normally, when Todd Winograd left his office in Cohasset after his last appointment of the day, he would pause for a proud glance at what he had built in a few short years. A large and growing family practice in a cutting-edge facility, maybe the best on the whole South Shore. His first practice had been as a junior partner in a large Weymouth clinic, but it took only two years among the established practitioners there, with their traditional ways and willingness to carry considerable dead weight on their staff, for him to know that he needed independence. When he left the clinic, a hundred and fifty families had followed him to Cohasset, and within three years his practice had tripled and his start-up investors had been paid off.

This Thursday night was different. He could not afford to be late for his meeting in Quincy. His financial status and perhaps his physical well-being depended on it. Despite the success of his practice, his credit at the bank had been stretched to its limit, his credit cards had been maxed out, and he had no access to other resources because they were now all in his wife's exclusive name.

The usual Hingham traffic held him up just enough so that he drove the rest of the way into Quincy with increasing anxiety, but he pulled past the golden arches into the parking lot of McDonald's at exactly the appointed time. And the maroon Fleetwood he'd been told was the trademark car of Carmine Solazzo was parked at the far corner of the lot. His instructions were simply to get into the front seat of the car, and so he did.

"Hiya, Doc." Solazzo was all smiles, shook his hand warmly, and gave a shrugging gesture meant to indicate a kind of self-deprecating welcome to his "office." They were of an age, might have been mistaken for former team-mates celebrating a twentieth reunion of some high school championship. But Carmine had lost a lot of what had been his fine head of dark black waves while putting on a lot of weight, while Todd still had his full crop of straight sandy hair and had maintained his athletic fitness and agility.

They had never met. Only an unlikely sequence of events had brought the loan shark and the physician together in this unlikely setting. The terms of their transaction had already been set, but Todd had no idea how to proceed. He squirmed around in his seat to face his congenial, burly companion, but it was Carmine who broke the silence before it got too uncomfortable.

"What do you need this for, anyway, Doc?"

Todd had not expected the question, had no cover story ready, hadn't thought he'd need one. Still, he answered quickly, "I want to get started right away on some building expansion at the office, and I wanted to cut through the red tape delays at the bank."

"Doesn't matter. You could have whatever you asked for, no questions asked, after what you did for Chin's sister."

"Who? What?" Now genuine confusion overtook the nervousness and anxiety.

"You really don't know why I'm here? It's because of what you did for Cynthia Capelli. Didn't you know she was Vincent Donato's sister? Hey, friends don't forget. And friends of friends look out for each other."

Now it all clicked into place. One Friday evening almost two years before, there had been a call at the office from a terrified Mrs. Capelli. Her little boy was sick, in pain, getting worse, and she was frantically trying to find a doctor to see him. Todd had actually seen the child once before, during a difficult infancy, when he had been moonlighting at the South Shore Hospital during his first year in the area. Cynthia had remembered the kindness of Dr. Winograd and called for his help when her regular family doctors were unavailable.

Todd had been reluctant to see them, suggested they go to the emergency room, but the woman's combination of hysterical begging and flattery had gotten to him and he'd agreed to have them come in right away. What made the timing awkward was that Friday was when he met with his bookie to settle on the week's tab and begin an action-filled weekend of a full football schedule with some early-season hoops games to boot.

Todd always began an appointment with a child by giving her or him a little gift, a small toy or piece of sugar-free candy. When he held it out to little Tony, the child reached for it—and missed it by a foot. "How long has he been blind?" he asked the young mother, who was shocked at the question. An immediate CT scan showed the brain tumor, which was removed that night in emergency surgery. Todd's timely diagnosis led to Tony's survival, and the doctor was now receiving an unexpected bonus fee, in the form of a loan, no questions asked—well, practically none. And Todd had come here thinking that he had been approved for the loan simply because they knew he was good for the money.

Carmine reached across and opened the glove compartment, removing a thick brown envelope. He casually thumbed through the neatly packed stacks of bills, six packets with rubber bands around them, each with fifty $100 bills.

"Thirty large," he said, handing the stacks over.

"Thanks," Todd said, finding it necessary to use three different pockets to stow the cash.

"You know the drill, Doc," Carmine said. "I'll see you here next week at this time, with the first payment."

"Right." He went to his car, sat, and watched the Cadillac cruise out of the lot. He felt suddenly drained of energy, unable even to start the car, all the anxiety of his situation eclipsed by a profound sense of exhaustion and guilt. He had sunk to a new low. For the first time, he realized, he had actually and directly used his profession, traded on his professional skills, compromised the great pride he took in his achievements as a physician, to support his gambling habit.

The urgency of this loan was prompted by a losing streak of astounding proportions. He had lost before, sometimes into five figures, but he now owed twenty-five thousand to his bookie, and he was supposed to settle, as usual, tomorrow night. He had borrowed thirty because he figured he needed five to play with after he had paid off the twenty-five. And obviously he had to stay in action to have any hope of making a comeback—and of meeting the terms for his new debt.

Why had Carmine asked why he needed the loan? Wouldn't a connected loan shark know that he was betting his lungs with a bookie? Well, maybe not. He had never worried about whether his bookies were connected, caring only whether they paid off when they lost, whether they'd continue to take his action when he was behind, and whether they were discreet about protecting his identity as a bettor—from his patients and especially his wife. If he had ever worried about bookies and organized crime it would have been in Philadelphia, since when he left medical school he had skipped town still owing his bookie there a four-figure debt—and he had never paid that off.

How had Dr. Winograd come to this? We can trace the path of his promising life, but while we may find patterns we will not reach comfortable conclusions about causes. Todd grew up in a middle-class home in Pawtucket, Rhode Island, long considered a blue-collar appendage to Providence, with an ethnically diverse population. Doted on by two older sisters and their mom, he was the proverbial fair-haired boy of the family. Outgoing, energetic, and excitable, he was the full-dimensional picture of juvenile success: popular, tall, good-looking, bright, and athletic.

No doubt Todd was his father's pride and joy, but this was not the kind of father who drew attention to himself by advising coaches and shouting at officials from the sidelines. The son was not spoiled in material ways, but he was indulged in the sense of having unconditional love and support at home. And he satisfied the family's expectations and aspirations—top student, class officer, team captain—throughout his school years. He was equally comfortable among his African American basketball teammates, the Italian guys from Federal Hill he played American Legion baseball with, the Jewish crowd at the JCC and Temple, and his affluent social crowd from Blackstone Boulevard on Providence's East Side.

By the time of semester break during his junior year, Todd had sharpened the focus of his life in certain ways. Academically, he had decided to avoid the competitive rat race of the Ivy League, whether or not he ended up valedictorian of his class, assured as he was that he could pick and choose among good small liberal arts colleges. In practical terms, he felt that this would be the better and probably easier path into medical school.

Basketball had become his sport of choice. He was playing year round now. The high school team was having a banner season, came within five points of upsetting a Durfee High team from Fall River that would go all the way to the New England championship game. A strong rebounder and streak shooter, at 6' 1" he had no illusions about big-time college hoops, not to mention pro ball, but as a solid schoolboy player he was thinking of Division III or maybe Division I-AA competition.

Todd's social life was a pleasant round of parties with an extended circle of friends. He had neither a steady girlfriend nor a clearly defined "type" among the casual connections he hooked up with. There was occasional drinking in this circle but virtually no evidence of hard drugs. Smoking pot, however, had become a regular part of his weekends and some weekdays as well.

It was a reliable source of mild pleasure, both solitary and in groups, but he believed that it never got in the way of his athletic or academic performance. His record gave no telltale signs of impairment.

One other activity had emerged as a prominent preoccupation. He was betting on sports. It had started at the end of the summer, during a Labor Day weekend basketball tournament, in the locker room at the JCC. A kid from Barrington had mentioned how excited he was about the start of the NFL season, because he expected to make a lot of money this year. An avid sports fan anyway, Todd had asked the right questions, gotten the necessary information including phone numbers to call and names to use, and had plunged right in.

Within a few weeks, Todd and two of his Providence buddies (one at Hope High and one at Moses Brown) made some intriguing discoveries. Alerted to the possibilities, they found that every locker room, every athletic venue they visited, every sports program in or out of the schools, had someone who would take or place a bet for them or set them up with a direct line. They also discovered a key to winning.

Though neophytes, they became "savvy" contrarians. The popular teams, the public choices, were the teams they wanted to bet against. When a point spread moved during the week, indicating one-sided action on a game, they wanted to bet the other side. And when a line seemed to be an "invitation," say, minus six and a half points on a team that seemed to be a clear touchdown better than its opponent, they would decline that invitation and bet on the underdog.

Two months into the NFL season, "the boys"—as their bookie was calling them—were betting up to five hundred dollars a week and winning consistently, two out of three, three out of five, one week an amazing six out of seven against the spread. It got so that "Red," the only name they had for the bookie, was asking for their opinions on games they weren't betting. It was coming so easy that they branched out into college games and began to look at the coming basketball season as opening new possibilities. When the college Bowl season was over and then the Super Bowl, they were sitting on thousands of dollars each, hardly knowing what to do with the money and hardly able to keep from telling people about their success.

Todd's father was an occasional gambler, who was known among friends as the "guru" because he seemed consistently to pick two out of three winners. The "boys," in fact, had learned the contrarian strategy from him. Wealthy acquaintances would often call for advice before making bets, but Mr. Winograd himself was a small bettor. No wonder Todd felt comfortable telling his father that he was making some bets. He even got some advice, not about picks but about how to maintain judgment and handle money when gambling. You could never make serious money by gambling, Mr. Winograd told his son, because as the amounts got bigger a gambler's judgment faded away. Todd wanted to be like him, but he also wanted to outdo him, prove that he was not so limited. The father had no idea of the extent of the son's action or the amount of money involved and later felt guilty, both for not knowing and for passing on bad habits, but Todd never blamed him.

During the spring, the boys found a constructive way of spending the money. They would go away on weekend trips, ostensibly to visit college campuses to prepare for the application process to come. They were in fact making the rounds of the better schools in the Northeast, even venturing as far south as Charlottesville and Chapel Hill, but these trips were basically partying escapades on which they lavished their seemingly inexhaustible funds. And, oh yes, they had a hidden criterion on which to base their choice of college: how easy it was to pursue sports betting on each campus.

That criterion, they discovered, provided no distinctions. Campuses large and small, state and private, nonsectarian and church-related, were all equal in offering outlets for the sports-minded gambler. And everyone knew it. Wherever they went, no matter who they asked, there was in answer a first-hand or secondhand referral by name to someone who could handle or direct their action.

The basketball season provided some sobering results. They barely broke even and had to back off somewhat during tournament and playoff time, but by then they were studying strategies for the baseball season to come. And they came up with another winning formula, what they called a "streak theory." Disregarding odds, disregarding relative overall strengths of teams, disregarding even the pitching matchups (that staple of baseball handicapping), they determined to bet that streaks (of three games) would continue and to stay with—or against—a streaking team as long as the streak lasted.

Their reasoning was that a streak could go on and on but could only end once, and since baseball was "a game of streaks" they would have to come out ahead. A team on a winning streak against a team on a losing streak, of course, was a double-up game. Again, it worked. Their success continued throughout the summer, gathered strength in the fall, augmented by the new football season. Their winter hoops losses and the indifferent results of the next summer were hardly significant. As they were having trouble hiding the cash they had amassed, it was almost a relief to pay back some of their stash before they went off in separate directions to start college.

Todd's college career was hardly the unblemished success he had known in high school. He chose Muhlenberg for a variety of reasons. He liked the small campus with its warm but distinguished architecture, the apparent coziness of the fraternity system, the liberal arts curriculum that was more liberal than he expected from a Lutheran school, the chance to play Division III college hoops, the decent scholarship package they offered him, and the attractive coeds. Besides, on his first visit the boys had discovered that blue-collar Allentown, Pennsylvania, provided ample opportunities for any type of gambling action their bettors' hearts desired.

The first two years did not go quite as planned. He handled his course work easily, but without distinction and with little enthusiasm or interest. He was becoming a run-of-the-mill B+/A- student—and he didn't care. He decided after only a couple of weeks of practice that he didn't want to devote that much time to basketball. Fraternity life, for him, became a daily round of pot smoking with less bonding or camaraderie than he had anticipated. His drinking increased, in large part because it was what his brothers and the girls at their parties expected. He had his first exhilarating tastes of cocaine. And he was losing his touch as a sports bettor. He had a losing season in football, but still had a slush fund to cover it.

Todd's sophomore slump began to feel almost like actual depression. At least, there was the unfamiliar sensation of being dissatisfied with himself, actually unhappy with his life. By the end of February, with the NCAA tournament looming ahead, he was in debt to his bookie and about to be cut off. He had to turn to his father to bail him out.

Sol Winograd was a relatively quiet, undemonstrative man, whose sensitivity and intelligence were hidden rather than shown. He had sensed for some time that things were not quite right with his "golden boy" but had no clue as to the nature or seriousness of the problems. It was almost a relief to attribute the malaise to gambling. It's only money, he thought to himself, not surprisingly defending himself with rationalizations and denial from the anxiety and guilt that were to emerge over time. For now it was enough to administer a sober rebuke to Todd, to pass along some wise advice, and to extract a promise that the habit would stop. The requisite promise was duly, glibly, offered, and Todd coolly began to produce some plus figures during March Madness.

Todd felt that he needed to get away from Allentown, quit the college scene, and terminate his dependence on his dad. This was the very end of the '70s, hardly the heyday of the drop-out generation, but he was ready to light out for the territories, that is, the West Coast, at the end of spring semester. It was not an impulsive act—he actually presented a plan to his family—and by Memorial Day he was en route to Seattle (the Pacific Northwest having replaced Big Sur and the Bay Area as the "in" place for those who had dropped out), promising to stay away from the more radical Eugene. Todd was interested in gambling—not political—action.

He yo-yoed between Seattle and Portland for the better part of fifteen months, working occasional jobs when necessary, making new connections and gambling successfully, cruising among a variety of communal scenes, and increasing his drug use. Somehow, his old level of energy was restored, his nature perhaps prevailing over his lifestyle and environment. He enjoyed occasionally tripping on LSD, but never came close to being an acidhead (despite his proximity to Dead country). Whether or not the acid had anything to do with it, his brain got cleared and he returned to school with a more positive attitude. He was more focused, and able to pay his own way.

For his last two undergraduate years, despite the continuation of his pot smoking, Todd abstained from gambling, focused on academics, and worked hard and well enough to graduate summa cum laude and Phi Beta Kappa and to earn admission to medical schools. The family may have been disappointed that he didn't get into Harvard or Yale, but Cornell and Case Western would do just fine. He never told them why he chose Hahnemann, but one deciding factor was that he had access to bookies in Philadelphia. Despite two years of abstinence, recovery had yet to begin.

In medical school, the stakes increased: not only the educational/professional stakes, but the gambling stakes and the narcotics stakes as well. Cocaine was plentiful, and with a bountiful college football season he could well afford it. In his second year, he fell in love for the first time in his life. Leslie was all he could ask for in a companion, friend, and future partner in life and perhaps practice as well. The courtship was a whirlwind of speed and intensity, as everything in med school tends to be, and within months they were discussing plans for conjoint internships, residencies, and specialities as well as marriage.

Socially and intellectually they were well-matched. With Leslie, Todd tried to moderate his substance use, sensing that she would not tolerate excess and would be difficult to fool. But instead of changing his behaviors, he was learning strategies for masking them. And he concealed the gambling from her. Up to a point. Even before they moved in together the next year, he had had to account for the lavish gifts, the odd phone calls, the excitement over sports events. He had to time his jogging precisely so that he could reach a place on the path near a wooded grove, where he would duck under cover, whip out his cell-phone, and get down for the day's action.

But he could not hide the fact that within a few months of their marriage he had to use the bulk of their wedding-present cash to pay off an unusual losing streak. Leslie learned first from a bank statement what had happened, and Todd told her the rest. It was his mother who came through for him then, playing the enabler's role by covering his debt, and Leslie stuck by him. In his eventual understanding of his condition, he has never attached any blame to either of these women.

Leslie's career was put on temporary hold a couple of years later for her first pregnancy. Meanwhile, Todd's aggravations at the Weymouth clinic were accompanied by increased cocaine use, growing alcohol intake, and escalating sports action. He celebrated his son's birth with a seventy-two-hour flight of snorting and betting. Their rosy prospects were being eclipsed by disproportionate debt. Leslie demanded that he get treatment, and he did: AA, GA, therapy, programs for impaired physicians. Nothing worked; he was talking the talk but really had no intention of walking the walk. There were episodes of relapse, periods when he abandoned even the pretense of working the program, but somehow he avoided major trouble.

The successful move into his own practice seemed to bring him into a stable, healthy place. But it was a cover. Pot, alcohol, cocaine, and gambling were virtual constants, but even during occasional periods of abstinence there was no recovery. It was amazing that he could be as effective a physician as he was, but he took great pride in his work, his diagnostic acumen, his steady hand in treatment, and his engaging manner with children and parents alike. He talked about how good family practitioners ought to be like loved and admired members of the families they served. Leslie's second pregnancy was in part the result of the good feelings engendered by the move to Cohasset, but by the time their daughter was born Todd's behavior was erratic rather than merely excitable. Leslie had to ask him to move out.

The next round of treatment included her attendance at Gam-Anon and couples therapy while he went from one psychiatric diagnosis and medication to another. Agitated on lithium, impervious to Prozac, alert on Xanax, anxious on Ativan, Todd went on with the rounds of appointments with patients and the flirtations with disaster of his habits. He adored his children, and that was why Leslie countenanced a reconciliation. He appeared to be working on abstinence, but he had learned many ways of faking urines for his impaired-physician program.

Meeting with the loan shark, as described at the beginning of this chapter, could have meant hitting bottom. But it wasn't. When he paid off his bookie, he was told that he now had a $10,000 limit, unacceptable for a gambler who has just lost $25,000. So he found two other bookies who gave him the same terms. A month later he owed thirty thousand (ten each). Even Carmine Solazzo, friend of Chin Donato, couldn't help him now. Out of resources, out of excuses, he was soon out of his home again as well.

No bookie anywhere would take his action. No dealer would give him coke on credit. Withdrawal symptoms made his daily professional practice a risky ordeal. Leslie was filing for divorce. Massachusetts could well revoke his license. He was probably going to have to turn his practice over to Leslie anyway, as part of a settlement agreement. He couldn't bear to lose his children. And it was at this low point that he discovered crack, the ultimate cut-rate escape vehicle of the downtrodden masses. Available, affordable, and deadly, crack cocaine was the vehicle that drove Todd Winograd to Hattiesburg, Mississippi, to an inpatient program, to abstinence, and to a new life.

As part of the intake interview at Hattiesburg, Todd presented his history of psychiatric diagnoses: manic-depression, major depressive episodes, chronic hypomania, general anxiety. (Oddly enough, no Axis II diagnosis, no personality disorder, was part of the record.) All this was greeted with laughter that was more indulgent than derisive.

"You're an addict," he was told, with the implicit corollary that any other diagnosis was totally unnecessary. From that moment on, he knew he was in the right place, with the right epithet attached to his identity. He followed a dual track in treatment for substance abuse and gambling addiction, and his recovery has proceeded from that day forward, without relapse.

At our last meeting, in a corner of the cafeteria in the large Midwestern teaching hospital where he is attempting to start a new life (he has a fellowship in child psychology with an emphasis on adolescent addictions), he had been abstinent from gambling for three and a half years, straight and sober for almost three. He's still an excitable, energetic, outgoing guy, who stays in good shape by running and working out. There's a new woman in his life, and they are cautiously optimistic about a future together. He sees his children every other weekend in Cohasset, where Leslie has maintained the practice and the home, and they spend five or six vacations with him every year. He is a regular at an AA chapter near the campus. One reason he likes that better than GA or NA, he says, is that AA people seem to be more comfortable with the spiritual component of the program, and it is his belatedly discovered spirituality that sustains him in his recovery. Besides, stories of alcoholics' experience seem to be told in a less arrogant tone than stories of gambling exploits.

"Addiction is addiction," he says, with a kind of grim smile at the incredulity with which that knowledge is sometimes greeted by others. "Making bets, smoking dope, snorting coke, drinking Jack Daniel's, it was all the same to me. I liked it, I craved it, I had to have more and more of it to make it work for me, and there was always the crash of withdrawal.

"All these behaviors meet what I think of as the three criteria for addictions, the things that push you across the line from a heavy user to an addict. First, there is the preoccupation with the behavior: all your associations revolve around it, and it fills up your mind time. Second, there is the compulsivity to continue despite any adverse consequences. And third, there is the cycle of relapse—failed attempts to cut back, the intention to stop and the desire to stop but you can't.[1]

"The greatest obsession of all is that we'll gain control, and there will be periods of control, but inevitably they end with pitiful and incomprehensible demoralization. This is the language of the Big Book, and I'd say they got it right. Immediately after a spell of abstinence it's as if you never stopped, and the escalation is dramatic. You have to raise the amount to get the same high—that's what tolerance means.

"I found that a twelve-step program worked best. And like any other addiction you did best when you really worked the program, getting a sponsor and working through the steps. That's probably why AA is just as helpful to me in recovery from gambling as GA, maybe better since GA tends to focus less on the steps. But there's one way that gambling is different from other addictions. Even though loss of trust is a regular component and consequence of addiction, trust can be regained in abstinence. But you can tell when other addicts have fallen off the wagon. How do you know when or whether a gambler has?

"We're going to learn a lot more than we know now about the biochemistry of addiction,[2] though we'll probably never be able to prove cause and effect. For someone like me, there must be something in the hardwiring of the brain that makes us susceptible. The number of people who are dually or multiply addicted is staggering, and too often only one of the problem habits is treated.

"My hope is to find a way to identify addiction-prone kids early. Prevention might be a whole lot easier than recovery. Lives can be saved, a lot of pain avoided, not to mention the savings of time and money. I was lucky. I learned that I was an addict when I could still have a second chance at a useful life, and I'm very thankful to my Higher Power for it."

Early in my clinical career, when I worked in a family service agency and a substance-abuse treatment facility, I got a good practical education in the frequency and complexities of dual diagnosis, comorbidity, multiple addictions. One case, typical in many of its features, may provide an enlightening example.

Aram was court-ordered to get counseling as part of a negotiated plea designed to keep him from serving time in jail for a first conviction on drug charges. With only this to go on, I was surprised to have his case assigned to me. Not that I had no experience with substance abuse cases; at the time I was still spending a couple of hours a week at the other agency, co-leading a therapy group for cocaine addicts. But here most of my caseload consisted of families or couples in crisis.

The agency's clinical supervisor, however, one of the wisest people I've ever known, had picked up on something from the report of Aram's intake session that suggested she should assign him to me. That decision, based on the appropriate premise that a good client-therapist fit facilitates treatment and on her intuition that he and I were well-matched, was probably a mistake for all concerned.

My first impression of Aram was quite favorable. In his mid-thirties, casually well-dressed and attractive, he seemed bright, energetic, and engaging. He had three young children to whom he was apparently devoted, and he took satisfaction in his relative success as a car salesman because of the way it allowed him to support his family. But that success was seasonal and cyclical, and it was anxiety and a need to escape from the pressures of the job and the family that had led to his occasional use of narcotics. His arrest for possession, he said, must have been the result of an anonymous tip from someone wishing to harm him, because he rarely *was* in possession of any more than a weekend's supply of *anything*. As for intent to distribute, that was nonsense, and he claimed that the police routinely made such a charge to justify arrests and facilitate pleas.

The legal and financial problems were, in his present state of mind, however, the least of his worries. His wife, Nora, had filed for divorce, charging that he spent too much time and money away from home gambling, that he was usually drinking when he was at home, and that he was so verbally abusive that she and the children feared his anger would escalate to physical abuse. He said all this was false, that she was angling for a favorable financial settlement, and that what he most feared was loss of custody of his children as a result of his "unfair" arrest and the distorted picture Nora was painting. It was to counter all this that he welcomed the opportunity for therapy to work on his anger, his anxiety, and his frustrations. But he resented having to go to NA meetings as part of the plea bargain, since he did not have a drug problem.

Part of my responsibility was to recommend a treatment plan that would be acceptable to the court as conditions for Aram's probation. And he knew that I was therefore in a position to impose my agenda on him, yet I appreciated that he was making no attempt to curry favor with me. On the other hand, even though therapy was mandated by an enlightened system of criminal justice, my primary responsibility was to the client, who seemed to me, in the bluesman's phrase, to be in a whole world of trouble.

Where multiple problems are presented, one tactic of practice is to go for the most accessible goal, to get an easy win at the outset, at the same time moving toward establishing a working alliance with a client, a relationship of mutual comfort and trust. I decided to address the element of gambling in Aram's behavior, in part, I acknowledge, because I sensed that that was the feature of the profile that led my supervisor to choose me as his therapist. It made sense. I could talk the gambling talk with him, quickly ascertain whether it was a problem, help him address it if it was, or supportively set it aside if it were not.

"Could you tell me about your gambling, Aram?"

"I've been a gambler ever since I was a kid. I'm known as a gambler, and I'm pretty good at it. Nora has always known about it; I never kept it from her. She never objected when I was bringing in the money, and it's only now she's decided it's a problem."

"Casino gambling?"

"No, I never got into that."

"Cards?"

"There's a regular poker game I play in, usually once a week."

"What kind of game?"

"Straight seven-card stud lowball."

"Stakes?"

"Buck, two, and five."

"Hm. You could win or lose a couple of hundred a night in a game like that, right?"

"No. I never lose more than fifty bucks. I play carefully when the cards are cold, but when I'm hot I've won two, three hundred."

"What about horses?"

"Yeah, I love to go to the track. If I work evenings, I can relax at the trotters for the last four or five races. And I like to catch a full card on the weekend at Charles Town."

"How much would you bet in an evening?"

"Maybe forty, fifty bucks."

"Bet every race?"

"Sure, otherwise it's a waste. But I don't bet much, two- or five-dollar tickets."

"Exactas?"

"What I like best."

"Then you're probably betting twelve to thirty a race, maybe more, right?"

"Well, it pretty much evens out. I'm a good handicapper. I win my share."

"What's poker night?"

"Friday. Why?"

"When you have a hot night, do you take your winnings to West Virginia on Saturday?"

"I guess so. If I have more to bet with, I can spread my action around and have a better chance to parlay my profits."

"Or not feel too bad when you lose?"

"It's always more fun to be playing with their money."

"Do you bet on sports?"

"Sometimes. Football, some hoops."

"With a bookie?"

"..."

"Don't worry. I'm not blowing a whistle on anyone."

"Yeah."

"How much?"

"I'll bet twenty-five or fifty on a game I like."

"How much would you guess your total action is in an average week?"

"Two fifty, maybe three hundred a week, give or take."

"And your net figures?"

"Close to even, I'd say, but the amount I've lost, it's worth it for the entertainment, the relaxation. It's always been fun for me."

"Doesn't compute, Aram. You can't play in that game without a couple of hundred in your pocket, and it sounds like you bet a bunch of ballgames a week—maybe up to a hundred each. You're probably gambling around two thousand a week."

"It's something I've always done. And it's not a problem. And it's not what I'm here for."

"Your wife says it's a problem, and it may come up in court."

"She's wrong."

"Okay. I'd like to be able to support you on this. Let's put it to a test. Let's see if you can quit gambling—of any kind—for two weeks, and let's see what happens if you do, or, perhaps, what's going on if you don't. And I think I'm going to include in my recommendations that, for now, you attend a GA meeting once a week, for purposes of assessment."

"I don't like it."

"Aram, let's get this one issue behind us and move on."

I had expected an angry client at this point, given his reported temper and the transparent testing I was laying on him. Instead, I got a subdued client, rather glum than sullen, and as I watched him over the final few minutes of the session, I wondered if I'd lost him.

"I'll have a report ready in a few days," I said finally, "and maybe we can get started by the end of next week. There's a lot to work on, I think you know, and I think I'd like to see you two maybe three times a week at first."

This jolted him; there was a flash of anger.

"I can't afford that!"

I tried a joking response: "At these prices? Or do you mean the time? Just think of all the extra time you'll have by not gambling, I mean, besides the extra cash flow."

He was not smiling when he left.

Aram's rationalizations were considerable, his denial massive, the symptoms of personality disorder manifold. I was sure, for one thing, that he did have a drug problem, for another that he had been intending to distribute to support his addiction. And if the gambling was out of control, I suspected that he could easily be drawn into illegal gambling operations to support that habit. Habits and patterns would feed on each other in a self-destructive spiral.

I wrote what I thought was a careful, thorough, constructive treatment plan, in which I felt that my genuine concern for Aram would come through. But his lawyer was too good (as I saw it, however, not in the best interests of his client). A plea bargain that traded probation for mandated counseling was appropriate in both legal and clinical terms—but not if the client was overly resistant to treatment, and perhaps not if the accused was guilty of worse than he had pled to. The attorney, in the week following my session with Aram, also skillfully negotiated a Voluntary Separation Agreement with Nora (with the consequence of obviating the need for work on anger management which I had included in my plan).

The attorney's letter to me should not have been a surprise. The recommendation for random urinalysis was apparently acceptable; addressing the gambling behavior was not. A close paraphrase of part of that letter follows: "My client acknowledges his gambling, but believes that his gambling activities are all legal. Whereas some may object to his habit, he feels that there is no reason for him to be receiving counseling on that issue since his gambling is neither outside the law nor in anyway related to the criminal matter for which he is under probation." Objecting, then, to the direction, time, and cost of counseling outlined in the treatment plan, Aram's attorney nevertheless claimed that his client was "openly willing to participate in whatever counseling you deem proper," an assurance he repeated at the close of his letter, which requested a response.

I would not dispute the legal arguments, though Aram's gambling extended beyond parimutuel wagering. In clinical terms, however, the denial that the gambling had anything to do with his need for psychiatric attention was itself symptomatic. My concern as a clinician was for the client, for the full range of his pathological condition, not the conditions of his probation, that is, not the letter of the law but the spirit of clinical care that could justify the judicial judgment.

The issue was rendered moot before I had a chance to respond when I was informed that the court had allowed Aram to enter treatment at another agency, where presumably his counseling would be limited to drug-related issues. Intensive attention to a specific addiction may often be effective, particularly in the short term, and I find it difficult to criticize even limited success in treatment, especially when allocation of limited clinical resources weighs heavily on the helping professions.

But in my view, short-term may be translated into short-sighted. Where addiction is a fact of life, one addiction may readily replace another, and multiple addictions may escape attention when one focuses narrowly on just one of them.[3] As a matter of public health and safety, necessarily involving the criminal justice system, no addicted individual should be deemed clean and sober without some attempt to discern or exclude the presence of accompanying conditions. Moreover, when the behaviors that signal addictions are symptoms of underlying pathologies, it should go without saying that symptom modification is hardly adequate treatment. These are some of the lessons that inform the discussion of diagnosis and treatment that follows.

When I use a word, it means
just what I choose it to mean—
neither more nor less.

Humpty Dumpty,
in Lewis Carroll's
Through the Looking Glass

All gamblers lie, to others and to themselves.

A woman speaking
to Shifty Lou Anderson
in William Murray's novel
When the Fat Man Sings

Dilemmas of Diagnosis and Treatment

The long-running series of Shifty Lou Anderson novels has elevated William Murray to a place of special distinction among writers of fiction involving gambling. Murray not only writes very well (as a longtime contributor to the *New Yorker* he has written the periodic column "Letter from Italy"), but he is exceptionally knowledgeable about many forms of gambling and brings a nonjudgmental attitude (amused, appreciative, even indulgent) to the subject. Anderson himself, the narrator/protagonist of these novels, is a close-up magician by trade and a horse racing devotee by choice, but his skill with cards and his keen awareness of probabilities attached to casino games and other vehicles of chance—along with his regard for the mysteries and magic that enrich an appreciation of life—make him an ideal commentator on the contemporary gambling scene.

The time that Shifty spends at the races (for example, he will not accept any work during his favorite season of the year, the seven-week summer meeting at Del Mar) gives ample opportunity for character vignettes, dramatic episodes, and conversational reflections of many types of gamblers. Most of them are habitual players, even "degenerates," and many of them are neurotics with constellations of idiosyncratic tics, traits, jargon, and behaviors. But even in this company the pathological gambler is hard to find, in large measure because the gambling either does not get in the way of normal functioning (it never does for Shifty himself) or is in fact central to a social and professional lifestyle (as for Shifty's closest associate, Jay Fox, a professional handicapper).

The case at hand, *When the Fat Man Sings* (third in the series), is exemplary of certain primary issues regarding diagnosis and treatment of pathological gambling, a consideration of which must be based—like all rational discourse—on a definition of terms. Shifty becomes involved with renowned opera singer Fulvio Gasparini, who may earn $50,000 a night for performing in a Las Vegas casino but may lose half a million during the week at the gaming tables. Fulvio's magnificent and generous voice is matched only by his mammoth exuberance for gambling and his monumental ignorance of any winning strategies. Shifty becomes his gambling guru, sharing the tenor's great delight in winning ventures and teaching him ways to minimize losses.

Without Shifty's steady hand or cautionary presence, Fulvio plunges giddily, preferring—by far—the thrill of the action, however negative the results, to the prospect of even short-term abstention. Fulvio's career and fortune may be seen to be at risk from his engrossing habit, and yet he does not qualify as pathological. His devotion to his art comes first. His preoccupation does not intrude on his occupation. He exhibits the symptoms of a condition for which he cannot be diagnosed. At-risk he surely is; liable to seek treatment he is not.

When Fulvio's manager expresses the conviction which serves as an epigraph to this chapter, she is focusing on a salient feature of the pathology that makes it resistant to treatment.[1] She mistakenly assumes that because Shifty gambles he must himself be a dissembler (by profession he practices deception but by avocation, lifestyle, personal values, and self-awareness he is as honest as the Belmont home stretch is long). But in seeking to protect her interests in her client she is appropriately aware of Fulvio's propensity to deny, rationalize, justify, and disguise his gambling "problem." She calls him "sick" and asserts that he "has this terrible compulsion to lose his money" (123).

Shifty does not disagree with her, but his "treatment plan" assumes that the behavior is not subject to change and that the compulsion is not to lose but to play, that the "problem" is ignorance of how to have a reasonable chance at winning. His plan is one of prevention through education, primarily practical but also philosophical and psychological. He knows that, barring sufficiently negative consequences of the gambling (big losses are insufficient to someone in Fulvio's position, just as they would be for an Albert Belle or a Michael Jordan), the best way to avoid the clinical emergence of the pathological condition is to cut losses and impose winning strategies.

In a climactic confrontation with Fulvio's manager, Shifty authoritatively answers her question about how long her client's behavior can continue with a single word: "Forever." He goes on to say, "You're not going to get Fulvio to join Gamblers Anonymous, you know that as well as I do. He's hooked, but it can be controlled" (201). Shifty makes a crucial distinction: Fulvio is a dedicated habitual gambler, but his habit has not become pathological because his singing is more important to him.

"Most gamblers substitute their habit for everything else in their lives" (202), but not Fulvio, he says. And then he lays out a long-term treatment plan that can delay or prevent the emergence of pathology. Education, vigilance, and control are the elements in the game plan, which might be compared to "maintenance drinking" by an alcoholic to minimize the liver damage and other medical consequences of drinking, on the one hand, and the physical and psychological devastation and trauma of withdrawal and abstinence on the other.[2]

The implications of Fulvio's "case" are germane to a number of the dilemmas about treatment. When does the habit become a problem? When does the problem become pathology? If gamblers lie about their habit, how can they be afforded treatment? If gamblers lie to themselves, how can they acknowledge their problem? If full-blown pathology is required for diagnosis and treatment, won't it be too late to arrest or reverse the consequences of the condition?

The case of Patrick the math teacher in chapter 10 is illustrative of several of those dilemmas, and it may be instructive for anyone attempting to deal with the enormous array of problems associated with pathological gambling. It is a characteristic of the condition, regardless of the assignment of primary and secondary diagnoses in a multiaxial system, that relapse is nearly universal and perhaps inevitable.[3] Patrick maintained his abstinence for less than two months after terminating therapy. He had already stopped attending GA metings (with his therapist's tacit agreement), and he found he could not tolerate the burden of his accumulated debts and the prospect of years of hard work (including side jobs that were beneath him) to pay them off.

He thought he could get even quickly by making just a few intelligent bets at the start of the new NFL season. Within weeks he was in as deep as ever, and with no other resources available, he forged Prudence's signature on a check—not to pay off the bookie but to go to the track to recoup. Back in the office, the therapist suggested the debt wasn't the *reason*; it was Patrick's *excuse* to gamble again. The problem was that intellectual acknowledgment of his disorder wasn't enough—it only permitted Patrick to use his intellectualizing power to return to action. Emotional acknowledgment was missing; Patrick never bought into GA membership, never felt at gut level that he belonged there. A second relapse brought him into an inpatient program, his best chance for total acknowledgment, remediation, and recovery.

One obvious dilemma regarding the treatment of pathological gambling is that existing clinical data are seriously skewed. Many of the cases that are diagnosed are diagnosed after the fact, that is, recognized retrospectively when it is too late. Either the subjects are dead (suicide rates are unusually high among serious gamblers[4]) or incarcerated, or the diagnostic profiles are provided by friends, families, and/or business associates whose lives have been ravaged by the dereliction of the gamblers. These are the extreme cases, to be sure, but the extremity is the predictable result of such conditions when unacknowledged, unrecognized, and untreated.

The second dilemma applies to the many cases that are recognized and reported—but go untreated nevertheless. The recognition (or at least strong suspicion) and the reporting are secondhand. In my own practice, for every problem gambler who has come into treatment, there are five or six whose problems have been described to me by spouses, siblings, close friends, or the like. Though I keep my practice small (at least while I continue to teach full-time), I always find time for a gambler strongly suspected of pathology. The next call, however, must be made by the prospective client. And more often than not that call never comes.

The third dilemma occurs when the call is made but my terms of admitting such clients—presented over the phone or declared at a first appointment (assuming the appointment is kept, which it often is not)—are unacceptable to them. There are only two nonnegotiable items: attendance at GA meetings at least once a week and abstinence from gambling "at least until we get a handle on the situation."

That first term is a way of asking for at least a token acknowledgment that a problem exists in their gambling behavior. At this point I do not require that they buy into a twelve-step program (and I would be very suspicious if they said they wanted to), only that they be willing to attend and listen. Sometimes this becomes a reason, or pretext, for not going forward into treatment: "I don't belong in the same room with a bunch of degenerate gamblers."

The second term is a way of saying to them, "If you don't have a problem, there's no reason why you can't stop gambling for a while; but if you do have a problem, we'll be able to examine it in the context of the difficulty—or impossibility—of your stopping at this time." In other words, it seems like too good a sporting proposition for them to *say* that they refuse temporary abstinence. No one, in my experience, has done so—and yet I suspect that among those who do not continue after the initial interview, there are some for whom this precondition is a reason—or excuse—to keep them out of treatment. More than a dilemma, it is a paradox that the inability to abstain from gambling, which by itself demonstrates the existence of a problem, keeps people from getting help for that problem.

The fourth dilemma almost goes without saying. It is, after all, financial crises that force acknowledgment of the existence of a problem. There are some who argue that the definition of the condition should specify financial crisis as the differentiating symptom. If a habitual gambler keeps winning or has ample resources to cover his losses, what's the problem?

By the time gamblers seek help for their problem, they usually cannot afford treatment. Insurors (for those who have managed to retain health coverage at all) typically do not reimburse for the condition. Debts loom overhead, creditors are everywhere, legal exigencies may be part of the picture, and all financial resources have been exhausted. Treatment may be the number-one priority for these people, but getting paid promptly may have to be the lowest priority for the treatment providers. Clearly, this is a neglected issue of public policy on gambling. In the most intransigent of cases, where inpatient treatment is indicated, the high cost often makes it unavailable.

What I find almost incomprehensible is the way treatment of and knowledge about the condition have lagged so far behind the prevalence of gambling and the attendant rise in the problem gambling population. Hailed as "the addiction of the '90s" and proclaimed an "epidemic" in the December 1995 issue of the APA's *Monitor*, pathological gambling remains outside the understanding and competence of the public and most practitioners alike. There are some who doubt the very existence of a diagnosable disorder.[5]

Attempts to remedy the discrepancy between need and knowledge, to bridge the gap between myth and methodology, have too often been led into unproductive or even counterproductive channels (perhaps tunnels, as in vision, would be the appropriate metaphor[6]). Much effort has been devoted, for example, to attempts to delineate the personality characteristics of pathological gamblers. Reviewing no fewer than nine separate studies on this subject,[7] Mark Dickerson succinctly summarizes their common conclusions that compulsive gamblers score high on scales of extraversion, neuroticism, and intelligence. But Dickerson concludes, "The measurement of the personality characteristics of compulsive gamblers (i.e. those seeking treatment) in the absence of a comparison group of regular or high-frequency gamblers has lead [sic] to the unjustified assumption that people with certain personality traits are more likely to gamble excessively" (43).

There are other problems with those studies. For one, it seems obvious that pathological gamblers who do seek treatment are likely to rank higher on those very scales than pathological gamblers who do not seek treatment. For another, those studies significantly fail to include people seeking treatment for other psychiatric conditions, but who are also involved in pathological or habitual gambling (whether or not it has emerged in treatment).[8] Both practical and clinical experience teach that pathological gamblers come in all shapes and sizes of personality and character.

Rosecrance, another observer who has challenged the prevailing conventional wisdom, chose to explore "problem gambling from the participants' perspective" (Gambing without Guilt, 136). His conclusions include two "findings [that] have particular significance for those trying to comprehend inappropriate gambling behavior: (1) the process of becoming involved in problem gambling is reversible rather than inexorable, and (2) other gamblers can provide help in coping with gambling problems. These findings belie the traditional contentions" (135).

Rosecrance's second finding has become self-evident in the considerable success of Gamblers Anonymous. The first finding, however, depends on an assumption that full-blown pathology may be anticipated: that warning signals may be recognized, reported, and acknowledged in time to reverse the projected course. I agree that there is a possibility of early detection and remediation (preventative prophylaxis, if you will), and I reject the absolute necessity of "hitting bottom" as a precondition for recovery (as some would have it). But it is more accurate to call this "finding" a hope, and it is my hope that this book will provide some assistance, to gamblers and their families and associates as well as to therapists, in transforming that hope more often into a finding in reality.

Typically cautious about making broad generalizations, I would nevertheless offer an observation about typical defense mechanisms among pathological gamblers. I do so in order to anticipate obstacles likely to retard, impede, or subvert treatment. These gamblers, in my judgment and experience, are commonly and strongly defended by denial, accompanied by elements of distortion; by intellectualization; by rationalization; by splitting (assignment of "all-good" and "all-bad" projections onto the same object); by cleverness, with concomitant deviousness; and by verbal dexterity— the ability, in twelve-step jargon, to talk the talk without walking the walk. Treatment providers must resist the charm of such patients and clients, must avoid being taken in by them, and must be willing to accept the frustration that comes with the likelihood of relapse.

The very mechanisms of defense that characterize the typical pathological gambler are what make relapse prevalent, just as their symptoms of personality disorders make a clear diagnosis of pathological gambling problematic. Let me offer two examples from my own practice, contemporaneous cases where relapse occurred at times of apparent progress in recovery. One client's backsliding was discovered and reported by her spouse, and when confronted she was fully prepared with "reasons" for renewing her gambling and "justifications" for lying about it to her husband and her therapist. The other client called to cancel successive sessions and offered as the "reason" that since he had ceased to be abstinent, it was inappropriate for him to continue treatment. There was also the factor of his indebtedness to me, approaching the figure at which we had agreed on settlement (just as he had arranged with his bookie to "settle on a dime"). These strategies were polar opposites in a sense—one contrived to continue therapy while renewing gambling, the other to terminate treatment while renewing gambling. In both cases, however, whether through concealment or candor, the contrivance was in the service of an excuse to gamble. What their intelligence and charm allowed them to get away with in relationships with others (including their therapist), their proficiency at denial and rationalization permitted them to get away with in their own gambling behaviors.[9]

The characteristic defenses that obstruct diagnosis and treatment also obstruct acknowledgment of pathology. Consequently, too few pathological gamblers enter treatment at all, too few remain in treatment, too few are effectively treated (raising substantial questions regarding quantifying studies of treatment). Fully effective treatment is difficult to access, rare in administration, demanding in commitment, and costly to the point of general unfeasability. In the most severe cases the condition requires hospitalization. But even in outpatient settings, it is advisable to combine group therapy and individual therapy, augmented by regular attendance at GA meetings.[10] Moreover, given the frequency of dysfunction in the marriages and families of pathological gamblers, couples or family therapy is usually called for.

I am a great supporter of Gam-Anon, which is to GA as Al-Anon is to AA. If anything it is *more* important than GA to the possibility of recovery. More than simply a learning experience about enablers, codependency, and the separation of normal anger from crippling resentment, Gam-Anon provides a supportive context for dealing with the disruption, disgust, disillusionment, and despair, the frustration, depression, and anxiety that go with the emotional experience of living with a pathological gambler in the home. Reduction of marital and familial dysfunction is second only to restoration of satisfactory professional performance as a positive factor of recovery.[11]

My own approach to treatment of pathological gamblers is eclectic. I am

as leery of rigidly distinct treatment modalities as I am of the rigid constraints of exclusive diagnosis. And I suspect that most practitioners, dealing
pragmatically with patients or clients on a case-by-case basis, cannot afford
the theoretical luxury (a requirement of researchers conducting clinical trials) of one exclusive modality or another.

Typically, treatment would begin with a cognitive approach (I sometimes
feel like I'm wearing one of my other caps, that of my pedagogical profession)
in an attempt to break through irrational notions concerning gambling. Reality testing is a basic tactic, and a comprehensive knowledge of gambling is a
prerequisite for the role of teacher here. But I must acknowledge a primary
limitation of the cognitive component: intellectual understanding of gambling
realities and acceptance of the condition of pathological gambling, however
genuine, are not always accompanied by gut-level grasp and acceptance. Gamblers can *learn* about the irrationality of gambling and *know* their gambling
behavior is pathological, but if they don't *feel* it, relapse is inevitable. (This is
where GA can be most helpful because, other than demonstrable abstinence,
the best indication of emotional acknowledgment of pathology is actively
working a GA program.)

Cognitive awareness shades over into insight therapy, a psychodynamic
strategy. (My use of the language of defense mechanisms, of ego psychology
in general, has clearly revealed this aspect of my orientation.) When a gambler becomes aware of the contexts, circumstances, occasions, and effects of
his gambling behaviors, he is on his way toward understanding its appeal, its
functions, its triggers, perhaps even its etiology for him.[12]

I would acknowledge one other implication of the cognitive/psychody-
namic approach in the question of the viability of "maintenance gambling."
If one believes, as I do, that gambling is intrinsically neither criminal nor
immoral (though dangerous) and that understanding and acknowledgment
of the condition provide a legitimate fail-safe mechanism for prevention of
pathology or its recurrence, then a limited return to gambling ought to be
allowed. The practice may be questionable, but I cannot in good conscience
rule out a resumption of gambling by a client for whom it may be manageable, pleasurable, affordable, and acceptable to spouse, family, colleagues,
and employers. If it meets those criteria, I can countenance resumption of
gambling, under six additional conditions: the gambler must have (1) a sufficiently developed observant ego to be aware of changes in his/her own
behavior, (2) a clear understanding of the distinctions between habitual and
pathological gambling, (3) a well-placed warning system among family and
friends about changes in his/her gambling, (4) a demonstrated ability to be

abstinent in response to warning signals, (5) a comprehension of his/her own gambling nature and history that includes possible origins of the habit and possible triggers for that habit crossing over the line into pathology, and, perhaps most important, (6) no indication that the pathology has ever reached the point of addiction where any bet would trigger an uncontrollable escalation of action.

Finally, consider the possibility of medication. A few clinical trials have been reported, but rarely does the notion of pharmacological remedy occur in general recommendations for treatment of pathological gambling. Whether depression and/or anxiety is cause, effect, or correlated symptom, wouldn't a prescription for antidepressant or antianxiety medication be in order to complement therapy?[13] Relief of disturbed affect might even be accompanied by relief of impulses or disturbances related to gambling. Gambling may largely be learned behavior; it would be very difficult to disregard environmental factors, given the presence of gambling all around us and in everyday awareness. But strong correlations between pathological gamblers and the incidence of alcoholism in their families suggest a genetic component of susceptibility to addictions or addictive behavior. At-risk populations are generally, perhaps globally, at risk.[14]

At least one study (Roy et al., "Extraversion in Pathological Gamblers," 1989) has strongly suggested a biochemical component: a sample group of pathological gamblers, who coincidentally score high on a scale of extraversion (validating the conclusions of Custer and others), have an abnormally low level of production in the noradrenergic system.[15] That is, lacking specific by-products of norepinephrine, people may seek the excitement ("action") of gambling to stimulate secretion and raise those levels. Characteristically subject to boredom,[16] they must stimulate their "juices" (the common metaphor of juice in gambling parlance is thus given literal meaning) to counter anomie, to create a feeling of involvement or aliveness. This study, then, tends to support the idea that gambling can be an addiction, a chronic, progressive condition, following a typical course of increased tolerance, loss of regard for consequences, and precipitous decline into depression upon withdrawal.

A case recently came to my attention twenty years after the fact. A woman reported to me that when her father was hospitalized for depression, her mother took the occasion to tell her (among many other things) that her father was a compulsive gambler. He had been an expert card player, but his gambling was on horses and football.

"He was in his sixties, I was twenty, and for the first time I had an explanation for a lot of things I had always accepted without questioning: why, though both my parents worked and were well-paid for what they did, we lived so modestly. We never were deprived, I don't mean that, but there was always a sense that there was nothing extra, no frivolous spending.

"He used to take me with him to the racetracks, and I remember he was always very sweet to me. My favorites were the state and county fairs, where after the races were over I could do whatever I wanted at the fair. And I loved watching the trotters pull those sulkies around the track. I could never tell whether he won or lost. Even during the races, he'd never give any indication.

"The other thing I loved was watching football games on TV with him. He'd explain every detail to me, talk about strategy, and anticipate what was going to happen. He had all these insights and theories about the game, but I had no idea he was betting on them. It seemed to be an intellectual exercise with him, and he'd never show any emotion."

"Who handled the finances for the family?"

"My mother, but I don't think it had always been that way. I remember there was one major refinancing of the house, and maybe that was when she took over."

"I knew her as a strong, intelligent, energetic woman. Was she also an enabler?"

"Yes, I think she was. She wanted to make sure that we were all taken care of, that they maintained their status quo, and I suppose that Dad was able to continue with what he was doing—as long as it didn't get out of control. Even in hindsight, I can't see that there were any signs that gambling interfered with his professional or social life."

"Was he ever treated for pathological gambling?"

"I don't think that was ever part of the program. I don't know if they even knew about it in the hospital or treatment afterward. I know he was on medication, but I don't know anything else about how his case was handled."

"What happened after he came home?"

"That's when he began showing symptoms. He was withdrawn, wouldn't go out, just stayed around the house. He was clearly depressed, but also somewhat phobic and maybe a little paranoid."

"Was he still gambling then?"

"I don't think so. I don't think he could."

"It's possible, I think, that he had been experiencing depression and anxiety for a long time, that those inner feelings weren't explicable to his logical, analytical mind, so that he masked them with the gambling. Even though he never showed those feelings outwardly—and even was stoic in the event of wins and losses—the mounting losses would account for both the depressive and the anxious components of his inner life. When he could no longer gamble, for whatever reason, the masked symptoms became graphically visible."[17]

I'm not sure that I convinced her that my scenario accounted somehow for her father's behavior, and I told her that at best I could only guess about it. Given the orientation of the psychiatric hospital where he was treated, I doubt that the gambling behavior ever became an issue. And at that point perhaps no useful purpose would have been served anyway.

Yet I can't help but speculate on earlier stages of his depressive illness. If his gambling had been recognized as pathological, if it had then been attended to, and if the behavior had been recognized as masking an underlying and progressing disorder, it is just possible that the major episode, the hospitalization, and the subsequent withdrawal from normal functioning could all have been avoided—along with losses of considerable sums of money.

My final example is another kind of cautionary tale, the story of a young friend of mine who has had a gambling problem but gave up the habit without any professional counseling. Scooter, as I'll call him, began gambling when he was eleven or twelve years old, picking the winners of NFL games in a season-long pool with his family. Sunday afternoon was an occasion of family togetherness, all five watching all the games and keeping track of their picks. Two dollars a week from each went into the pot and it was winner take all at the end of the season.

"Gambling was never frowned on in our house," he said, early in our longest interview. "My father and my grandfather were both seriously involved in card playing, and they spoke freely about it, maybe even bragging about their skill and success. I wasn't into cards, but—sports junky that I am, been watching football since I was four—when the opportunity came, I jumped into betting against the spread on NFL games.

"I was a sophomore in college, a lot of guys in my fraternity were betting, and I met a guy on campus who introduced me to a local businessman who booked a lot of action on the side. Almost right away I was betting five to ten thousand dollars every weekend. And I killed it that first year, had more money than I'd ever seen before. I was a contrarian. I knew that if everyone in the house was betting the Redskins, then the Cowboys were sure to cover.

"I had become a broadcasting major, wanting to make a career of it, but in sports, not news. By the time I graduated I had done some baseball play-by-play, color on women's hoops, been assistant sports director at the station, and even got on for a time at the local TV station. But my favorite time of the week was Friday night, when I would sit down to study the matchups on the weekend schedule of games and make my picks against the spread.

"It was all about being justified, being right, and I guess I wanted to show my father I could do it. Besides, the rush was there. I was on top of the world. But I still kept my grades up and had a normal social life as well."

"Did your folks know what you were doing?"

"Not until senior year, when I started losing, and I had to go to them for help. They bailed me out, but my dad was furious, thought I was the dumbest thing walking. It was understood that I would quit, but as soon as I paid off I was back in action.

"After graduation, with no offers in broadcasting, I was back living at home, just working occasional odd jobs, hanging around the house, and betting football and basketball through this seventeen-year-old kid in the neighborhood who was into it big time. I was not doing well, and it was a struggle to hide what I was doing from my parents. One thing I learned was that you can't win when you can't afford to lose.

"When I got down about three thousand, I was thinking a lot of crazy things—robbery, even suicide, but mostly about running away, just pulling a disappearing act. But the next weekend I won five thousand. It was all about money, I thought during those days, but I was gambling on borrowed time.

"Then I made a decision to pursue what I really wanted to do. I went back to my college town to work for free at the local TV station, to do whatever they wanted me to do, to give it my best shot to get started in the business. I was a news photographer, then reporter and photographer, even got a chance as weekend sports anchor. And the job offer I was hoping for came through, TV sports production, my chance to be a little fish in a big pond.

"I was working really hard at a career, but I was playing hard at the betting, too. A month into the job, on New Year's Day, I had the biggest day of my life. My alma mater won the biggest game in its history in a major bowl, against their traditional rival even, and I had it straight up, in parlays, in teasers—a clean sweep."

"You're excited all over again, just telling me about it, aren't you?"

"Sure. There's no question that the betting enhanced my enjoyment of games, helped me focus on strategy of play, too. The worst part was watching a great game but losing a bet. I would get sky-high after a win, but that never lasted. And after a loss I would be majorly depressed. The most frustrating thing, though, was learning that knowledge or inside information didn't matter, and that took some of the fun out of it."

"Never helped Chet Forte."

"Right. I think the main difference between us is that he was already a big success in the business, had a lot of money, before he got into it. Lucky for me I wasn't making much money or I might have gotten buried. Yeah, you're probably right when you say that a lot of it is about ego satisfaction. I thought pretty highly of myself as a smart winning bettor, but I came to measure my own worth in terms of working toward a successful career in the business.

"I remember my roommate saying to me, 'You just don't get it, do you, that this is not how it's supposed to be?' I think I knew that but I didn't do anything to change things. And then one weekend about two years after that big bowl win I got killed, lost five thousand, and I had to get help from my parents again. They had no idea I was back into it, though after that year and a half at home I don't know how they could have missed the signs. Maybe they didn't want to see it, or maybe they were in denial themselves, or maybe they were enablers.

"But this time, when they bailed me out, my mom put a condition on it—I had to promise to start going to GA. And I did. She saw to it that I kept the promise, made some calls, and the guy that became my sponsor called me.

"I'll never forget what he said to me at that first meeting. 'How many times have you been watching a game, and the team you're betting on is ahead 55-0 and you turn the channel to a game where your bet is in doubt?' 'All the time,' I said. 'You can't enjoy the win, can you? You got to go for something else.'

"I knew exactly what he was talking about. It wasn't the money or the win that gave the rush. It was the action, the juice, the undecided outcome. That was what I was addicted to. I didn't stay with GA very long. I didn't think I had to. But I took a good look around me at those meetings and saw what I was heading for, where I'd be if I didn't quit. Seven and a half years I had been into it, and that was enough."

"Was it, Scooter? Are you sure?"

"Yes."

"It's been, what, four or five years? Have you made any bets since?"

"Just once, one Sunday afternoon, when I bet a couple of hundred dollars on the games on TV."

"What was going on?"

"It was depression. My ex-girlfriend had just got married, I was feeling lonely, my father had had a stroke. So I thought I'd pass the time that way. It didn't help, really."

"Was the action too small?"

"That wasn't it. I just couldn't get into it. And I don't think I'll do it again."

I hope so, Scooter, but I take that small relapse as a warning signal. Your story has elements of what we've seen in earlier chapters—Vinnie's depression, Patrick's ego-driven personality, Forte's high-profile profile in *potentia*, a touch of the void-filling behavior—but no coherent pattern. I don't really know you well enough to make an informed guess about what the appropriate diagnosis or treatment might have been had you gone into therapy, or what it would be should you seek help at some point in the future.

What I do know is that you are at risk. That is the word of caution I send your way and to anyone else who has reason to take it in. Once the gambling habit has become part of your experience, you may use it, revert to it, embrace it, plunge into it again, whenever you encounter the difficulties or downturns inevitable in everyone's life. You may be stressed by external or environmental conditions from which you feel the urge to escape.[18] You may feel the internal effects of conditions you may not even be consciously aware of, and you may be tempted to self-medicate or self-justify or self-validate. And you already have gambling in your repertoire of behaviors to satisfy any or all of those inclinations.

You may get to the point where your feelings of loss or despair or sadness are too deep for words, and you know that when words cannot suffice, then action is the answer. Or you may get to the point where you conclude that it doesn't matter what you do or refuse to do. What you must understand is that to allow any such thinking to give you license to gamble again means precisely that you have found an excuse to gamble. So if one of those bells should ever ring for you, let it be a sound of alarm. The call to self-destruction may not be far removed from any of us. For you, my friend, the vehicle to take you there, your old gambling habit, is ready and waiting.

Gamblers Anonymous has developed a twenty-question instrument to test the appropriateness (and promote the willingness) of people who may have problems with gambling to join the group. It has had such widespread use and influence that I consider it important to reprint it here:

1. Do you lose time from work because of gambling?

2. Is gambling making your home life unhappy?

3. Is gambling affecting your reputation?

4. Have you ever felt remorse after gambling?

5. Do you ever gamble to get money with which to pay debts or to otherwise solve financial difficulties?

6. Does gambling ever cause a decrease in your ambition or efficiency?

7. After losing, do you feel you must return as soon as possible to win back your losses?

8. After you win, do you have a strong urge to return to win more?

9. Do you often gamble until your last dollar is gone?

10. Do you ever borrow to finance your gambling?

11. Have you ever sold any real or personal property to finance gambling?

12. Are you reluctant to use "gambling money" for normal expenditures?

13. Does gambling make you careless of the welfare of your family?

14. Do you ever gamble longer than you have planned?

15. Do you ever gamble to escape worry and trouble?

16. Have you ever committed or considered committing an illegal act to finance gambling?

17. Does gambling cause you to have difficulty in sleeping?

18. Do arguments, disappointments, or frustrations cause you to gamble?

19. Do you have an urge to celebrate any good fortune by a few hours of gambling?

20. Have you ever considered self-destruction as a result of your gambling?

There are some obvious problems with this list of questions as an instrument of diagnosis.[19] They refer in an unstructured way to motivations, contexts, practical consequences, and emotional consequences of gambling, giving equal weight to each question and category. For an accurate count, they assume that the person answering has a highly functioning observing

ego, that he has overcome the defense mechanisms of denial and rationalization that characterize most gamblers' mentality, and that he will not lie to
himself or others about his gambling. Nevertheless, they have value in showing people that they belong in GA and that their own experience is shared by
others. (The threshold of "proof" is in some dispute: GA says seven affirma-
tive answers qualify one for appropriate membership; studies cite ten to
twelve as necessary to diagnose pathology.)

The questionnaire has proven useful over time, though it seems to me
that while it may not be necessary to persuade people who fill it out that
they belong in GA, it would be unlikely to persuade people who believe they
do not belong. The trouble with the list is that by the time people qualify for
GA by getting "passing" grades on the quiz they have already fallen prey to
the pathology; it's too late for preventative measures, the remedial measures
being far more difficult to prescribe and administer.

Custer, who reprints the list of questions (Custer and Milt, *When Luck
Runs Out*, 188) as a confirming diagnostic tool, recognizes this difficulty. He
therefore precedes it with his own list of thirty-nine indicators (185–87)
that reveal "soft signs" or preexistent suggestions that pathology is developing or is a danger in the future. At the end of the list he repeats a caveat:
"These 'soft' signs are not in themselves diagnostic. They may be useful to
reinforce a diagnosis that is in the making, based on the 'hard,' diagnostic,
signs." What they reinforce, however, is the profile of a compulsive gambler
as Custer has extrapolated it from his clinical evidence.

To take a few examples, I cannot see how superior intelligence (sign 1),
history of excellence in athletics (3), absence of alcohol- or drug-use when
gambling (6), absence of other hobbies (8), boredom in social situations
(18), preference for cash over traveler's checks (28), absence of record-keeping
(36), and/or distrust of the gambling industry (39) can possibly be consistent indicators of pathology in the making. Indeed, the opposite of each of
these characteristics shows up in case histories of pathological gamblers,
while in some cases their presence may defend habitual gamblers from becoming pathological.

The one generalization I am comfortable in making is this: people who
habitually gamble run the risk of becoming pathological gamblers—regardless of whatever quirks of behavior, personality, interests, mental capacities,
or emotional patterns may characterize them. The key to identifying, recog-
nizing, or realizing that a gambler is heading toward pathology is awareness
of change—by the gamblers themselves or those close to them. I offer four
general questions to ask, with specific examples of each:

1. Have there been changes in gambling habits?
   a. gambling more often?
   b. increasing stakes?
   c. trying new, additional gambling vehicles or sites?
   d. altering old or experimenting with new gambling practices, strategies, principles, "systems"?

2. Have there been changes in attitudes toward gambling?
   a. becoming a more important part of life (for example, on Sunday, thinking "it's only three days until the Wednesday night poker game" or on Wednesdays, "only three days until college football Saturday")?
   b. starting to schedule other activities or plan trips around possibilities for gambling?
   c. increased ruminating about past gambling, obsessing about future gambling, or being preoccupied with ideas about gambling, gamblers, gambling institutions, gambling policies and philosophies and ethics and the like?

3. Have there been changes in emotional responses to gambling?
   a. greater anxiety? anxiety lasting longer? (look for changes in sleeping, drinking, eating, exercising)
   b. more serious depression? depression lasting longer? (look for changes in sleeping, drinking, eating, exercising)
   c. less patience between gambles? greater impatience with activities (and people) not connected with gambling?
   d. markedly greater anger over losses? muting of anger at losses?
   e. increased exhilaration at wins? dulling of enjoyment of wins?

4. Are there new environmental or external stressors in the gamblers' lives (factors likely to require major adjustments)?
   a. major life-cycle markers (for example, fortieth birthday, empty nest, graduation, promotion, birth of second child, explosion into adolescence of oldest child)?
   b. traumas (for example, illness, injury, loss of job, move to new home or neighborhood or town)?
   c. emotional losses (for example, death of parent, divorce)?

Awareness of change is one crucial thing. Another is being aware that changes may very well occur. Think of the gambling habit as a kind of brown mole (whether you call it a blemish or a beauty mark), familiar, symmetrical, and smooth. It's always been there; one is comfortable with it. But any sign of change in color, shape, or texture calls for vigilance, attention, and examination, with the possibility of treatment in view. Often it takes someone other than the bearer of the mole to perceive the change, just as it may take someone other than the gambler to call attention to the changes or even to be alert to a context for possible change.

I would offer, finally, another set of guidelines or questions regarding people who have the good fortune or intelligence to be in treatment. These are suggestions for those treatment providers who may not be familiar with gambling pathologies at all or, at the other extreme, may be too narrowly focused on the particular gambling behaviors that have brought someone into treatment.

For patients or clients who present with other addictions or other impulse-control problems, ask about gambling. It is common for such people to have dual or multiple sets of symptoms.

For patients or clients who have mood disorders, ask specifically if their depression, anxiety, or manic episodes are ever enacted in gambling.

For patients or clients with problems of self-destructive behaviors, suicidation, or reality testing, ask specifically if gambling is ever part of their thinking or acting out.

For patients or clients who seem to be struggling with what Yalom calls "existence pain" or what I have called "void-filling" behavior, ask if gambling is part of their lifestyle.

For patients or clients who exhibit symptoms of personality disorders, ask specifically whether their characteristic defenses are ever enacted in gambling behaviors. This may be one area where self-defeating expressions of grandiosity, omnipotence, splitting, and so forth may be modified or limited.

Conversely, when patients or clients are seeking treatment for pathological gambling, it is important to address—or eliminate—elements of the various types of disorders listed above. To approach successfully an understanding of these concomitant issues, it is necessary to take a complete history of the gambling behaviors, paying particular attention to the context in which, at each stage, the behaviors have been exhibited. And in examining the present manifestations, it is important to get a handle on the immediate context of the gambling practices, the triggers for the impulse to gamble, and the effects—at every level of experience—of the gambling. By all means eliminate the possibility that the gambler is divesting him/herself of unwanted baggage.

A cognitive approach implies the development of an "observing ego" in the gambler, that part of the self that can stand back and watch what he is doing and what is going on around him.[20] Group therapy, as Custer recommends, can be very useful in this process, cutting through denial and rationalization. But even when there is an intellectual acceptance by the gambler of a pathological condition in himself, it doesn't necessarily follow that he has emotionally identified himself as disordered. And that's where GA is most useful, accomplishing a gut-level acceptance of pathology and the knowledge that no one can achieve recovery alone.

Good luck.

Notes

Introduction

1. In *Gambling and Speculation*, Reuven Brenner has attempted to distinguish between the two terms. "The word 'gamble,'" he says, "refers to an act where the participant pursues a monetary gain without using his or her skills. It is therefore appropriate to use this word for games of chance only" (90). "'Speculation' . . . refers to carrying out an act where one backs one's own opinion. . . . This situation is in contrast with a gambling situation. The latter refers to situations that have been and can be repeated many times and where the probabilities, as well as the monetary gains and losses, are the same for everybody and well known" (91). These distinctions, though useful in a defense of gambling in general, seem to limit gambling per se to lotteries, simple slot machines, "wheel of fortune" devices, and perhaps roulette. With most card games and any sports-related, skill-influenced, or game-playing action, apparently (i.e., the majority of gambling as we know it in this country today), all bets are off for Brenner's definition of gambling.

See Goodman, chapter 7, where a discussion of at-home electronic betting reads eerily like a prediction of the development of at-home electronic day trading.

2. In "Busted Flush," David Plotz has neatly narrated the story of the modern-day mismatch of politics and gambling in South Carolina. The struggles among the electorate, the legislature, the judiciary, and the executive (not to mention the gaming industry, the churches, tourism, property owners, and other special interests) go on furiously. See Sue Anne Pressley's more recent summary in the *Washington Post*, June 11, 2000. This note is being written on the eve of the state's shutdown of 32,000 video poker machines, an estimated $3 billion a year business. Given the past performances of the voters and the politicians in South Carolina, the odds are that the ban will be temporary.

3. Why do we continue to accept the propagandistic jargon of talking about the "horse racing industry" as a self-contained enterprise dedicated to "the improve-

ment of the breed," when it is primarily a vehicle for gambling, both legal and illegal?

4. Except for a note on comorbidity studies, I will not address in this book the problematic issues regarding the gambling establishments on Native American reservations and tribal grounds. There is a kind of ironic or poetic justice in the remarkable enrichment of Native Americans at the expense of gambling-hungry Americans at large. Part of the irony resides in the historical fact that long-standing traditions among many tribes honored or even venerated certain forms of gambling. Impoverished by the imperial impositions of foreign cultures, Native Americans have now found a way to benefit materially from aspects of those cultures that mesh with their own. At Mohegan Sun, in Connecticut, to take the best example I have seen, they have found a way to celebrate their own culture in the very design and ambience of the casino. While one may rejoice in the material improvements on some reservations with regard to health care, housing, education, and employment opportunities, one may also raise issues with respect to level playing fields in terms of licensure, taxation, public oversight, and jurisdictional authority: separate but equal makes no better sense here than in such an area of public concern as education. The value placed on the land, on the natural environment, has typically not been subverted in Native American gambling establishments, rendering moot the intelligent proposal of Jerome Skolnick for a "zoning merit model" of casino planning (in Frey and Eadington, 48–60). Thompson and Gazel's application of the "Prisoner's Dilemma" analogy, however, may yet apply (in Eadington and Cornelius, 183–205). But there is apparently an increased risk for pathology or addiction in the Native American population (see chapter 12, note 14), which has yet to be appropriately addressed in provisions for prevention or treatment. Finally, I feel that we are too close to the Holocaust experience to be comfortable with some form of genetic quantification in measuring the legitimacy of membership in a tribal community. See Goodman, chapter 6.

5. What do these states think the cockfights are for, improving the breed? See Burkhard Bilger's "Enter the Chicken" for enlightenment on the cultural aspects of cockfighting in the bayou country. Until 1998, cockfighting was also legal (and betting winked at) in Arizona, probably due to the significant influence of a Mexican cultural heritage. When Arizona's voters determined overwhelmingly in 1998 to ban cockfighting, would many generations of cultural practice be terminated by a tyranny of a majority of voters? Would criminalization end the practice? One answer might have come, just four months before that election, from Alabama. There, where cockfighting has been illegal for some time, a raid in Gadsden "unearthed" a pit with a 250-seat theater, a restaurant, and air-conditioned trailers for the roosters. Incidentally, the only American jurisdiction where it is legal to bet on cockfights is Puerto Rico.

6. I say "may" and "often" because gambling in any form is illegal only when the particular form is identified or described as such by statute. Unless and until the game or device is specified in a statute, whether local, state, or federal, it is not

illegal. I. Nelson Rose in *Gambling and the Law* has deftly skewered the attempts at precise legislation and the sometimes ludicrous results thereof.

7. Randy Roberts and James Olson, in a chapter called "Scandal Time," tell the story of the invention of the spread in Chicago in the early 1940s by "Charles K. McNeil, a former math teacher in a Connecticut prep school" (81). They cite no source for this attractive, but I believe apocryphal, tale. I rely on my research with Gerald Strine that points to Minneapolis and the group associated with the Gorham Press and its "Green Sheet" for the origin of the spread, probably a full decade ahead of McNeil's "invention."

8. From the review's chapter on the prevalence of gambling: "It is important to emphasize how inadequate that research base is for drawing confident conclusions about the prevalence of pathological and problem gambling in the U.S. population or in important subpopulations" (National Research Council, 100). From the chapter on the origins of gambling pathology: "More and better research on the etiology of pathological gambling is needed" (140). From the chapter on social and economic effects: "In most of the impact analyses of gambling and of pathological and problem gambling, the methods used are so inadequate as to invalidate the conclusions" (185). From the chapter on treatment: "What is known about the treatment of pathological gambling lags behind even what is known about its prevalence and etiology" (220).

9. This is the main point of Brian Castellani's *Pathological Gambling: The Making of a Medical Problem*. This book appeared too late for careful integration into my argument, though I have been able to cite it in several footnotes. It is not a book about the condition itself but about how the condition has been politicized (in what he calls processes of "discursive strategies" and "discursive negotiations"), in effect replacing an old myth with a new. While I may question his focus on a particular court case (*United States v. John Torniero*, which resulted in precluding pathological gambling from insanity defenses) and his insistence on describing the process by which his reading of and thinking about Derrida, Foucault, Anselm Strauss, and others led him to his approach, these are mere quibbles. His considerable contribution, particularly in his recommendations for policy, practice, and research in the epilogue, should earn our respect and attention.

Castellani's premise that many of the flaws in our thinking about gambling stem from a historical context in which all gambling was considered "morally and legally illegitimate" (27) seconds the persuasive, vigorous rhetoric of Abt et al. in *The Business of Risk*: "This comfortable hypocrisy, that gambling is deviant and pathological, is the root cause of our inability to deal rationally with gambling behavior" (15) and "The time is long past when taking refuge in the myth of gambling as deviance and relegating commercial gambling to the status of a pariah industry can pass for meaningful responses to the phenomena of gambling" (16).

10. Elsewhere (10), Knapp adds Rabelais, Marivaux, Casanova, Pushkin, Ts'ao Hsueh-chi'in, Dickens, Mallarmé, and Cocteau to her list, saying, "Creative artists through the centuries have not only enriched our understanding of the problematics

of gambling, but have added to the subject a world of philosophical and psychological speculation as well." I would add that the very labels we give to the phenomena of problematic human experience are derived from literary sources, from Narcissus, Oedipus, and Job to Quixote, Uncle Tom, and the catch-22, to name a few. Literature offers great untapped resources for clinical analysis, and I am appreciative and confident in relying on analysts from Dostoevsky to DeLillo for some of the best "treatments" on record.

1. Seven Other Myths about Gambling

1. Wang's explanation was careful, if technical:

If we call the number of flips n, then as n increases, the *number* of heads is likely to move farther and farther away from the expected $n/2$. Rather, it is the *percentage* of heads that gets closer and closer to the expected 50. . . .

This distinction between the simultaneous divergence away from $n/2$ in absolute number but convergence toward 50 percent in percentage may be subtle, but it is also crucial.

2. Despite the historical references in this chapter, there is no pretense that this book offers a historical account of gambling. Interested readers are referred to any of the several general histories of gambling, such as Herbert Asbury's *Sucker's Progress. An Informal History of Gambling in America from the Colonies to Canfield* (New York: Dodd, Mead, 1938) or Henry Chafetz's *Play the Devil: A History of Gambling in the United States from 1492 to 1955* (New York: Potter, 1960) (but Stephen Longstreet's unreliable *Win or Lose: A Social History of Gambling in America* [Indianapolis: Bobbs-Merrill, 1979] only for anecdotal amusement). Nor is there any pretense here of presenting a survey of the academic scholarship on pathological gambling. I will make reference to a number of specific studies, but the interested reader would do well to start with the National Research Council's *Pathological Gambling: A Critical Review* (1999).

3. When Gregory the Great incorporated the seven into official Catholic teaching in his fifth-century *Moralia*, sloth (*acedia*) was merged with, and eventually replaced, *tristitia*, also known as *taedium cordis*, a condition in which one does not or cannot worship the Lord with proper joyfulness. Sloth becomes, basically, the sin of neglecting one's religious duties (presumably because of laziness). By the thirteenth century of Aquinas's *Summa Theologica*, sloth had long since been moved to seventh or lowest position in the hierarchy of the sins (and in the Old English Haltigar's *Penitential*, sloth was not even mentioned in a treatise listing thirteen sins). By the sixteenth century, the medieval conventions had lost sway, and in the anonymous *Complaynt of Scotlande* (1549) sloth is omitted from a chronicle of the sins. See Morton Bloomfield's thorough history of the development, use, and passing of this whole set of ideas—where reference to gambling as a sinful behavior begotten of sloth is rare indeed. Sloth had a hard time carrying its weight or keeping up with the other six.

4. See Olmert, 97.

5. The inherent hypocrisy in such persistent historical attitudes and societal biases is ironically suggested by Joyce Carol Oates in *The Mysteries of Winterthurn* when she comments about Perdita Kilgarvan that "she had been overheard to murmur, in one or another Winterthurn drawing room, that, had she a 'stake' with which to begin, she might as readily make her fortune by betting on the horses, like the gentlemen, as by seeking out someone to marry. 'For if gambling be a sin against God,' the impetuous woman said, 'is it not a far more grievous sin to gamble one's very *self*, than merely with money?'" (208).

6. One of Reuven Brenner's conclusions contains another form of refutation. "Does gambling *cause* an appetite for wealth without effort that undermines the work ethic?" he asks. "The answer, as we saw, was NO" (135). The context for this generalization, however, must be kept in mind. The Brenners' book is called *Gambling and Speculation*, and it contains both a general justification for much gambling as reasonable application of entrepreneurial attitudes and a refutation of the idea that much capitalistic speculation is a form of gambling. The problem with these positions is that they are based on rather idiosyncratic definitions of terms (see note 1 to the introduction above).

7. There are some who believe that buying a lottery ticket is the only way to achieve economic relief, a meaningful redistribution of wealth whereby a very poor person may on rare occasions become rich. In this way, the most egregious victims of a capitalistic system accept its values, and in this sense it is a rational, pragmatic choice. But see chapter 2, note 1. Gambling at long odds as a last resort, the only way to achieve a happy ending in a scenario of inevitable violence and tragedy, is wittily portrayed in the Tom Tykwer film *Run Lola Run*.

8. The best overview of legal and forensic issues associated with gambling is I. Nelson Rose, *Gambling and the Law*. See also Lesieur, "Gambling, Pathological Gambling, and Crime"; Burglass, "Compulsive Gambling"; Brenner; and Wolfe.

9. This is apparently a demi-myth in itself. According to Rose, the legal issue is "not whether a particular game is one of skill or chance," an issue having "no bearing whatsoever on whether a game is prohibited by the state Penal Code" (40) in California. A memorandum issued by the state's attorney general's office in 1983 was erroneously based on that issue (and included other errors of fact), but the state's penal code is clear: unless a game is specifically prohibited it is legal.

10. A vivid portrait of Texas Hold 'Em as played in the Las Vegas World Series of Poker—a competition involving a number of demonstrable skills—is found in Alvarez's "No Limit," which appeared under the *New Yorker*'s departmental rubric "The Sporting Scene."

11. See Kaplan, "The Social and Economic Impact of State Lotteries." The first time any jurisdiction tried to counter widespread illegal gambling by legalization was in Venice in the seventeenth century. The plan for the Ridotto was implemented in 1638, and it sounds like something out of *Dune* or *Star Wars*, with the management—including dealers—limited to a particular noble family, the Barnabots, who were required to wear a specific (and bizarre) costume. At various times renowned for world-class accomplishments and innovations in trade, banking, painting, archi-

tecture, and pleasure, Venice instantly became the great holiday/festival/convention/carnival center of Europe, with the Ridotto as its major tourist attraction. It thus provided the model for Las Vegas's current quest to become a destination site for tourists. The institution lasted until 1774, its black-robed, white-wigged, long-haired dealers presiding over the basset, biribi, and panfil tables for almost a century and a half. See Barnhart for a fuller relation of this colorful narrative.

12. See David Dixon's concise comparison of the British and Australian experiences in this regard.

13. See Kaplan and Blount, for example, for a test case in Florida.

14. Several examples are presented with a kind of self-startled eagerness by Peter Alson in *Confessions of an Ivy League Bookie*. See also Reuter, 26–29.

15. According to the Council on Compulsive Gambling of New Jersey, in 1998, for the first time since such records were begun in 1983, average gambling debts of callers to their helpline exceeded their average annual income—by thousands of dollars.

16. Kusyszyn, for example, asserts, "During gambling, money loses its economic value," and that the "gambler is seen to be playing with money rather than for it" [134]).

17. Surprisingly, Freud was not the first psychoanalytical theorist to associate gambling behaviors with sexuality (see Von Hattingberg, Simmel, and Stekel). But Freud's suggestions of oral fixation and masochism were given substantial amplification in Bergler's *The Psychology of Gambling* (1957). Halliday and Fuller, however, in 1974 countered notions of orality in their identification of an underlying anal fixation, and they pointed to such gambling terminology as "pot" and "craps" (Leonard Ashley's 1990 reverie on the use of gambling vernacular in mainstream language provides a context for that argument). This view seems to be supported by Thorstein Veblen in *The Theory of the Leisure Class*, by Goffman, and by Kusyszyn.

Lesieur, who realistically took into account the perspectives of gamblers themselves, argued for the centrality of *excitement*, whether pleasurable or painful, in gamblers' motivation (*The Chase*). This view finds support in Kusyszyn's conclusions that humanistic-existential theories of motivation see gambling as healthy adult play and that people gamble in order to "confirm their existence and affirm their worth" (136).

It is important to note that Custer, as well as Moran ("An Assessment"), Chapman, Dickerson, and Brenner have all argued that neurotic behavior and gambling are not necessarily directly linked at all. The most persuasive presentation of this position is in Abt et al., in both their book *The Business of Risk* and its succinct recapitulation ("Misconceptions Abound"). They make useful distinctions between conventional and nonconventional gambling (they see all conventional gambling as "play"), and between obsessive and compulsive gambling. Obsessive gambling, while it is nonconventional behavior and "perversion of play," is "not sick in a clinical sense. Control is a fundamental characteristic of *all* obsessive behavior" (*The Business of Risk*, 123). "For most people," they conclude, "gambling is a healthy recreation. It provides escape from both the uncertainty and the boring routine of modern life by reinforcing, in familiar and highly ritualized surroundings, conventions and roles that let gamblers feel, at least for the duration of the game, that they are the masters of their fates" ("Misconceptions Abound," 417).

Their argument seems to be supported by Oldman's; their research by Wagenaar's. Oldman isolates a need to win money and a hope to win money, along with the long-shot possibility of hitting a jackpot of money, as factors that contribute to a "hopeless optimism" (368) in the face of expectations of losing money because of house odds. Wagenaar's studies have led him to question the "truth . . . that gamblers do not generally consider amusement more important than winning." Like most contemporary observers, he also rejects the "wish to lose" as a significant motivation: "gamblers continue to gamble and to lose, even though they want to win, and hate losing" (103).

Where Lesieur points to the gambler's *concentration on money,* Wagenaar suggests that "it is true that money constitutes one of the most potent rewards, sought by all gamblers" (85). Note the phrase "one of"; in the same study, Wagenaar devised experiments to test Lesieur's thesis that "*the major objective* of gambling is amusement and excitement" (43, emphasis mine); although he failed to find majority support among those tested, it is important to note that he was testing a different sample of a different population from those of Lesieur.

18. The possibilities are seemingly endless for symbolic interpretation of gambling. To take a novel example from the fiction of the irrepressible Jack Butler, he has a character theorize—at a group therapy session, no less—that "gambling is a psychological orgasm, because money, if you lose you're the man spraying it out, and if you win they're coming in you and making you pregnant so that's your wish to acknowledge your feminine side and yet at the same time be a winner" (138).

19. This is a premise of Findlay's *People of Chance,* which he begins by quoting Tocqueville, who observed in 1835, "Those who live in the midst of democratic fluctuations have always before their eyes the image of chance; and they end by liking all undertakings in which chance plays a part" (3).

20. Congressional proposals typically ignore this recommendation. A case in point is Lindsey Graham's H.R. 3575 "Student-Athlete Protection Bill," a well-intentioned initiative to ban all betting on college sports (currently stalled in the Judiciary Committee). One unintended consequence of such legislation would be to provide a bonanza for illegal bookies, especially in Nevada, and for on-line offshore betting operations (other proposed legislation would outlaw the latter—but how it could be enforced is a major question). The NCAA supports this legislation, presumably because it shares with its congressional supporters the wish to protect student-athletes from the pressures of having their activities the subject of wagering, plus the desire to send a message to the athletes that betting is illegal. But if zero tolerance of gambling by its athletes is the goal, it is hard to see how driving further underground an activity in which most of them—and a substantial portion of athletic staffs as well—are involved could be successful. Why make it even more difficult than it is now to identify the participants? Loss of eligibility and scholarships by athletes who gamble on sports could be clearly mandated and should be consis-

tently enforced by the NCAA and its member institutions. The *appearance* of actively opposing a practice that is widely tolerated is unlikely to reassure or disarm an increasingly savvy public.

2. Gambling and the Irrational

1. I would agree with Abt et al. that there is a kind of rationality that informs the behavior of most gamblers: "gamblers are realistically aware of their chances of winning and conduct their wagering with deliberation and disciplined concentration." Again, "each gamble is evaluated according to odds, expected return, alternative betting opportunities, and a number of other structural characteristics" ("Misconceptions Abound," 405).

But some arguments for the "rationality" of gambling are spurious. David Ramsey Steele, for example, puts the case that for someone needing a million dollars to be "saved from a painful and potentially fatal disease" to play the lottery would be rational, while not to would be "contemptible" (233). Would holding up a Brink's truck, then, also be rational, and not to do so also contemptible? What makes either act irrational is that one has about as much chance of getting away with the holdup as of winning the lottery.

2. The way we use language may be the best indication of the way the human brain/mind works. See the remarkably readable work of Steven Pinker, for example, *How the Mind Works* and *The Language Instinct*.

3. Knapp discusses how Balzac, in *The Wild Ass's Skin*, symbolically equates entering a gambling den with losing one's "thinking faculties" (47). The irrationality of gambling is necessarily a focus of cognitive-learning and cognitive-behavioral treatment and theory. See, e.g., Walker, *The Psychology of Gambling*; Ladouceur et al.; Blaszczynski and Silove.

4. The sexual charge of much gambling experience, not to mention the erotic ambience of many gambling settings, has often been dramatized but rarely analyzed. It may always be found in scenes where James Bond goes to a casino, for example, and is brilliantly enacted in the London casino scene from John Cassavetes's *Husbands*, where a wrinkled but wealthy crone attempts a seduction with the line, "You want girls, I'll get you girls; you want boys, I'll get you boys." The erotics of gambling is a subject crying out for exploration.

5. In more technical terms, the house seems to be relying on perceived empirical evidence of recursive sets and stochastic patterns, rather than on the demonstrable unpredictability of Poisson distributions.

Downes et al. cite the unpublished dissertation of a student of Talcott Parsons, Edward C. Devereux (also cited by Rosecrance, *Gambling without Guilt*), to the effect that "while gamblers affect the cognitive detachment of rational, economic man, as in the attention paid to odds and probabilities, and in the cold-blooded reaction to success or failure, the façade hides the fact that each stake placed at hazard subjects the gambler to a 'veritable emotional shower bath . . . to the flesh and blood gambler, the situation is full of promise, but it is also full of mystery, and danger, and meaning

... it is also fraught with strain: the conflicting valences and ambivalences of hope versus fear, risk versus security, power versus helplessness, and faith versus doubt are playing complicated melodies within his consciousness. The result is an intolerable, but not necessarily wholly unpleasant, state of tension'" (20). Downes goes on to list eight irrational motivations for gambling:

1. protest against budgetary constraints
2. protest against rationality
3. protest against ethics
4. thrill-seeking
5. competitiveness and aggression
6. problem-solving (as game-playing)
7. teleological motivations (counter-religious, testing luck, imbued with cosmic significance)
8. extrinsic or contextual behavior (social pressures, symbolic associations, preceding intrinsic interest in event as justification) (24–26)

To the extent that these motivations provide for social, emotional, and psychological needs, their irrationality may be said to have a rational, not merely rationalized, basis. See also Abt et al., "Misconceptions Abound."

6. The relationships between specific personality disorders and pathological gambling will be addressed in some detail in chapter 10. A case like Riche's, specifically, would primarily be labeled with Antisocial Personality Disorder (and very likely, if treated as a child or adolescent, would have been diagnosed with Oppositional Defiant Disorder). Not just antiestablishment but resistent to any kind of authority, this sort of person is also characteristically a loner with no allegiance even to antiestablishmentarian groups. Like other personality-disordered types (especially in the Narcissistic and Borderline Personality Disorders), he has few if any intimate or enduring personal relationships and relates to others as if they exist only as partial extensions of himself.

7. The trickster figure is examined in books by Lewis Hyde, *Trickster Makes the World: Mischief, Myth, and Art* (New York: North Point Press, 1998), and by Fred Allen Wolf, *The Spiritual Universe: One Physicist's Vision of Spirit, Soul, Matter, and Self* (Portsmouth, N.H.: Moment Point Press, 1999), but the seminal work is Paul Radin's *The Trickster: A Study in American Indian Mythology* (New York: Schocken Books, 1987), which includes commentaries by C.G. Jung and by Karl Kerenyi.

8. The role of aggression in gambling behaviors is addressed by Lindner. See chapter 9, note 3.

9. In treatment of pathological gambling, strict adherence to "normal time" may be a useful focus. Taber, Ingersoll, and McCormick say, "In a good therapeutic milieu the gambler who judges time, for example, by his own needs rather than the needs of anyone else is forced to adjust to a rigid schedule and is confronted with his egocentric clock" (148).

10. The phrase is George T. Wright's, as lucidly presented in his award-winning essay, "The Lyric Present."

3. The High-Profile Profile

1. Indeed, as Corky reported to me with considerable chagrin, Pete was within hours of entering a Custer program when his agent made the deal with the commissioner that would keep him out of baseball, out of the Hall of Fame, and out in the freedom to continue his gambling. Pete Rose's characteristic, overdefended denial thus deflected his best hope for change, for a chance to redeem himself and his reputation. That would have had to begin with acknowledgment of pathology. Both his denial and his cultivation of the company of enablers apparently persist to this day, to the frustration and sadness of baseball fans throughout the world. He continues his campaign to end the lifetime ban and become eligible for election to the Hall of Fame but is not willing to pay the price of giving up his gambling activities.

2. For examples, see the feature story by Bill Brubaker in the *Washington Post* and the article by Geoffrey Norman in *Sports Illustrated* in April and May of 1991, respectively.

3. The phenomenal growth of day trading is producing a whole new generation of pathological gamblers. For far too many, electronic expertise facilitates Internet gambling that encompasses both traditional forms of gaming and market speculation. The same sets of symptoms, from preoccupation to addiction, mark both activities, and for many "players" they alternate and overlap. Treatment providers must recognize and include these activities in their understanding of the contemporary epidemic of pathological gambling.

4. Memoir writing may provide valuable data for the understanding and treatment of pathological gambling, but it presents problems of reliability, depending in part on the context. For example, is the memoir a response to questions with an implied agenda, an approach to the art form of the nonfiction novel, a "confession" or *apologia pro vita sua*, a presentation structured by the format of presentation (as in GA meetings)? The "autobiography" so highly valued in Custer-style treatment is likely to be informed by a variety of devices and material conventional to such narratives.

5. Brian Castellani attributes this preponderance to the "discursive strategies used by researchers to understand exactly how the medical model is applied" (49); he finds that 76 percent of the articles published over a thirteen-year span in the *Journal of Gambling Studies* support the medical model's dominance, while the others discussed epidemiological, demographic, policy, political, social, economic, and sociological issues. He concludes, "Researchers situate pathological gambling this way because of its DSM diagnosis" (52).

6. Other significant factors may be overlooked or disregarded: differentiating symptoms, underlying conditions, et al. This is an entropic process, in which the energy devoted to diagnosis is lost or diverted in the effort to force symptoms to fit into a preconceived pattern. Treatment is inevitably weakened or undercut by such dissipation of energy.

7. The DSM's multiaxial system is designed to support a biopsychosocial model of evaluation, to provide a convenient format for citing clinical information, to capture "the complexity of clinical situations," to "describe the heterogeneity of indi-

viduals presenting with the same diagnosis," and above all to "facilitate comprehensive and systematic evaluation with attention to the various mental disorders and general medical conditions, psychosocial and environmental problems, and level of functioning that might be overlooked if the focus were on assessing a single presenting problem" (DSM-IV, 25). Its five axes are (I) clinical disorders and other conditions that may be a focus of clinical attention, (II) personality disorders and mental retardation, (III) general medical conditions, (IV) psychosocial and environmental problems, and (V) global assessment of functioning.

8. In another context I would call this case a miscarriage of justice. Herman was the only gambler caught in a sting operation that had gone on for two years (and netted dozens of petty criminals). Yet, as he knew, any serious bettor with gambling contacts could have been directed to major bookmaking operations in Herman's city and county. In any case, the extension of RICO laws to incorporate small-time bookmaking is like shooting at flies with an elephant gun and it goes against the explicit original intent of the legislation.

9. I am reminded, incidentally, of a column written by Courtland Milloy, an African American columnist for the *Washington Post*, after a visit to Tunica County, Mississippi. Milloy praises the riverboat casinos as a place where tensions and discriminations of race and class are overcome by the shared play of gamblers rubbing shoulders: in social terms, large and small, apparently, gambling can be beneficial, can facilitate a clearing of barriers.

5. Gambling and Anxiety

1. Though there has been debate over the *degree* of correlation between anxiety disorders and suicide, Jamison's profound *Night Falls Fast: Understanding Suicide* cites eight recent studies to support her conclusions: "Anxiety disorders . . . definitely increase the chances of suicide. . . . Panic attacks are also associated with an increased rate of suicide and suicide attempts. . . . [Frequent] panic attacks . . . may lead to a sense of despair and hopelessness. . . . Severe anxiety, like severe agitation, is a potent predictor of suicide" (121). Despite these conclusions and the abnormally high rate of suicide among pathological gamblers, it is surprising to find only a single mention in Jamison's book of gambling as a factor: "For those with a short wick, a savage temper, and impulse-laden wiring, life's setbacks and illnesses are more dangerous. For them, it is as though the nervous system had been soaked in kerosene: a fight with a lover, a gambling loss or a run-in with the law, or an irritable flash from a mental illness can ignite a suicidal response" (197).

2. The National Research Council reports, "Little is known about the association of anxiety disorders and problem gambling. Only two studies of pathological gamblers in treatment have reported an increased prevalence of anxiety . . . , yet the numbers are so small that the meaning is questionable" (138). Nevertheless, Valerie Lorenz, Executive Director of the Compulsive Gambling Center in Baltimore, has told me that it is very important at intake of pathological gamblers to assess the level of anxiety they are experiencing.

A possible example of an anxiety disorder in a gambler is the case of Stephan Jarvis, whose "medical confession" (as Castellani calls it) was published in 1988. "If Jarvis was admitted to the psychiatric ward instead of a prison," Castellani says, "he would probably be diagnosed with Post Traumatic Stress Disorder. Watching his father die [in a boating accident when Jarvis was ten] was too much. Jarvis broke down and never fully recovered" (154). Instead he was living out—for the sixth time—a cycle of gambling, check kiting, and imprisonment.

There is, however, no clinical record of OCD sufferers exhibiting pathological gambling behaviors. By far the largest ongoing study of OCD is being administered at NIH. I have been checking periodically with people engaged in that study, and I have been assured that they have found *not one single* case in which OCD had been manifested in gambling behaviors. Hollander disagrees, inferring that pathological gambling and OCD are closely related (see, especially, Hollander and Benzaquen).

Arguing inferentially against Hollander's minority view is Jamison's report, *Night Falls Fast*: "Surprisingly, and uniquely among the major mental illnesses, obsessive-compulsive disorder seems not to put those who suffer from it at an increased risk for suicide" (121–22), with ample citations for support (349).

For generally well-informed laypersons, a major source of confusion is the overlapping terminology of another condition, Obsessive-Compulsive Personality Disorder, which may well include symptoms of maladaptive gambling behavior. Incidentally, the most effective tricyclic antidepressant for the treatment of OCD is also highly effective in treating Trichotillomania. This provides a hint that over time some forms of pathological gambling may be found to be responsive to medication, particularly if Hollander is right.

6. Gambling and Depression

1. See John Russell's definitive analysis of this artistic prose genre, *Reciprocities in the Nonfiction Novel*. The blurring of boundaries among genres is another reason to reject the rigid rule of certain social scientists who will accept the validity of reportage or autobiography (regardless of distortions and self-deception) and reject all fiction (regardless of profound and comprehensive portraits).

2. See chapter 2, note 4.

3. E.g., Crockford and el-Guebaly, and McCormick et al., "Affective Disorders." Cunningham-Williams et al. found problem gamblers significantly more likely to report depressive symptoms.

4. For the always troublesome transliteration of Russian names, I have in most cases simply adopted Frank's spellings.

5. Dostoevsky continues to be a fascinating figure for imaginative recreation, as the novels of Tsypkin and Peri Rossi demonstrate. J.M. Coetzee's 1994 *The Master of Petersburg* is yet another impressive example. Coetzee places Dostoevsky in St. Petersburg in the fall of 1869, following the death of his stepson, Pavel Ivanaev, probably by suicide. It is a wholesale invention: Pavel did not die until many years later, and

Dostoevsky apparently left Germany during this time only for brief sojourns in Italy. Coetzee's invention serves the purpose of imagining the origins of The Devils in this "experience" (Coetzee's last chapter is called "Stavrogin" and contains not only a sketch of the Lebyakins, who play a significant part in Dostoevsky's novel, but also two passages purporting to be "drafts" of material for that novel, material I have not been able to locate in any translation). Coetzee focuses on Doestoevsky's eroticism, including a tendency toward pedophilia, and delves into his epilepsy, mysticism, and religious and political thinking.

Though the period in question marks the acme of Dostoevsky's gambling fixation, Coetzee refers in only four brief passages to that preoccupation. These fragments, however, are instructive for our purposes. In the first, numbers on gravestones trigger superstitious thoughts that he attempts to block (suggesting obsessive-compulsive symptoms), giving way then to a philosophical speculation: "he thinks: there are no final numbers, all are provisional, otherwise the play would come to an end. In a while the wheel will roll, the numbers will start moving, and all will be well again" (8). The anarchist Nachaev, whom Coetzee imagines as a transvestite, taunts Dostoevsky for his cheapness, saying he can't believe he is really a gambler because "I thought gamblers didn't care about money. But there is a second side to gambling, isn't there? . . . You must be the kind who gambles because he is never satisfied, who is always greedy for more" (158). Coetzee's Dostoevsky, however, meditates on the metaphsyics of gambling. Wondering if betting on all the numbers is still gambling, he speculates, "Without the risk, without subjecting oneself to the voice speaking from elsewhere in the fall of the dice, what is left that is divine? Surely God knows that, and will have mercy on the gambler-at-heart!" (84). Finally, he relates other problematic behaviors to gambling: "He is in the old labyrinth. It is the story of his gambling in another guise. He gambles because God does not speak. He gambles to make God speak. But to make God speak in the turn of a card is blasphemous. Only when God is silent does God speak. When God seems to speak God does not speak" (237). I need hardly say that Coetzee's Dostoevsky is yet another depiction of the internal turbulence of a manic-depressive.

6. Richard Rosenthal, for one, expresses dismay at Freud's focus and at the subsequent misunderstandings to which it has led ("Psychodynamics").

7. "Dostoevsky: The Idea of The Gambler," an essay by the British poet D.S. Savage, long held sway as the prevailing interpretation. Published in the Sewanee Review in 1950, it could be included, virtually verbatim, in a 1984 volume called Dostoevsky: New Perspectives. The "idea" was that Aleksey's experience enacted a crisis of faith, representative of Dostoevsky's own and his major theme in the major novels. Joseph Frank, noting that a single remark in a letter describing a conception that would evolve into The Gambler could hardly be persuasive when the text itself provides no support for that interpretation, overthrew Savage's interpretive hegemony. Frank's essay focuses on the novella's ethnic stereotyping as its essential thematic concern, as his title suggests ("The Gambler: A Study in Ethnopsychology"). As a biographer, Frank rejects the notion of the book as mere autobiographic projection, arguing for its artistic accomplishment in transmuting autobiographical material. In his view,

Aleksey's pathological gambling is more chronic than Dostoevsky's own, though it expresses the author's view of roulette as perfectly suited to the Russian temperament and nature, as opposed to the French or the German.

Frank makes much of the fact that Dostoevsky gambled only when abroad and of his wife's report that when his gambling had exhausted all available funds he would plunge into redemptive periods of intense literary productivity (321–22). What Frank fails to understand is the nature of Dostoevsky's pathological gambling (and to a certain extent Aleksey's as well), so he accepts rationalizations of and pretexts and justifications for gambling. Neither Dostoevsky himself, nor his wife (a textbook enabler), nor his protagonist fully understood this, either. Feodor and Aleksey would always find reasons or excuses for their gambling; that is in the nature of the pathology.

Inevitably, the *Journal of Gambling Studies* would have to present a "book review" of *The Gambler.* So, in 1991, 135 years after its publication, Dostoevsky's novel was "reviewed" by Robert Wildman, who concluded that its "empirically discovered facets of problem gambling" have been ignored by previous commentators (who focus on "signs of psychodynamic causes [that] are almost totally lacking in the work"). Wildman found those facets "so clearly present as to literally jump off the page" (*sic*, 174).

8. My view (diagnosis) is substantially supported by Knapp. Aleksey's "mood swings are dramatic and increasingly frequent," she says (104), and again: "Even his mood swings are no longer predictable. To add to his anxieties are the nightmarish fantasies that haunt him—most overtly, that he might be insane and incarcerated in a lunatic asylum" (119). I depart from her analysis, however, in several ways: her assessment of Granny is more positive; she omits Astley from the cast and its love relationships; and she insists (98, 119) that Aleksey is a writer intent on publishing his diary to recoup his gambling losses. Since he never explicitly states this in the diary, and since the timeline strongly suggests that the diary begins before he even starts gambling, Knapp's unlikely inference seems to be yet another conflation of author and character—perhaps not unlike my own.

9. Jamison (*An Unquiet Mind*) and Styron provide riveting accounts of such experience. Another case in point is presented in *The Loser,* billed as "The Confessions of a Compulsive Gambler," by William S. Hoffman Jr. Hoffman narrates his extended ventures into self-destructive gambling, supported by his extraordinary ability to get people to cash his worthless checks. From racetrack to casino, from poker parlor back to the track, Hoffman kept coming close to winning enough to satisfy his creditors, only to blow his whole stake in a desperate and grandiose gamble to accelerate the process. Along the way he suggests causative factors for his pathological behavior: a hateful mother who continually threatened reform school and once punished him by not talking to him for four years; a father who was a legendary four-sport coach, whose focus on winning was internalized by his unathletic son into a hunger for quick success; a strict Catholic education that somehow convinced him that failure, disaster, and damnation were inevitable despite his intellect, talents, and charm. On the final page of the book, Hoffman says he is "now . . . getting the

help it seems was badly needed. The gambling seems to be a thing of the past. . . . I suppose it is just possible . . . that I was the victim of something I didn't cause; it is certain that in my confused and uncoordinated and frantic quest for mental tranquility that what happened is the last thing I could have wanted" (181). Just what that help is, he doesn't say. He had tried GA without commitment, without success. He had tried to engineer a reconciliation with his wife and children but never met the conditions she had demanded (now newly determined to try yet again). He had tried repeatedly to plunge into work, multiple jobs providing occupation and preoccupation but inevitably new opportunities to gamble and new sources for cashing checks. What is missing from this account is a proper diagnosis, though the symptoms leap (figuratively) floridly from the page.

Hoffman's manipulativeness seems transparently an exercise in resentful revenge since he regularly targets people connected either directly with the church and Jesuit educational institutions or with former employers. Finally, he uses the cash from kited checks not for gambling but to support dirty tricks directed at his rejecting wife. Still, the personality disorders suggested by this behavior seem secondary to a more essential primary disorder. As a friendly boss once said to him, "There's a demon in you" (61). That "demon" is manic-depressive disease.

The depression is apparent throughout, in the lack of self-worth, the sense of hopelessness, the pervasive anxiousness. The manic features are even more obvious: the false sense of omnipotence, the boundless energy when gambling despite not eating or sleeping, the episodes of "generosity" even when gambling. The brief glimpse of himself as standing "on the corner of a D.C. slum . . . a strange sight, clothes wrinkled and soiled, passing out twenty-dollar bills" (178) is a textbook illustration of a full-blown manic episode.

Compulsive gambler? Sure, as a symptomatic expression of bipolar disorder. J. Livingston, however, in *Compulsive Gamblers: Observations on Action and Abstinence*, apparently accepts Hoffman's as a representative case, and this, for me, supports my supposition that pathological gambling symptoms *often* mask manic-depressive illness. See Niederland for an earlier account of gambling masking depression.

7. Gambling and Psychosis

1. The brief scene (213–19) takes place in Denmark's "most prestigious casino," where the "gambling bug" is called a "parasite . . . a little animal [that] takes up residence inside you" as soon as you buy your chips. Smilla observes that the "room is tense with deep concentration" and the players' faces "absorbed, enraptured . . . like empty shells. At that moment it's practically impossible to imagine that they have any life outside this room. Maybe they don't." She is told that all the different people there "have one thing in common. They're losers, Smilla. In the long run they all lose." As for Captain Lukas, his "parasite . . . has eaten him up from the inside and now takes up more room than he does." He gambles every night at the casino, until he is broke, then goes to sea for six months to make enough money to play again.

2. Joseph Frank, in *The Miraculous Years* (73f), sees "The Queen of Spades" as a forerunner of *Crime and Punishment*.

3. In Tchaikovsky's derivative opera, *Pique Dame*, both Hermann and the Countess are habitual gamblers, and he is in love with Lisa, who is the Countess's granddaughter. More melodramatically, that is, operatically, Lisa kills herself when Hermann refuses to carry out the betting scheme, and Hermann kills himself when the scheme fails. The passion is magnified—and diminished; there is neither madness nor psychological insight into gambling, but instead passion and greed. For a musical appreciation of Pushkin, probably Prokofiev's incidental music for "The Queen of Spades" is more nearly satisfactory. But musical genius is not necessarily incompatible with problem gambling, as we have seen in William Murray's character Fulvio Gasparini, and as we find in no less a personage than Richard Wagner, who said of his youthful gambling excesses, "The despair over my lack of good luck flared my passion into an insane craving."

4. Knapp's illuminating discussion of this Poe story thoroughly probes its symbols of and associations with psychosis. This can go too far, I think, when the mirror in the climactic scene is taken as a far-reaching, polysemous symbol (93–94), when in the text it is primarily just a mirror. I also object to the assertion, "To conceal cards in one's sleeves is not unusual for inveterate gamblers" (90), which leads to symbolic interpretations of the sleeve as a "dark, tubelike space." Most gamblers are not cheats; the odds are that gamblers with cards up their sleeves will not survive to become inveterate.

5. Knapp notes, "Stephan Zweig's 'The Gambler' is, for some, a metaphor of his obsessive suicidal tendencies" (11). Freud's conflation of Zweig and Dostovesky here extends to their titles.

6. In "Taking Chances: Problem Gamblers and Mental Health Disorders—Results from St. Louis Epidemiologic Catchment Area (ECA) Study," Cunningham-Williams et al. report a 3.9 percent correlation of problem gambling and schizophrenia (6 of 161), compared to 1.1 percent among nongamblers (15 of 1543) and 0.7 percent (12 of 1250) among recreational gamblers. In this sample, schizophrenia occurred twice as often as manic episodes, more often than obsessive-compulsive disorder (4) or panic disorder (5), but significantly less often than generalized anxiety disorder (13), major depression (15), phobias (32), and antisocial personality disorder (64). See chapter 10, note 2.

7. As an example of the relative strength and persuasiveness of clinical literature vis-à-vis creative literature, I suggest the following. See Frieda Fromm-Reichmann's lucid and illuminating published accounts of a case of schizophrenia, all interpolated into theoretical discussions (Bullard, 192f, 190, 196f, 204, 206f, 213); then read the imaginatively reconstructed accounts of the *same* case by Joanne Greenberg (*I Never Promised You a Rose Garden* [New York: Holt, Rinehart and Winston, 1964], published originally under the name Hannah Green—the author was the patient) and J.R. Salamanca (*Lilith* [New York: Simon and Schuster, 1961]), both of which provide the reader, I believe, with richer, multidimensional versions of the schizo-

phrenic experience. Evelyne Keitel, who compares Fromm-Reichmann's and Greenberg's versions of the "story" (apparently unaware of Salamanca's), argues that "psychoanalytical case histories contain features of literary discourse," including a "convention . . . of inserting short fragments of actual cases into theoretical treatises [with] the use of a different typeface" (58).

8. In *The Facts* (1988), Roth credits ex-GIs as his "only real tutors" in his adolescent education in gambling: "Under the bleachers in the playground [near Weequaihic] they taught us how to shoot craps and to play five-card stud with change stolen from our mothers' purses and our fathers' trouser pockets" (37).

8. Filling the Void

1. In Kevin Canty's *Rounders*, a novel based on the screenplay, Mike says, "I felt alive for the first time since. . . . Can't you understand that?" And Jo says, "Understand? You just said you felt alive for the first time sitting at a card table. What's that supposed to make me understand?" (83). Much is lost in the attempt to render the nuanced and textured film narrative as first-person narration, though the dialogue on the page occasionally makes the points more clearly explicit.

2. The language of "object relations" theory gives us another way to describe the process by which "existence pain" leads to what I call void-filling behaviors. I take my example from Althea J. Horner's *Psychoanalytic Object Relations Therapy*, in a passage where she is discussing a patient with problematic patterns of sexual behavior:

> As with any obsession or with a compulsive acting out, one asks, "What is the psychological function of the symptom? Why is it necessary?" As we can construct a sense of the internalized chaos that would evolve out of the early interpersonal matrix, Charlie would have to find a way to contain and bind anxiety and a way to give him a sense of himself as existing. For Charlie the issues are primarily existential, with a constant fight against the terror of annihilation of the self. How can he convince himself that he exists? The use of the body is often the only anchor in the presence of annihilation terror. Charlie felt very powerful after a sexual experience, but as a chronically needed antidote to feelings of terror and nonexistence, his symptoms were in the nature of an addiction that could quiet his fears but not resolve them. (249)

Substitute habitual gambling behaviors for this patient's sexual, addictive, "compulsive acting out," change the use of the body to the risking of stakes for external verification of self by chance or fate or luck, and you have a viable description of how gambling serves in the struggle against "internal chaos" or existential angst that characterizes the gamblers discussed in this chapter.

3. See Zinberg for a brief discussion of the usefulness of adapting the AA model to "other compulsive behaviors."

4. McCormick and Taber report a case in language which indicates the overlapping of concerns between this chapter and chapter 10: "By now life really consisted

of endless attempts to fill a keenly sensed internal void," they say. "Unfortunately, the inner void, the empty socket where no self had grown, required constant filling, but was unfillable" (33). They associate this patient's behavior and his "perfectionistic strivings" with "a narcissistic personality disorder" (34).

5. Knapp discusses the significance of archetypal numbers as ordering devices for humans since ancient times (110–12).

6. I can testify to the persistence of the gambling/sex metaphor surviving in common street parlance. As a young man in Venice, when I politely rebuffed the solicitation of a prostitute who accosted me as I was crossing the little bridge leading toward the Bauer Grunwald away from the Piazza San Marco, I explained that I could not afford to partake of her pleasures because I had lost all my money at the casino. It was, in fact, true; my friends and I had pooled our money at the Lido for one last play on the black at the roulette table, only to see the number fourteen come up—"*rouge, pair, et passe.*" Her sympathy was voluble, but it soon became apparent from her vehement diatribe against the "casino" that for her the word meant "brothel." See chapter 2, note 4.

9. Gambling and the Brothers Barthelme

1. Coincidentally, Elizabeth Spencer's elegant 1984 novel, *The Salt Line*, is also set in the Mississippi Gulf Coast, but at a time when the only organized gambling is in the windowless rooms of a mob-connected restaurateur's establishment. Struggling to rebuild after Hurricane Camille (1969) has devastated it, the Coast is reproducing the very detritus that Ray laments: "The Coast now is nothing but the bones of itself" (10), Spencer's protagonist says, and he has a number of projects going with an architect partner in an attempt to salvage something more worthy of the natural beauty and heritage of the area. What Spencer calls Southern Pines University in Hartsville is apparently in large part a version of Southern Mississippi State University in Hattiesburg, where the Barthelmes teach. Of course, the Barthelmes' father was an architect, so there should be no suspicion of "influence," though the novels have common themes of generation and rebirth.

2. The boredom of a gambler's life is captured brilliantly, that is to say, dully, in Paul Thomas Anderson's movie *Hard Eight*. The life of the protagonist (Philip Baker Hall) is one of unremitting, fastidious tedium, and even the presence of Gwyneth Paltrow and Samuel L. Jackson in the cast cannot relieve the somber, depressive atmosphere of a de-glamorized, tarnished-glitzy Las Vegas. That superficial glamour is what prevails in Andres Martinez's *24/7: Living It Up and Doubling Down in the New Las Vegas* (New York: Villard, 1999). See Blaszczynski, McConaghy, and Frankova's report on "Boredom Proneness in Pathological Gambling."

3. Mike Hodges and his writer Paul Mayersberg run an interesting variation on this theme in their recent movie *Croupier*. The title character is a would-be novelist, Jack Manfred (Clive Owen), who works as a dealer in a London club while composing a fiction based on his firsthand experience there. His protagonist, Jake, takes on an identity of his own, and Jack becomes aware that sometimes he is acting unlike

himself, that Jake is living Jack's "life" in ways that Jack would avoid. When his novel, "I, Croupier," is published and becomes a best-seller, Jack, knowing he's a one-book writer, takes great satisfaction that it was published anonymously, that only he knows who Jake is—and he has fused Jake upon Jack (and vice versa) without anyone knowing.

The movie depicts the gambling scene as well as any I have seen. Among Jack's/Jake's voice-over observations is the notion that most gamblers don't, as many believe, want to lose or hurt themselves by losing, but instead really want to punish everyone else (or the house) by beating them—a long-shot proposition, but worth the chance because the satisfaction of that aggressive wish would be the more delightful for being perceived as benign luck and not malignant triumph. We get no sense that such an idea has occurred to Ray and Jewel, or to Rick and Steve.

10. Gambling and Personality Disorders

1. I cannot overemphasize the importance of the distinction between Obsessive-Compulsive Disorder (OCD) and Obsessive-Compulsive Personality Disorder. The former, like its biochemical sibling Trichotillomania (and its consanguineous cousin Tourette's Disorder), is usually responsive to medication. Its symptomatic behaviors are not only involuntary but *unwanted* (ego-dystonic); moreover, the behavior is a significant, often crippling obstacle to normal functioning. Paradoxically, though the more severe of the two conditions, it is far more readily accessible to treatment.

2. This diagnostic problem was addressed by Alida Mixson Glen in the very first issue of the *Journal of Gambling Behavior* (1985), and has received continued attention (e.g., by Blaszczynski and Steel). Another dimension of the problem, however, has not been addressed. The criminal behavior considered symptomatic of Antisocial Personality Disorder in pathological gamblers is typically the *result* of the desperation that accompanies excessive losses. Fraud, forgery, and larceny are last-resort remedies for otherwise unpayable debts—and of course a last hope to stay in action with *restitution of illegally obtained funds* as a conscious intention (or pretext). Habitual cheating is so rare among habitual gamblers that any correlation of APD with pathological gambling would seem to be the result of a strongly skewed sample. The gambling having become pathological, the gambler *begins* to exhibit symptoms of APD, primarily among those pathological gamblers who have been apprehended for the criminal behavior and diagnosed as pathological gamblers. Strong correlations of APD and pathological gambling are commonly recorded; see, e.g., Cunningham-Williams et al. and *Brown University Digest*, but see chapter 12, note 8 for discussion of problems with statistical demonstrations of correlation.

3. It has been pointed out to me that the gross distortions of reality in the generation of a fantasy world in this movie resemble those of the "fantasy world" GA members talk about (See, e.g., the GA pamphlet "The Combo Book"). Rather than disqualifying *The Gambler* from consideration, these corresponding distortions

give us illuminating insights into the gamblers' own experiences of fantasy and distortion. In another movie, Ron Moler's *The Runner* (1999), the bizarre fantasy world of a pathological gambler in Las Vegas enacts a paranoid projection of a world controlled by a maniacal but all-knowing gambler (a bravura performance by John Goodman), a world in which the metaphor of "losing wife and child to the disease" takes on a literal reality.

4. One of my students, Paul Monusky, has suggested another indication of narcissism. After the fixed basketball game, Hips assumes the corrupted player will be willing to do business again; but Axel tells him he won't, because, "He only did it for me." The idea that there could be a direct connection between *his* student and *his* bookie, without himself as the hub of the wheel, is inconceivable to him.

5. I called this the Icarus Syndrome long before I came across Jack Richardson's observation, upon arrival in Las Vegas, that "millions of dollars waited for the one who could confound the laws of probability—*the Icarus in every gambler* was beginning to slip on his wings" (37, emphasis mine).

6. This dialogue appears intact in Jim Mortimore's novelization of the first episode (*Cracker: The Mad Woman in the Attic* [New York: St. Martin's, 1994]).

7. This analysis is based entirely on the original English series, not the American spinoff—or ripoff—that has cannibalized whole scenarios and even dialogue from the English version without apparent comprehension of the material.

Is it possible to "diagnose" a fictional character at all? Consider that the ten episodes under consideration constitute about as much time spent "with" the individual as ten fifty-minute-hour sessions in treatment, not to mention the advantage of being able to re-view videotapes. Any therapist so informed of the life story of a "client" or "patient" had better be able to arrive at a diagnosis—or find some way to finesse the next examination for licensing or certification. Nor is it necessary for the character to be portrayed in the process of psychiatric treatment, like Tony Soprano in many episodes of *The Sopranos* series on HBO.

8. It seemed to me that Yalom's naming technique might have been a bit heavy-handed here: Ernest Lash, an earnest self-flagellator, vs. Marshal Streider, a martial strider, a dogged exerciser who in college was a tenacious linebacker. But Yalom was kind enough to read a draft of these pages and wrote me that I had it wrong, that what he had in mind was "an old-time U.S. Marshal riding into town" and "lash to the mast of reason like Ulysses to resist the siren's call." There are lessons here for onomastic presumption in literary criticism.

9. The plot of *Rounders* revolves around this element of the game, which is the key to winning and losing in Texas Hold 'Em, the game played in most big-league poker tournaments, including the World Series of Poker. See Seth Stevenson's "A Straight Face" for a brief account of the psychology of tells and bluffing.

10. See R. Victor and C. Krug, "'Paradoxical Intention' in the Treatment of Compulsive Gambling"; more generally, Seltzer's *Paradoxical Strategies in Psychotherapy*. Paradoxical approaches, in my view, are for the most part misguided, desperate, dangerous, and perhaps unethical, particularly in treating gamblers who may well

take a "paradoxical" instruction as yet another excuse or justification to gamble and lose even more. Behavioral approaches including imaginal desensitization and aversive therapy are discussed in McConaghy et al.

11. Gambling and Addiction

1. The value of treating pathological gambling as if it were addiction per se is addressed by Jacobs ("A General Theory of Addiction: Application"). But Dr. Winograd's careful application of criteria should serve as a caution against casual use of the term, lest it lead to trivializing the condition (and diminishing public concern). Brenner, for example, speaking of "the hope and opportunities for the casualties of dynamic societies" (140) provided by progressive legalization of gambling, acknowledges "the presence of addicted players. But gambling is a mass phenomenon," he goes on to say, "and its study must not be confused with that of a pathological minority of compulsive gamblers, just as the examination of a few workaholics, alcoholics, obese people, womanizers, addicted TV watchers, and addicted exercisers is irrelevant for a social judgment on the behavior of the billions who work, drink, eat, love and/or have sex, watch TV or enjoy exercising with customary frequency" (141).

2. See, e.g., Carlton and Goldstein for developments in research along these lines. The evidence grows that there may be a biological/genetic predisposition to addictions in general in certain people. See also Blum et al.; Comings; and Comings et al.

3. This appears to be one of the lessons dramatized in Keith Ablow's first novel, *Denial* (New York: Pantheon, 1997). The narrator/protagonist is a forensic psychiatrist battling addictions to cocaine, alcohol, sex—and gambling. Ablow is a psychiatrist.

12. Dilemmas of Diagnosis and Treatment

1. The narrator of *Croupier* extends this globalizing cliché to "All gamblers are born liars."

2. Rosecrance ("Controlled Gambling") argues for "a promising future" for "controlled gambling," at least in some cases of "troubled" or "problem" gamblers. Castellani (171ff) strongly supports this view.

3. Castellani argues (193–98) for an "indexical diagnosis" to supplement the "categorical nomenclature" of the DSM's taxonomy (which sets patients up for relapse, in his view) and for a biopsychosocial framework to *replace* the medical model (as if they were mutually exclusive).

4. Many studies have shown an unusually high suicide rate among pathological gamblers consistently throughout the world. See, e.g., Sullivan (New Zealand), Schwarz and Linder (Germany), Moran, "Taking," (England), and McCormick et al., "Affective Disorders," (U.S.). "Gaming . . . appears to increase the suicide rate," concludes Rob Stein in a brief report of a study by sociologist David Phillips et al. "While the average U.S. county had a suicide rate of less than 1 percent of all deaths

among out-of-state visitors, the suicide rates among both visitors and residents were significantly higher in the gambling communities." Las Vegas has the highest suicide rate in the country, and unusually high suicide rates followed the opening of casinos in Atlantic City. Stein quotes the researchers as saying, "Our findings suggest but do not prove that gamblers experience abnormally high risks of suicide," and they added that increased suicides "do not seem to result merely because gaming settings attract suicidal individuals."

I would like to see a study measuring a correlation between rates of teenage suicide and the alarming reports of dramatic increase of teenagers diagnosed with pathological gambling. See, e.g., Shaffer et al. (*Estimating the Prevalence* and "Pathological Gambling") and the National Research Council's general conclusion that "the proportion of pathological gamblers among adolescents in the United States could be more than three times that of adults" (89).

For a brilliant fictional account of the progression of a gambling habit to pathology and ultimate suicide, I refer the reader to Eric Rolfe Greenberg's novel *The Celebrant* (New York: Penguin, 1986). Even more persuasively than Brendan Boyd's *Blue Ruin* (New York: Norton, 1991) or Eliot Asinof's *Eight Men Out* (New York: Holt, 1963), both of which dramatize the connections between baseball and gambling in the context of the "Black Sox" scandal of 1919, Greenberg's historical novel brings to life the cultural and philosophical issues that bind sports and gambling. But Art Schlichter, who lost his NFL career, wife, children, and freedom to his gambling addiction, may have said it best when he told *People* Magazine from prison in 1996, "When you start stealing from your family and friends, you know that it's only a matter of time before you're put in jail or you put a gun to your head" (cited in *Sports Illustrated*, May 29, 2000, 30).

5. See Barbieri for the notion of trendiness, Freiberg for the notion of epidemic. Sadly but perhaps not surprisingly, there are still some skeptics who reject the notion that alcoholism is a disease, others who insist that "mental illness" is an empty or wrongheaded concept, not only unprovable but therefore untenable. I call these true believers a latter-day branch of the Flat Earth Society. One possible source of confusion is the common phrase "medical model." The crucial word is *model*, which implies that certain conditions, like alcoholism and other addictions, may be effectively treated *as if* they were medical conditions (on models of medical treatments). It is not a wrongful application of the model simply because the conditions lack one or more elements of a technical definition of "disease" or "illness"; application of medical model has proven to be the most effective treatment of such conditions. Still, writers like Vatz and Weinberg ("Keno Krazy?") argue that since "there is no credible evidence of any neurochemical or neurophysiological status causally linked to heavy gambling," it cannot be called a disease and isn't even an addiction. Theirs is a clear example of argument by assertion, a spurious attempt to prove a negative. Nor is the argument strengthened by repetition ("Refuting the Myths" and "Heavy Gambling"). A full explication of that position, the rejection of problem gambling as addiction, disease, or pathology is found in Michael Walker's "The Medicalisation of Gambling as

an 'Addiction.'" Castellani, arguing from analyses of discourse, substantially concurs. Walker speaks of "the mistaken belief that drug abuse and heavy gambling are similar" and attributes dysfunctional and self-destructive gambling behavior to "personal failure." On the other hand, "personal failure" is not far removed from the concept of "personality disorder." Abt et al. state flatly, "Compulsive gambling is a manifestation of personality disorder" (*The Business of Risk*, 135), but this begs the question of whether personality disorders themselves are indeed diseases.

Andrew Beyer, who ranks with Audax Minor and Joe Palmer among the great chroniclers of horse racing in America, accepts without question the Vatz-Weinberg pronouncements. The headlines over a Beyer column said, "Compulsive Gamblers Are Not Victims" and "The Odds Are, Compulsive Gambling Is Not a Disease," but as my response said, "You cannot treat pyromaniacs, kleptomaniacs, bulimics, or addicts [other impulse-control disorders] by telling them to stop fooling around and just say 'no'" ("Compulsive Gambling Afflicts Millions"). A main problem with these nay-sayers is that nowhere in their rejections of a mental health/mental illness approach to problem gambling is there an alternative to the effective "medical model" therapies and the *as-*if implications of their application. It works. It really does. Keep coming back unless and until you find a better way.

6. This is not to suggest a concurrence of metaphors, but William Gass's encyclopedic novel, *The Tunnel*, contains a passage (577–82) in which the narrator recounts how, at ten or twelve years old, he would steal change from his parents to play the punchboards at the corner store. This "brief gambling career" ends with his father's discovery of the penny-pinching and his confession of the motivation—to gamble—is proved, after initial disbelief, because he has saved all his losing slips!

7. The samples come either from polled GA members or clinical cases diagnosed as compulsive or pathological gamblers; the studies cited are those by Moran ("An Assessment of Gambling"), Wong, Seager, Blaszcynski et al. ("Behavioral Treatment"), Moravec, Malkin, Custer and Milt, and McGlothin. McCormick and Taber join Dickerson in rejecting the notion of a "profile" (36–37), and Castellani's humane plea for case-by-case treatment clearly opposes profiling. *Gamblers Anonymous*, GA's compact statement of principles candidly derived from AA's *Big Book*, precedes the twelve steps with its own streamlined profile. Livingston, too, sketches a profile, not based on "some completely internal, immutable set of characteristics but rather a preference for certain behaviors in certain situations—that is, particular 'role enactments'" (25). Perhaps the most cogent argument against the monolithic profile is presented by Abt et al., who characterize the "binge" of popular and professional writing about gambling as "a marathon writing jag . . . a fog of verbiage, a wordy miasma of misconceptions, stereotypes, loaded buzzwords, and simple misinformation, through which the reality of gambling situations and gambling behavior has been almost wholly obscured" ("Misconceptions Abound," 395f).

8. Studies of pathological gambling may show a variety of limitations or weaknesses. They may be entirely anecdotal, involving one or two cases, or be severely biased by small samples carefully chosen. Even large samples may be skewed; the "Berkson bias" (from his 1946 study) may skew studies of comorbidity, since mul-

tiply diagnosed patients are more likely to be in treatment and therefore accessible for inclusion. Even the best of epidemiological studies, e.g., Cunningham-Williams et al. or *Brown University Digest*, may be skewed by the tendency of respondents in a general population to be suggestible, to associate symptoms of one condition with those of another.

9. Rosenthal's analysis of "The Pathological Gambler's System for Self-Deception" adds the mechanisms of *idealization, devaluation,* and *projective identification* to three I have listed (*denial, omnipotence,* and *splitting*). His comments on blaming and self-destructive fantasies suggest a sadomasochistic component in the disorder, a suggestion that could be supported by Novick and Novick's persuasive presentation in *Fearful Symmetry* of the essential connection between sadomasochism and fantasies of omnipotence.

10. An interesting outpatient approach reported by Walter Miller addresses the common occurrence of a "self-induced and self-escalating crisis" (95) that leads to treatment, and then the need to process the "loss of gambling" in terms of grieving. Miller implies a comprehension of concurrent psychiatric conditions that may be enacted in aberrant gambling behaviors. The difficulty in assessing treatment options for multiple conditions is addressed by Gambino.

11. These assertions are strongly supported in the lucid report of Clark Hudak et al. See also Lorenz, Franklin and Thoms, and Gaudia.

12. To complement the eclectic mix of modalities, or rather, treatment strategies, where spouses or families are engaged in the process, I also would apply general systems theory.

13. I ask the question in the spirit of Kay Redfield Jamison's remarks: "The very success of psychopharmacology in treating serious mental illness has had the unfortunate effect of minimizing the importance of psychotherapy in healing patients and keeping them alive. . . . Despite the extensive and elegant series of studies conducted by Myrna Weissman and Gerald Klerman at Yale University, which showed that the combination of pyschotherapy and antidepressants was more effective in treating depression than either treatment alone, and despite convincing recent work . . . demonstrating better outcomes in bipolar and schizophrenic patients who receive a combination of medications and psychotherapy rather than drugs only, there remains a pervasive belief in many psychiatric and research quarters that medication by itself is sufficient to deal with serious mental illness" (*Night Falls Fast*, 252).

14. Many studies point to a high rate of comorbidity for alcoholism and pathological gambling, e.g., Wendy S. Slutske et al. See especially Elia and Jacobs' study of comorbidity among Native Americans. Zitzow's analysis of gambling problems for Native Americans is also instructive. Another interesting account of gambling problems in a particular population is Hanan Sher's article in the *Jerusalem Report*, calling gambling "The Jewish Vice" and "our drug of choice" (26).

15. Ever vigilant, the *New York Times* took notice of this report: over Daniel Goleman's byline, the headline read, "Biology of Brain May Hold Key for Gamblers," with the subhead, "When the casino becomes an addiction, the condition may be chemical." Case studies of pharmacopsychiatric treatments include the use of lithium

carbonate (Moskowitz), carbamazepine, i.e., Tegretol (Haller and Hinterhuber), clomipramine (Hollander et al., "Treatment"), and fluvoxamine, an SSRI (Hollander et al., "Pharmacological Approaches"). Moskowitz's single case was a bipolar patient; where there is comorbidity or an underlying or preexisting condition, it is not clear whether the pathological gambling per se is what is being medicated.

16. See Blaszczynski et al., "Boredom Proneness."

17. Wolfe warns how, in a forensic context, such masking may cause problems. She says, "Although compulsive gambling is an identifiable disease, the presence of other problems . . . often masks its presence" (66). The issue of comorbidity is addressed by Crockford and el-Guebaly; by McCormick et al., "Affective Disorders"; and Specker et al. with a focus on depression; and by Blaszczynski and McConaghy, "Anxiety," who consider anxiety along with depression.

18. Bolen and Boyd long ago suggested a correlation of life crises and stressors with pathological gambling behavior: "our patients often began to gamble compulsively after a life crisis or a major stress" (627). "One of the most frequent stresses related to the outbreak of pathological gambling," they go on to say, "is the death of the gambler's father" (628). For readers of the Ray Kaiser, Bill Barich, and Barthelme brothers cases described above, this observation resonates strongly.

Bolen and Boyd's suggestion was corroborated (but without acknowledgment to them) twenty years later by Taber et al. in "The Prevalence and Impact of Major Life Stressors among Pathological Gamblers." They explain their findings by saying, "Gambling offers many things to an individual seeking escape from his own emotional trauma and its resulting chronic dysphoria" (78), and go on to list several of those "numbing" or "escape" mechanisms, including the possibility of a need for "self-punishment" for "irrational guilt."

19. A modified, refined version, Lesieur and Blume's "South Oaks Gambling Screen," has recently become the instrument of choice.

20. The use of pschodynamic terminology to describe a significant aspect of cognitive approaches reinforces my point about the permeability of boundaries among therapeutic modalities.

Bibliography

Abt, Vicki, James F. Smith, and Eugene Martin Christiansen. *The Business of Risk.* Lawrence: Univ. Press of Kansas, 1985.

————. "Misconceptions Abound in the Debate over Legalized Gambling." In Evans and Hance, 392–434.

Alson, Peter. *Confessions of an Ivy League Bookie.* New York: Crown, 1996.

Alvarez, A. "High Rollers." *New York Review of Books,* Mar. 9, 2000, 24–26.

————. "No Limit." *New Yorker,* Aug. 8, 1994, 56–63.

Anderson, Paul Thomas. See *Hard Eight.*

Annie. See Strouse and Charwin.

Armstrong, Gillian. See *Oscar and Lucinda.*

Ashley, Leonard R.N. "'The Words of My Mouth, and the Meditation of My Heart': The Mindset of Gamblers Revealed in Their Language." *Journal of Gambling Studies* 6 (1990): 241–61.

Banks, Russell. *Continental Drift.* New York: Harper and Row, 1985.

Barbieri, Susan M. "The Addiction of the '90s." *Washington Post,* Nov. 30, 1992, D5.

Barich, Bill. *Laughing in the Hills.* New York: Penguin, 1981.

Barnhart, Russell T. "Gambling and Giancomo Casanova and Lorenzo Da Ponte in Eighteenth-Century Venice—The *Ridotto:* 1638–1774." In Eadington and Cornelius, 451–66.

Barthelme, Frederick. *Bob the Gambler.* New York: Houghton Mifflin, 1997.

Barthelme, Frederick, and Steven Barthelme. *Double Down: Reflections on Gambling and Loss.* New York: Houghton Mifflin, 1999.

————. "Personal History: Good Losers." *New Yorker,* Mar. 8, 1999, 46–61.

Bergler, Edmund. *The Psychology of Gambling.* New York: Hill and Wang, 1957.

Berkson, J. "Limitations of the Application of Fourfold Table Analysis to Hospital Data." *Biometrics* 2 (1946): 47–53.

Beyer, Andrew. "Compulsive Gamblers Are Not Victims." *Washington Post,* Feb. 10, 1999, D1, D10.

Bilger, Burkhard. "Enter the Chicken." *Harper's Magazine,* Mar. 1999, 48–57.

Blaszczynski, A.P., and N. McConaghy. "Anxiety and/or Depression in the Pathogenesis of Addictive Gambling." *International Journal of the Addictions* 24 (1989): 337–50.

Blaszczynski, A.P., N. McConaghy, M.S. Armstrong, and C. Allcock. "The Behavioural Treatment of Compulsive Gamblers." Brisbane: Fifth National Conference on Behaviour Modification, 1982.

Blaszczynski, A.P., N. McConaghy, and A. Frankova. "Boredom Proneness in Pathological Gambling." *Psychological Reports* 67 (1990): 35–42.

Blaszczynski, A.P., and D. Silove. "Cognitive and Behavioral Therapies for Pathological Gambling." *Journal of Gambling Studies* 11 (1995): 195–220.

Blaszczynski, A.P., and Z.P. Steel. "Personality Disorders among Pathological Gamblers." *Journal of Gambling Studies* 14 (1998): 51–71.

Block, Lawrence. *Eight Million Ways to Die.* New York: Avon, 1991.

———. *Even the Wicked.* New York: Morrow, 1997.

Bloomfield, Morton W. *The Seven Deadly Sins.* 1952. Lansing: Michigan State Univ. Press, 1967.

Blum, K., J.G. Cull, E.R. Braverman, and D.E. Comings. "Reward Deficiency Syndrome: Addictive, Impulsive and Compulsive Disorders Including Alcoholism, Attention-Deficit Disorder, Drug Abuse and Food Bingeing May Have a Common Genetic Basis." *American Scientist* 84 (1996): 132–45.

Bob le Flambeur (Bob the Gambler). Jean-Pierre Melville, dir. Triumph, 1955.

Bolen, D.W., and W.H. Boyd. "Gambling and the Gambler." *Archives of General Psychiatry* 18 (1968): 617–30.

"Born under a Bad Sign." See Jones and Bell.

Brenner, Reuven, with Gabrielle A. Brenner. *Gambling and Speculation.* Cambridge, Eng.: Cambridge Univ. Press, 1990.

Brown University Digest of Addiction Theory and Application 18 (1999): 7–10.

Brubaker, Bill. "He Gambled and Lost." *Washington Post,* Apr. 28, 1991, A1, 24.

Bukowski, Charles. *Hollywood.* Santa Rosa, Calif.: Black Sparrow, 1989.

Bullard, Dexter M., ed. *Psychoanalysis and Psychotherapy: Selected Papers of Frieda Fromm-Reichmann.* Chicago: Univ. of Chicago Press, 1959.

Burglass, Milton Earl. "Compulsive Gambling: Forensic Update and Commentary." In Shaffer, Stein, et al., 205–22.

Butler, Jack. *Living in Little Rock with Miss Little Rock.* New York: Knopf, 1993.

Caillois, Roger. *Man, Play, and Games.* New York: Schocken Books, 1979.

Canty, Kevin. *Rounders.* New York: Hyperion, 1998.

Carey, Peter. *Oscar and Lucinda.* New York: Vintage, 1997.

Carlton, Peter L., and Leonide Goldstein. "Physiological Determinants of Pathological Gambling." In Galski, 111–22.

Cassavetes, John. See *Husbands.*

Castellani, Brian. *Pathological Gambling: The Making of a Medical Problem.* Albany: State Univ. of New York Press, 2000.

Castiglione, Baldassare. *The Book of the Courtier.* 1528. Trans. Sir Thomas Hoby, 1561. New York: AMS Press, 1967.

Chapman, Sanford R. "An Argument Against the 'Unconscious Need to Lose' Concept in the Compulsive Gambler." Second National Conference on Gambling and Risk Taking, Lake Tahoe, 1975.

Chicago Hope. CBS, Mar. 18, 1998.

Coetzee, J.M. *The Master of Petersburg*. New York: Viking Penguin, 1994.

Coover, Robert. *John's Wife*. New York: Simon & Schuster, 1996.

"The Combo Book." Gamblers Anonymous pamphlet. Los Angeles.

Comings, D.E. "The Molecular Genetics of Pathological Gambling." *CNS Spectrums* 3 (1998): 20–37.

Comings, D.E., R.J. Rosenthal, H.R. Lesieur et al. "A Study of the Dopamine D_2 Receptor Gene in Pathological Gambling." *Pharmacogentics* 6 (1996): 223–34.

Core, George. Introduction to *The Old Army Game*, by George Garrett. Dallas: Southern Methodist Univ. Press, 1994.

Cracker. Paul Abbott, Jimmie McGovern, Jim Mortimore, and Ted Whitehead, screenwriters. BBC, 1993.

Crist, Steven. "ATM Act Would Punish Players." *Daily Racing Form*, Oct. 3, 1999, 5.

Crockford, D.N., and N. el-Guebaly. "Psychiatric Comorbidity in Pathological Gambling: A Critical Review." *Canadian Journal of Psychiatry* 43 (1998): 43–50.

Cronley, Jay. *Good Vibes*. Garden City, N.Y.: Doubleday, 1979.

Croupier. Mike Hodges, dir. Paul Mayersberg, screenwriter. Shooting Gallery, 2000.

Cunningham-Williams, Renee M., Linda B. Cottler, W.M. Compton, and E.L. Spitznagel. "Taking Chances: Problem Gamblers and Mental Health Disorders—Results from the St. Louis Epidemiological Catchment Area (ECA) Study." *American Journal of Public Health* 88 (1998): 1093–96.

Custer, Robert, and Harry Milt. *When Luck Runs Out*. New York: Facts on File, 1985.

Dahl, John. See *Rounders*.

Defoe, Daniel. *The Gamester*. London: 1719.

DeLillo, Don. "Total Loss Weekend." *Sports Illustrated*, Nov. 27, 1972, 99–114.

———. *Underworld*. New York: Scribner, 1997.

Diagnostic and Statistical Manual of Mental Disorders, 4th ed. (DSM-IV). Washington, D.C.: American Psychiatric Association, 1994.

Dickerson, Mark G. *Compulsive Gamblers*. London: Longman, 1984.

Dixon, David. "Illegal Betting in Britain and Australia: Contrasts in Control Strategies and Cultures." In McMillen, 86–100.

Dostoevsky, Fyodor. *The Gambler*. 1866. *Great Short Works of Fyodor Dostoevsky*. Trans. Constance Garnett. New York: Harper and Row, 1968.

———. *Letters of . . .* New York: Horizon, 1961.

Downes, D.M., B.P. Davies, M.E. David, and P. Stone. *Gambling, Work and Leisure: A Study across Three Areas*. London: Routledge, 1976.

DSM (see *Diagnostic and Statistical . . .*).

Eadington, William R., and Judy A. Cornelius, eds. *Gambling: Public Policies and the Social Sciences*. Reno: Institute for the Study of Gambling and Commercial Gaming, 1997.

Elia, C., and D.F. Jacobs. "The Incidence of Pathological Gambling among Native

Americans Treated for Alcohol Dependence." *International Journal of the Addictions* 28 (1993): 659–66.

Evans, Rod L., and Mark Hance, eds. *Legalized Gambling: For and Against*. Chicago: Open Court, 1998.

Faust, Irvin. *The Year of the Hot Jock and Other Stories*. New York: Dutton, 1985.

Ferré, Rosario. *The House on the Lagoon*. New York: Farrar, Straus and Giroux, 1995.

Findlay, John M. *People of Chance*. New York: Oxford Univ. Press, 1986.

Frank, Joseph. *Dostoevsky: The Miraculous Years, 1865–1871*. Princeton: Princeton Univ. Press, 1995.

———. "*The Gambler*: A Study in Ethnopsychology," *Hudson Review* 46 (1993): 301–22.

Franklin, Joanna, and Donald R. Thoms. "Clinical Observations of Family Members of Compulsive Gamblers." In Shaffer, Stein, et al., 135–46.

Freiberg, Peter. "Pathological Gambling Turning into Epidemic." *APA Monitor*, Dec. 1995, 1, 32.

Fresh Air. Terry Gross, host. National Public Radio.

Freud, Sigmund. "Dostoevsky and Parricide." 1928. *Collected Papers*, vol. 5. Ed. James Strachey. New York: Basic Books, 1959.

Frey, James H., and William R. Eadington, eds. *Gambling: Views from the Social Sciences*. Beverly Hills: Sage, 1984.

Fromm-Reichmann, Frieda. See Dexter Bullard.

Galski, Thomas, ed. *Handbook of Pathological Gambling*. Springfield, Ill.: Charles Thomas, 1987.

Gambino, Blase. "The Search for Prescriptive Interventions." In Shaffer, Stein, et al., 293–314.

The Gambler. Karel Reisz, dir. James Toback, screenwriter. Paramount, 1975.

Gamblers Anonymous. Los Angeles: G.A. Publishing, 1973.

Garrett, George. *Which Ones Are the Enemy?* 1961. Rpt. in *The Old Army Game*. Dallas: Southen Methodist Univ. Press, 1994.

Garrick, David. Prologue to *The Gamester*. See Edward Moore.

Gass, William. *The Tunnel*. New York: Knopf, 1995.

Gaudia, Ronald. "Effects of Compulsive Gambling on the Family." *Social Work* 32 (1987): 254–56.

Gibson, William, and Bruce Sterling. *The Difference Engine*. New York: Bantam, 1992.

Glen, Alida Mixson. "Diagnosing the Pathological Gambler." *Journal of Gambling Behavior* 1 (1985): 17–22.

Goffman, Erving. "Where the Action Is." In *Interaction Ritual*. Chicago: Aldine, 1967.

Gogol, Nikolai. *Gamblers*. 1836–42. Trans. Eric Bentley. *Inspector and Three Other Plays*. New York: Applause, 1987.

Goleman, Daniel. "Biology of Brain May Hold Key for Gamblers." *New York Times*, Oct. 10, 1989, C1, 11.

Goodman, Robert. *The Luck Business*. New York: Free Press, 1995.

Grant, James. *The Great Metropolis*, 2 vols. 1837. New York: Garland, 1985.

Gross, Terry. See *Fresh Air*.

Haller, R., and H. Hinterhuber. "Treatment of Pathological Gambling with Carbamazepine." *Pharmacopsychiatry* 27 (1994): 19.

Halliday, J., and P. Fuller, eds. *The Psychology of Gambling*. New York: Harper and Row, 1974.

Halperin, James. *The Truth Machine*. New York: Ballantine, 1996.

Hammerstein, Oscar, II, and Jerome Kern. "Why Was I Born?" *Sweet Adeline*. P.B. Harms, 1929.

Hard Eight. Paul Thomas Anderson, dir. Columbia TriStar, 1997.

Hart, Lorenz, and Richard Rodgers. "I Wish I Were in Love Again." *Babes in Arms*. Chappell, 1937.

Hershey, Robert L. "Why the Lottery Is a Bad Bet." *Washington Post*, Aug. 13, 1997, H8.

Hoagland, Jim. "America—The Big Casino." *Washington Post*, July 23, 1998, A19.

Hodges, Mike. See *Croupier*.

Hoeg, Peter. *Smilla's Sense of Snow*. New York: Farrar, Straus and Giroux, 1993.

Hoffman, William S., Jr. *The Loser*. New York: Bantam, 1969.

Hollander, Eric, T. Begaz, and M. DeCaria. "Pharmacological Approaches in the Treatment of Pathological Gambling." *CNS Spectrums* 3 (1998): 72–82.

Hollander, Eric, and Stephanie D. Benzaquen. "The Obsessive-Compulsive Spectrum Disorders." *International Review of Psychiatry* 9 (1997): 99–109.

Hollander, Eric, M. Frenkel, C. DeCaria, S. Trungold, and D.J. Stein. "Treatment of Pathological Gambling with Clomipramine." *American Journal of Psychiatry* 149 (1992): 710–11.

Hopkins, Anne Yearout. "Uptown Down." Unpublished performance piece, ca. 1973.

Horner, Althea J. *Psychoanalytic Object Relations Therapy*. Northvale, N.J.: Jason Aronson, 1995.

Hudak, Clark J., Jr., Raju Varghese, and Robert M. Politzer. "Family, Marital, and Occupational Satisfaction for Recovering Pathological Gamblers." *Journal of Gambling Behavior* 5 (1989): 201–10.

Huizinga, Johan. *Homo Ludens: A Study of the Play Element in Culture*. 1938. Boston: Beacon Press, 1955.

Husbands. John Cassavetes, dir. Columbia Pictures, 1970.

The Hustler. Robert Rossen, dir. Twentieth Century-Fox, 1961.

Huston, John. See *Under the Volcano*.

Ignatin, George. "Sports Betting." In Frey and Eadington, 168–77.

Isaacs, Neil D. *All the Moves: A History of College Basketball*. Philadelphia: Lippincott, 1975.

———. "Compulsive Gambling Afflicts Millions." *Washington Post*, Feb. 13, 1999, D3.

———. *The Great Molinas*. Bethesda, Md.: WID Publishing Group, 1992.

———. *Jock Culture, U.S.A.* New York: Norton, 1978.

Israeli, Nathan. "Outlook of a Depressed Patient, Interested in Planned Gambling, Before and After His Attempt at Suicide." *American Journal of Orthopsychiatry* 5 (1935): 57–63.

Jacobs, Durand F. "A General Theory of Addiction: Application to Treatment and Rehabilitation Planning for Pathological Gamblers." In Galski, 169–94.

———. "A General Theory of Addiction: Rationale for and Evidence Supporting a New Approach for Understanding and Treating Addictive Behaviors." In Shaffer, Stein, et al., 35–64.

Jamison, Kay Redfield. Night Falls Fast: Understanding Suicide. New York: Knopf, 1999.

———. An Unquiet Mind. New York: Knopf, 1996.

Jarvis, Stephan. "From the View of a Compulsive Gambler/Recidivist." Journal of Gambling Behavior 4 (1988): 316–19.

Jones, Booker T., and William Bell. "Born under a Bad Sign." East/Memphis Music, 1970.

Jones, Laura. See Oscar and Lucinda.

Kaplan, H. Roy. "The Social and Economic Impact of State Lotteries." In Frey and Eadington, 91–106.

Kaplan, H. Roy, and William R. Blount. "The Impact of the Daily Lottery on the Numbers Game: Does Legalization Make a Difference?" Journal of Gambling Studies 6 (1990): 263–74.

Kavanagh, Thomas M. Enlightenment and the Shadows of Chance. Baltimore: Johns Hopkins, 1993.

Keitel, Evelyne. Reading Psychosis: Readers, Texts, and Psychoanalysis. Trans. Anthea Bell. Oxford, Eng.: Basil Blackwell, 1989.

Knapp, Bettina L. Gambling, Game, and Psyche. Albany: State Univ. of New York Press, 2000.

Koppelman, Brian. See Rounders.

Kusyszyn, Igor. "The Psychology of Gambling." In Frey and Eadington, 133–45.

Ladouceur, Robert, Jean-Marie Boisvert, and J. Dumont. "Cognitive-Behavioral Treatment for Adolescent Pathological Gamblers." Behavior Modification 18 (1994): 230–43.

Lesieur, Henry R. The Chase: Career of the Compulsive Gambler. Rev. ed. Rochester, Vt.: Shenkman, 1984.

———. "The Compulsive Gambler's Spiral of Options and Involvement." Psychiatry 42 (1979): 79–87.

———. "Gambling, Pathological Gambling, and Crime." In Galski, 89–110.

Lesieur, H.R., and S.B. Blume. "The South Oaks Gambling Screen (SOGS): A New Instrument for the Identification of Pathological Gamblers." American Journal of Psychiatry 144 (1987): 1184–88.

Let It Ride. Joe Pytka, dir. Ernest Morton, screenwriter. Paramount, 1989.

Levien, David. See Rounders.

Lightfoot, Gordon. "Sundown." Moose Music, 1973.

Lindner, R.M. "The Psychodynamics of Gambling." Annals of the American Academy of Political and Social Science 269 (1950): 93–107.

Livingston, Jay. Compulsive Gamblers: Observations on Action and Abstinence. New York: Harper and Row, 1974.

Lorenz, Valerie C. "Family Dynamics of Pathological Gamblers." In Galski, 71–88.

Lowry, Malcolm. *Under the Volcano*. 1947. New York: Penguin, 1971.

Malkin, D. "An Empirical Investigation into Some Aspects of Problem Gambling." Master's thesis, University of Western Australia, 1981.

Martin, Bob. Cited in Strine and Isaacs.

Max, D.T. "House of Cards." *New York Times Magazine*, Mar. 28, 1999, 34–39.

Mayersberg, Paul. See *Croupier*.

McConaghy, N., A. Blaszczynski, and A. Frankova. "Comparison of Imaginal Desensitization with Other Behavioral Treatments of Pathological Gambling. *British Journal of Psychiatry* 159 (1991): 390–93.

McCormick, Richard A., A.M. Russo, L.F. Ramirez, and J.I. Taber. "Affective Disorders among Pathological Gamblers Seeking Treatment." *American Journal of Psychiatry* 141 (1984): 215–18.

McCormick, Richard A., and J. Ingersoll Taber. "The Pathological Gambler: Salient Personality Variables." In Galski, 9–39.

McGlothin, W.H. "A Psychometric Study of Gambling." *Journal of Consulting Psychology* 18 (1954): 145–49.

McMillen, Jan, ed. *Gambling Cultures: Studies in History and Interpretation*. London: Routledge, 1996.

Melville, Jean-Pierre. See *Bob le Flambeur (Bob the Gambler)*.

Mercer, Johnny, and Harold Arlen. "That Old Black Magic." *Star-Spangled Rhythm*. Famous Music, 1942.

Miller, Walter. "Individual Outpatient Treatment of Pathological Gambling." *Journal of Gambling Behavior* 2 (1986): 95–107.

Milloy, Courtland. "Cash, Not Race, Rules in Casinos of Mississippi." *Washington Post*, Mar. 1, 1998, B1, 5.

Moler, Ron. See *The Runner*.

Moore, Edward. *The Gamester, a Tragedy*. 1753. Dublin: Bell's Edition, 1983.

Moran, E. "An Assessment of the Report of the Royal Commission on Gambling, 1976–1978." *British Journal of the Addictions* 74 (1979): 3–7.

———. "Gambling as a Form of Dependence." *British Journal of the Addictions* 64 (1970): 425.

———. "Pathological Gambling." *British Journal of Psychiatry* 9 (1975): 416–28.

———. "Taking the Final Risk." *Mental Health* (winter 1969): 21–22.

Moravec, J.D. "Professional Response to the Pathological Gambler: The Miami Experience." American Psychological Association Meeting, Montreal, 1980.

Morton, Ernest. See, *Let It Ride*.

Moskowitz, J.A. "Lithium and Lady Luck: Use of Lithium Carbonate in Compulsive Gambling." *New York State Journal of Medicine* 80 (1980): 785–88.

Murder One. Steven Bochco, prod. ABC, 1996–1997.

Murray, William. *The Getaway Blues*. New York: Bantam, 1991.

———. *The Hard Knocker's Luck*. New York: Penguin, 1986.

———. *Now You See Her, Now You Don't*. New York: Holt, 1994.

———. *Tip on a Dead Crab*. New York: Penguin, 1985.

———. *When the Fat Man Sings*. New York: Bantam, 1987.

The National Gambling Impact Study Commission, Executive Summary. Washington, D.C.: N.p., June 1999.

National Research Council. Pathological Gambling: A Critical Review. Washington, D.C.: National Academy Press, 1999.

Niederland, William. "A Contribution to the Psychology of Gambling." Psychoanalytic Forum 2 (1967): 175–85.

Norman, Geoffrey. "After the Fall." Sports Illustrated, May 20, 1991, 72–84.

Noverr, Douglas A., and Lawrence E. Ziewacz. The Games They Played: Sports in American History, 1865–1980. Chicago: Nelson-Hall, 1983.

Novick, Jack, and Kerry Kelly Novick. Fearful Symmetry. Northvale, N.J.: Jason Aronson, 1996.

Oates, Joyce Carol. The Mysteries of Winterthurn. New York: Dutton, 1984.

O'Brien, Timothy L. Bad Bet. New York: Random House, 1998.

Oldman, David. "Compulsive Gamblers." Sociological Review 26 (1978): 349–71.

Olmert, Michael. Milton's Teeth and Ovid's Umbrella. New York: Simon and Schuster, 1996.

O'Neill, Eugene. Hughie. In Complete Plays 1932–1943. New York: Library of America, 1988.

Oscar and Lucinda. Gillian Armstrong, dir. Laura Jones, screenwriter. Twentieth Century-Fox, 1997.

Ozick, Cynthia. The Pagan Rabbi and Other Stories. New York: Dutton, 1983.

Palliser, Charles. The Quincunx. New York: Ballantine, 1989.

Peri Rossi, Cristina. Dostoevsky's Last Night. New York: Picador, 1996.

Playing to Win. "A Moment of Truth Movie." NBC, Feb. 11, 1998.

Plotz, David. "Busted Flush." Harper's, Aug. 1999, 63–72.

Poe, Edgar Allan. Complete Tales and Poems of Edgar Allan Poe. New York: Vintage, 1975.

Pressley, Sue Anne. "S.C. Knows How to Fold 'Em." Washington Post, June 11, 2000, A3.

Profiler. NBC, Mar. 14, 1998.

Pushkin, Alexander. "The Queen of Spades." In A Treasury of Russian Literature, ed. and trans. Bernard Guilbert Guerney. New York: Vanguard, 1943.

Pytka, Joe. See Let It Ride.

Quigley, Lillian. The Blind Men and the Elephant. New York: Scribner's, 1959.

Reisz, Karel. See The Gambler.

Reuter, Peter. Disorganized Crime: The Economics of the Visible Hand. Cambridge, Mass.: MIT Press, 1983.

Richardson, Jack. Memoir of a Gambler. New York: Simon and Schuster, 1979.

Roberts, Randy, and James Olson. Winning Is the Only Thing: Sports in America since 1945. Baltimore: Johns Hopkins Univ. Press, 1989.

Rose, I. Nelson. Gambling and the Law. Hollywood: Gambling Times, 1986.

Rosecrance, John. "Controlled Gambling: A Promising Future." In Shaffer, Stein, et al., 147–60.

———. Gambling without Guilt: The Legitimation of an American Pastime. Pacific Grove, Calif.: Brooks/Cole, 1988.

Rosenthal, Richard J. "The Pathological Gambler's System for Self-Deception." Journal of Gambling Behavior 2 (1986): 108–20.

———. "The Psychodynamics of Pathological Gambling: A Review of the Literature." In Galski, 41–70.

Rossen, Robert. See The Hustler.

Roth, Philip. The Facts. New York: Penguin, 1989.

———. Sabbath's Theater. New York: Vintage, 1995.

Rounders. John Dahl, dir. David Levien and Brian Koppelman, screenwriters. Miramax, 1998.

Roy, Alec, Judith De Jong, and Markku Linnoila. "Extraversion in Pathological Gamblers." Archives of General Psychiatry 46 (1989): 679–81.

The Runner. Ron Moler, dir. D.E.J. Productions, 1999.

Runyon, Damon. "A Nice Price." In The Bloodhounds of Broadway and Other Stories. New York: William Morrow, 1981.

Russell, John. Reciprocities in the Nonfiction Novel. Athens: Univ. of Georgia Press, 2000.

Savage, D.S. "Dostoevsky: The Idea of The Gambler." Sewanee Review 58 (1950): 281–98. Rpt. in Dostoevky: New Perspectives, ed. Robert Louis Jackson. Englewood Cliffs, N.J. Prentice-Hall, 1984. 111–25.

Schwarz, J., and A. Lindner. "Inpatient Treatment of Male Pathological Gamblers in Germany." Journal of Gambling Studies 8 (1992): 93–109.

Seager, C.P. "Treatment of Compulsive Gamblers Using Electrical Aversion." British Journal of Psychiatry 117 (1970): 545–53.

Seltzer, Leon F. Paradoxical Strategies in Psychotherapy. New York: Wiley, 1986.

Shaffer, Howard J. "Strange Bedfellows: A Critical View of Pathological Gambling and Addiction." Addiction 94 (1999): 1445–48.

Shaffer, H.J., and M.N. Hall. The Emergence of Youthful Addiction: The Prevalence of Pathological Gambling Among Adolescents at Agawam High School. Boston: Massachusetts Council on Compulsive Gambling, 1994.

Shaffer, H.J., M.N. Hall, and J.V. Bilt. Estimating the Prevalence of Disordered Gambling Behavior in the United States and Canada: A Meta-Analysis. Cambridge, Mass.: Harvard Medical School Division of Addictions, 1997.

Shaffer, H.J., R. LaBrie, K.M. Scanlan, and T.N. Cummings. "Pathological Gambling among Adolescents: Massachusetts Gambling Screen (MAGS)." Journal of Gambling Studies 10 (1994): 339–62.

Shaffer, Howard J., Sharon A. Stein, Blase Gambino, and Thomas N. Cummings, eds. Compulsive Gambling: Theory, Research, and Practice. Lexington, Mass.: Heath, 1989.

Sher, Hanan. "The Jewish Vice." Jerusalem Report, Aug. 16, 1999, 26–33.

Simmel, Ernst. "Psychoanalysis of the Gambler." International Journal of Psychoanalysis 1 (1920): 352–53.

Skolnick, Jerome H. "A Zoning Merit Model for Casino Gambling." In Frey and Eadington, 48–60.

Slutske, Wendy S., Seth Eisen, William R. True, Michael J. Lyons, Jack Goldberg, and Ming Tsuang. "Common Genetic Vulnerability for Pathological Gambling and Alcohol Dependence in Men." Archives of General Psychiatry 57 (2000): 666–75.

"South Oaks Gambling Screen (SOGS)." See Lesieur and Blume.

Specker, S.M., G.A. Carlson, K.M. Edmonson, P.E. Johnson, and M. Marcotte. "Psychopathology in Pathological Gamblers Seeking Treatment." *Journal of Gambling Studies* 12 (1996): 67–81.

Spencer, Elizabeth. *The Salt Line.* Baton Rouge: Louisiana State Univ. Press, 1995.

Steele, David Ramsay. "Gambling Is Productive and Rational." In Evans and Hance, 224–33.

Stein, Rob. "Sociology: Gambling Sites Show High Suicide Rates." *Washington Post,* Dec. 12, 1997,

Stekel, Wilhelm. "The Gambler." 1924. In *Peculiarities of Behavior,* vol. 2. Ed. and trans. S. Van Teslaar. New York: Liveright, 1943.

Stevenson, Seth. "A Straight Face." *Newsweek,* May 17, 1999, 76–78.

Strine, Gerald, and Neil D. Isaacs. *Covering the Spread.* New York: Random House, 1978.

Strouse, Charles, and Martin Charwin. "Tomorrow." *Annie.* Edwin H. Morris Co. and Charles Strouse Co., 1977.

Styron, William. *Darkness Visible.* New York: Random House, 1990.

Sullivan, S. "Why Compulsive Gamblers Are a High Suicide Risk." *Community Mental Health in New Zealand* 8 (1994): 40–47.

"Sundown." See Gordon Lightfoot.

Taber, J. Ingersoll, and Richard A. McCormick. "The Pathological Gambler in Treatment." In Galski, 137–68.

Taber, J. Ingersoll, Richard A. McCormick, and Luis F. Ramirez. "The Prevalence and Impact of Major Life Stressors among Pathological Gamblers." *International Journal of the Addictions* 22 (1987): 71–79.

Taber, Julian I., Angel M. Russo, Bonnie J. Adkins, and Richard A. McCormick. "Ego Strength and Achievement Motivation in Pathological Gamblers." *Journal of Gambling Behavior* 2 (1986): 69–80.

Tevis, Walter. *The Hustler.* New York: Dell, 1961.

"That Old Black Magic." See Mercer and Arlen.

Thompson, William N., and Ricardo Gazel. "*The Last Resort* Revisited: The Spread of Gambling as a 'Prisoner's Dilemma.'" In Eadington and Cornelius, 183–205.

Toback, James. See *The Gambler.*

"Tomorrow." See Strouse and Charwin.

Tsypkin, Leonid. *Summer in Baden-Baden.* Trans. Roger and Angela Keys. London: Quartet, 1987.

Under the Volcano. John Huston, dir. Ithaca, 1984.

Vatz, Richard E., and Lee S. Weinberg. "Keno Krazy?" *Washington Post,* Jan. 10, 1993, C5.

———. "Refuting the Myths of Compulsive Gambling." *USA Today,* Nov. 1993, 54–56. Rpt. as "Heavy Gambling Is Not a Disease" in Evans and Hance, 54–63.

Verghese, Abraham. *The Tennis Partner.* New York: HarperCollins, 1998.

Victor, Ralph G., and Carolyn M. Krug. "'Paradoxical Intention' in the Treatment of Compulsive Gambling." *American Journal of Psychotherapy* 21 (1967): 808–14.

Von Hattingberg, Hans. "Analerotik, Angstlust, and Eigensinn." *Internationale Zeitschrift fur Psychoanalyse* 2 (1914): 244–58.

Wagenaar, Willem Albert. *Paradoxes of Gambling Behavior*. Hove and London: Lawrence Erlbaum, 1988.

Walker, Michael. "The Medicalisation of Gambling as an 'Addiction.'" In McMillen, 223–42.

———. *The Psychology of Gambling*. Oxford, Eng.: Pergamon Press, 1992.

Wang, Ferdie. "Reality Breaks the 'Law of Averages.'" *Washington Post*, Aug. 20, 1997, H2.

Whitaker, Rick. "One Last Chance." *New York Times Magazine*, Nov. 28, 1999, 162.

"Why the Lottery Is a Bad Bet." See Robert Hershey.

"Why Was I Born?" See Hammerstein and Kern.

Wildman, Robert W., II. "Book Review of *The Gambler*." *Journal of Gambling Studies* 7 (1991): 169–75.

Wolfe, Joy. "It Won't Be Easy to Hold Casinos Legally Responsible for Patrons' Losses." In Evans and Hance, 64–79.

Wong, G. "The Obsessional Aspects of Compulsive Gambling." Society for the Study of Gambling Meeting. London, 1980.

Wrangel (Vrangel), Baron Alexander. Cited in Dostoevsky, *Letters*. . . .

Wright, George T. "The Lyric Present: Simple Present Verbs in English Poems." *PMLA* 89 (1974): 563–79.

Yalom, Irvin D. *Existential Psychotherapy*. New York: Basic Books, 1980.

. *Love's Executioner*. New York: Basic Books, 1989.

———. *Lying on the Couch*. New York: Harper, 1997.

———. *Theory and Practice of Group Psychotherapy*. 4th ed. New York: Basic Books, 1995.

Zinberg, Norman E. "The Applicability of the Twelve-Step Model to Compulsive Intoxicant Use and Other Compulsive Behaviors." In Shaffer, Stein, et al., 91–99.

Zitzow, D. "Comparative Study of Problematic Gambling Behaviors between American Indian and Non-Indian Adolescents within and near a Northern Plains Reservation." *American Indian and Alaskan Native Mental Health Research* 7 (1996): 14–26.

Zweig, Stefan. "Four-and-Twenty Hours in a Woman's Life." In *Conflicts*. Trans. Eden and Cedar Paul. New York: Viking, 1934.

Index

Note: Books, plays, and short stories appear under authors; movies and television shows appear by title.

268